What to Ask
When You Don't
Know What to Say

WHAT TO ASK WHEN YOU DON'T KNOW WHAT TO SAY

555 Powerful Questions to Use for Getting Your Way at Work

SAM DEEP · LYLE SUSSMAN

PRENTICE HALL
Englewood Cliffs, New Jersey 07632

Prentice-Hall International (UK) Limited, *London*
Prentice-Hall of Australia Pty. Limited, *Sydney*
Prentice-Hall Canada, Inc., *Toronto*
Prentice-Hall Hispanoamericana, S.A., *Mexico*
Prentice-Hall of India Private Limited, *New Delhi*
Prentice-Hall of Japan, Inc., *Tokyo*
Simon & Schuster Asia Pte. Ltd., *Singapore*
Editora Prentice-Hall do Brasil, Ltda., *Rio de Janeiro*

©1993 *by*
PRENTICE-HALL, Inc.
Englewood Cliffs, NJ

10 9 8 7 6 5 4 3 2 1

Library of Congress Cataloging-in-Publication Data

Deep, Samuel D.
    What to ask when you don't know what to say /
Sam Deep, Lyle Sussman.
        p. cm.
    Includes index.
    ISBN 0-13-953985-9—ISBN 0-13-953977-8
    1. Career development.   2. Managing your   boss.
3. Interpersonal relations.   4. Employees—Life skills
guides.   I. Sussman, Lyle, 1944–   . II. Title.
HF5381.D422   1993   93-9657
650.1'3—dc20   CIP

ISBN 0-13-953977-8
ISBN 0-13-953985-9 (pbk)

PRENTICE HALL
Career & Personal Development
Englewood Cliffs, NJ 07632
Simon & Schuster, A Paramount Communications Company

Printed in the United States of America

Dedication

This book is dedicated to those of you whose teaching, coaching, guidance, and support over the years have meant so much to us. Each of you in your own way either challenged our minds, shaped our values, polished our technique, or strengthened our resolve and some did all four! We are eternally grateful to each of you: Bernie Bass, Ken Frandsen, Frank Dance, Jim Derry, Rich Enos, Don Henderson, Pete Jones, Mark Knapp, Phil Long, Chet Lucido, Jack Matthews, Robert Moore, Rick Meyers, Dave Raymond, W. Charles Redding, Robert Taylor.

How to Use
This Book

Regardless of how good a book is, you eventually have to put it down. The same is true with *What to Ask When You Don't Know What to Say*. Our goal in writing it, however, was to make sure that when you do put it down you'll keep it close by.

We hope that this book will find a permanent place on your desk, in your briefcase, or on your night stand. We also hope you wear it out, filling its margins with notes and stuffing its pages with bookmarks reflecting your successes in making it work for you. Its cover should be tattered from being passed back and forth with friends and colleagues. The spine should begin to fail as you prosper from the advice it ties together. We want this book to become one of your prized possessions.

How can we justify such high expectations? Because we believe that here you will find solutions to some of life's most perplexing problems. You see, it's more than just a book of questions. It's a way out, a tool for getting off the spot. It tells you what to say when you either can't or don't know what to say. It enables you to win when you're dealt an unplayable hand at work. It empowers you with the magic of questions.

You'll never again be at a loss for words if you follow one basic piece of advice: Stop looking for what to *say* and start looking for what to *ask*. This simple yet powerful thesis is developed in the first two chapters, where you learn why questions have the power to turn confusion into clarity, desperation into decisiveness, and trial into triumph. More important, you'll learn *how* to ask questions that achieve these turnabouts.

Then the real help begins. In the remaining nineteen chapters you'll read about 181 of the most difficult situations that might slam you down at work. You'll find the questions, 555 in all, that we believe will enable you to dust yourself off and get back up again. In most cases, we even tell you what answers to expect to your questions and how to counter each one.

Here's some advice on how to get the most out of the book. It's in the form of the steps you should use in Chapters 3 through 21.

1. *Read the book through, cover to cover.* Even though you'll be reading situations you may never face and going over questions you may never need, you will gain valuable and generalizable insights into getting out of your own particular tight spots.

2. *Go back to reread the scenarios that have been, or may become, real for you.* Chapters 3 through 21 each contain several lifelike vignettes on particular topics. You can expect to encounter events just like these on your job. Each scenario places you in a dilemma from which we suggest you extract yourself by posing a question. Cover up the questions while you study the scenario. Test yourself. Using the advice of Chapter 2, come up with at least one question you believe would work magic for you in that situation.

3. *Study the questions we recommend for that scenario.* Compare your question with ours. Does it appear to be as or more effective? If so, write it in your book. Read our questions carefully. They may suggest more questions that will work for you.

4. *Adapt questions to your situation.* In some cases, our scenario will be related to but different from what you encounter. For example, we might describe a boss who doesn't get back to you on

an idea of yours, when you may be frustrated by that same behavior on the part of a coworker. When the roles of the players are other than what we have established, adapt our questions with revisions that fit your situation.

5. *Flesh in the questions as needed.* If you inject our questions into your conversations exactly as phrased, they may be too abrupt for your conditions. Feel free to preface your questions with appropriate transitions from what has been going on with the other person. For example, prior to saying, "How does that comment relate to the third agenda item?" a meeting leader might say, "That's a creative suggestion."

6. *Revise questions to fit your language.* Some questions as presented in the chapters may be too formal or too informal for the context of your conversation, or when repeated verbatim they might not sound like your words. Modify our vocabulary as needed to bring the questions in line with the tone you wish to establish and maintain.

7. *Be careful not to revise the muscle out of questions.* Before you make *any* changes in wording, thoughtfully consider the impact those changes may have on the potency of the question. For example, we have avoided the word "you" or "your" in certain questions to minimize defensiveness in the person to whom you pose them. We have carefully expressed each question to get the desired impact. Study each to understand the source of its power before you revise it for any of the reasons suggested above.

8. *Continue to use statements when they work best.* Do not be misled by our zeal in recommending the use of questions in tough situations. There *are* many cases where a straightforward de-clarative statement is more appropriate and more potent than a question. We were moved to write this book not because we believe that questions are always superior to assertions, but because we observe so many cases where the power of inquiry is totally overlooked. But choose your opportunities well. When the situation calls for you to assert your needs and your intent, do so with clarity and aplomb. But when you aren't quite empowered to say what you feel, or when you expect poor results if you do, *ask a magic question.*

A Final Piece of Advice

Francis Bacon said, "A prudent question is one half of wisdom." We believe the other half is listening to the answer. We've provided you with one half of the wisdom, the questions. Please provide the other half by opening your eyes and your ears when people answer them.

When you put both halves together you'll discover what wise people have always known: *Questions are magic.*

Contents

Chapter

3

Managing
Your Workload 21

Chapter

4

Satisfying Bosses 35

Chapter

5

Surviving Plateaus, Layoffs, and Firings   55

Chapter

6

Getting Promotions and Raises 73

Chapter

7

Dealing with Difficult Employees 87

Chapter

8

Working Together 109

Chapter

9

Responding to Ideas of Others   129

Chapter

10

Selling Your Ideas   139

Chapter

13

Running Meetings 177

Chapter

14

Attending Meetings 191

Chapter

15

Negotiating 203

Chapter

16

Being Interviewed
for a Job 217

Chapter

17

Interviewing
Job Applicants 227

Chapter

18

Presenting
on the Podium 243

Chapter

19

Resolving Ethical
Dilemmas 259

Chapter

20

Handling Criticisms and Complaints 275

Chapter

21

Responding
to a Changing World 289

Chapter

1

The Magic
of Questions

We've written this book on the basis of a single underlying premise: Questions are magic. Questions have the power to turn confusion into clarity, resistance into acceptance, division into consensus, and the frustration of not knowing what to say into the satisfaction of having said it.

Think about the most effective communicators you know, those people who seem to say just the right thing at the right time. Unlike most people, they don't have to search for the elusive right phrase needed to make the sale or to win agreement. They are never at a loss for words. They don't walk away from an encounter wishing that they had said something they didn't or regretting saying something they did. They know what to say to get what they want, and the people they leave feel listened to and valued.

Would you like to fit this description? Everyone would. And the good news is that the capability to influence others successfully is easily within your grasp. Simply understand and accept what effective communicators already know: Questions are magic.

The Qualities of Magical Questions

The right question at the right time provides the power that you seek in your relationships. This power stems from eight qualities of well-timed and well-stated questions.

1
_____

The Right Question at the Right Time
Focuses Thought

You've been in meetings where much more was said than was accomplished. Similarly, you've engaged in conversations that simply wasted time, space, and energy. Wasted meetings and wasted conversations usually lack focus.

A good question is like a lens condensing sunlight on a small spot. Diffuse rays converge at a single point, creating intensified light and energy. A good question does the same thing. Diffuse thoughts converge with increased clarity and power. Consider a few examples:

- A committee member listening to six colleagues debate myriad specifications of computers brings the discussion to a point by asking, "What exactly do we want to have that we don't have now without computers, and which model gives that best?"

- The architect evokes clarity by asking this question of a couple who have trouble describing their dream house: "What are the five most important characteristics for your house to possess?"

- An advertising agency account executive overcomes writer's block by asking himself, "What three features distinguish this product from the competitor's?"

- The Watergate investigation committee vowed to ask Richard Nixon one question: "Mr. President, what did you know and when did you know it?"

- During the 1980 presidential campaign, Ronald Reagan riveted the electorate with a magical question: "Are you better off today than you were four years ago?"

2

The Right Question at the Right Time *Bridges Conflicting Views*

Divergent opinions are often polarized further by even the most well-intentioned statements from either the parties in conflict or from outside observers or mediators. It's easy for such comments to threaten or to escalate those who hold views that may appear to be in opposition to yours.

When you witness a disagreement, or when you are part of one, take your lesson from labor negotiators and marriage counselors. They earn their living by using questions to get conflicting parties to recognize the root causes of their differences and to develop mutually satisfying solutions.

- A supervisor defuses the antagonisms between two embroiled employees by asking, "What are the common goals you're both working toward, and how can you help each other achieve those goals?"

- A career counselor helps a frustrated college graduate sort out career options by asking, "Of all the jobs you've held—part time and full time—what have you liked the most about any of them and what have you disliked the most?"

- A sales rep closes a sale by asking a prospective buyer, "What additional information will help you make your decision?" or "If you decide to put in an order, what quantity would you need?"

- When arguing with your spouse, you may have the presence of mind to say, "How do you see that our needs differ in this situation, and can you see any possible way to meet both of them with one solution?"

3

The Right Question at the Right Time *Builds Rapport and Strengthens Relationships*

Communication scholars tell us that information is exchanged between people on two levels: content and process. The content level is what we say; the process level is how we say it. If you could see yourself on videotape throughout a given day and could examine both the content and the process of your encounters with others, you would see yourself doing a great job of building rapport—an emotional bond—with the people around you in some situations and not doing so well in others.

Whenever we say anything to anyone we must realize that the words we use (the content) and our tone of voice as well as our body language (the process) give us tremendous potential to both create and to destroy rapport. We can experience a mutually satisfying or a negative confrontation. We can enhance the self-esteem of others or we can destroy it. We can leave that person wanting more or hoping that we disappear.

Well-timed and well-stated questions have the potential to build relationships and to establish bonds. They show that we care and that we are interested. To borrow a line from a long-distance telephone advertisement, questions have the ability to "reach out and touch someone."

- A boss creates rapport when she walks over to an employee and sincerely asks, "I understand your mother is ill. Is there anything I can do to help?"

- A maitre d' creates goodwill and fulfills customer expectations when he approaches a table of diners and says, "We are committed to your total satisfaction. If we are in any way falling short of that goal, what may I do to correct that before you leave us?"

- You call your bank about an error you notice on your checking account statement. When you reach the bank's representative, her first words are, "How may I help you?" To your delight, she listens carefully to your problem, asking questions throughout to be certain you are understood. She concludes the conversation by asking, "May I get back to you this afternoon? I'll need that much time to get to the bottom of your problem."

4

The Right Question at the Right Time *Deflects Anger and Hostility*

The natural reaction when attacked is to defend and to counterattack. Anger begets anger, shouting begets shouting, and profanity begets profanity. Unfortunately, what comes naturally in the face of conflict isn't necessarily what will serve you well, especially if it escalates the conflict. When the two of you start thinking with your instincts rather than your brains, you start to disagree like wild animals rather than act as rational human beings.

When faced with the anger, hostility, and frustration of others, allow them to vent their emotions without rebuttal. Listen fully to their positions, acknowledge their concerns, and watch them calm down. Ask questions that keep them talking and venting. You'll win them over through the determination you show to hear them out.

The questions you ask will also calm *you* down. They serve as a preferred alternative to biting your lip or to counting to ten. They'll encourage you to contemplate the concerns of others, to consider the validity of their positions, and to become more empathetic to their needs. You cannot do all this and remain upset for long. Asking a question also postpones your need to respond, buying time you need to gain your composure and offer a solution with which you can both live.

Just as music has power to soothe the savage beast, so do the right questions at the right time.

- Your in-laws accuse you of being selfish and insensitive. Rather than defending yourself, dredging up what you know to be *their* shortcomings, or discounting their indictment as nonsense, you ask a simple question: "What do I do to make you believe I'm selfish and insensitive?" You listen intently to their answer and continue the discussion by asking follow-up probes, such as: "When was the last time you saw an example of that?" or "What would you like to see me do differently?" Notice how this approach, in addition to defusing anger, puts you in control of problem solving.

- You're in a heated argument with your spouse. Your sensors tell you that he's about to lash out at you. You quickly and assertively intervene with, "I'm afraid you're about to say something we might both regret, something that might be hard to forget when we make up later. Do you still want to say it?" Even if he says yes and proceeds to criticize, you have probably blunted the worst of the attack.

- A customer looks you squarely in the eye, points his finger in your face, and punishingly says, "This is the worst store I've ever shopped in, and your service stinks!" You take a deep breath, stifle your desire to tell him where to go, and respond with, "I'm sorry you feel that way. What happened and how can I make it right?" You keep coming back with questions until the customer has flushed his system and you know exactly what you'll do to solve the problem.

5

The Right Question at the Right Time *Shows Your Commitment and Interest*

Someone once said that one of the easiest things in the world to fake is listening. By looking at someone's eyes, smiling, nodding affirmatively, and uttering a few "uh huhs," we can give the impression of listening when in fact our mind is somewhere else. More than one speaker has been thus deceived.

There are two reliable tests of having been heard. The first is seeing the person behave differently after our words than before: by complying with a request, obeying an order, or adopting a suggestion. The second is getting intelligent questions that seek to clarify your statement. Questioning, the most convincing of the two, shows you that your words not only made an impression but generated additional thought in the mind of your listener.

When you ask people questions about their assertions, you signal that you're plugged in to their needs and tuned into their feelings. By focusing on their ideas, you tell them that they are important to you. You demonstrate that you want to be absolutely sure you understand what's being said and why the person has a need to say it. You use your ears to say that you care, and you open the way for them to begin caring more about you and your ideas.

Learn to use "I care" questions like these:

- "Would you please repeat what you just said about . . . ? I'm not sure I got it all."
- "Are you saying that . . . ?"
- "How does that relate to what you said before about . . . ?"
- "If you're saying . . . , are you also suggesting that . . . ?"
- "A few minutes ago you said . . . Now I hear you saying . . . Isn't there a contradiction here?"

- "Do I understand correctly that . . . ?"
- "Does your statement about . . . mean that you . . . ?"

6

The Right Question at the Right Time *Turns Discomforting Silence into Clarifying Discourse*

There are two ways to impress people with your intellect and your insight. One is to be so intelligent and insightful that your actions naturally exude your brilliance. The other—and the one most of us rely on—is to communicate so effectively that your best side is always forward. Questions are the radar that keep you headed in the right direction.

With questions as your guide you'll never again be at a loss for words. You won't have to search the innermost recesses of your mind for the elusive bon mot. You'll never have to scan the skies hoping that a script will fall from the heavens. When you don't know what to say to someone you'll ask a question, and you'll let your trusty ears put the right words in your mouth. People will tell you where they are, how they feel, and what they expect. You'll start basing your success not on periods and exclamation points but on question marks.

- A management trainer starts a presentation skills seminar by asking, "What are the contexts in which each of you currently gives presentations?" The answers enable the trainer to target the seminar to the needs of this audience.
- An employee remains passive and nearly silent throughout a performance review meeting until the supervisor asks, "What can I do to help you achieve the performance level that I've just told you is expected?"
- Very little is said at a quality improvement meeting until the leader goes around the table to get answers to this question: "If you had one suggestion for how these meetings could become more valuable, what would it be?"
- A job interview becomes more lively and valuable when the interviewer asks, "What one question that I haven't asked you would you like to answer?"

7

The Right Question at the Right Time *Conveys Subtle Messages That Imply Rather Than Assert*

Sometimes the best response to a challenging encounter is to express your needs directly and assertively. For example, a subordinate who challenges your authority for the umpteenth time may simply need to be set in his or her place. However, it is not always wise to use such a heavy hand in getting your way. At times, stating your feelings and expressing your needs directly will add unwanted fuel to the fire. Gentleness is sometimes appropriate, depending on the vulnerability of the other person. In some settings, particularly with superiors, you may risk too much by insisting upon full recognition of your desires.

Yet, the consequences of inaction are often worse. The situation is unimproved and maybe worsened. To some you will mark yourself as an easy target for abuse. Or, the other person may grow to feel justified in continuing the offensive behavior and may grow accustomed to and comfortable with it.

Questions are wonderful substitutes for statements that might backfire on you. They enable you to communicate through the powers of suggestion rather than through intimidation. They soften the blow of potentially negative information. They reduce the level of threat to both of you. They follow the advice of a wonderful old Japanese proverb that says, "Never remove a fly from your friend's forehead with a hatchet."

Here are some examples of how to get your way by implying rather than asserting.

- You have reservations about your boss's new customer service policy. You raise concerns through this query: "Do you think there's a chance that this policy will give some customers an impression of us that we don't want them to have? And if they get that impression, might that not eventually depress sales?"

- A nurse is concerned that the attending physician may be overprescribing a medication for a certain patient. She approaches the physician with, "Is this the dosage you want for this patient? Since it's double what many of our other patients are on, I want to be certain I haven't made a mistake here."

Notice how statements that may need to accompany inference questions can be wrapped in an "it may be my fault" package.

▪ A boss has an employee who, probably due to low self-esteem, bridles at any form of criticism. Rather than confront the employee directly with the shortcomings of a recently submitted report, the boss asks this question: "As you look back over your report, what do you see as its three most distinctive strengths and its three most distinctive opportunities for improvement?" With the employee having first identified potential shortcomings, the path is cleared for the feedback that needs to be given.

8

The Right Question at the Right Time *Elicits Reflection, Contemplation,* and *Introspection*

Until you began reading this book you may have thought of questions mainly as tools for getting information. You may not have given them the credit they deserve for taking you beyond mere data collection. Of all the magical properties of questions, none is more powerful than their ability to cause an aggressive, insensitive, or rash person to start thinking about an issue. Indeed, well-timed, well-stated questions are remarkable in the way they can bring people to their senses, get them to see the impact of their behavior, and cause them to think twice about what they're doing or not doing.

With some of these magical questions, the asker is not looking for an answer. The resulting silent contemplation is enough. This type of probe is known as a rhetorical question. Here are some examples.

▪ During half time of a close football game, the coach concludes his pep talk with this question: "When the final numbers are put on the scoreboard will you be able to leave the field of play knowing that you gave your very best to your fans, your teammates, and yourself?" To turn the struggle into victory he wants them to reflect on their effort and their motivation.

▪ Two back-to-back questions have sold more insurance policies than any others: "If you were to die today would your family be taken care of? Would they have enough money in your absence to live the kind of life you want them to have?" These are simple and direct questions that have the power to get clients to consider how much more coverage they ought to purchase.

■ John F. Kennedy's most frequently quoted utterance is, "Ask not what your country can do for you, ask what you can do for your country." This syntactical variation of a question set the mood for his presidency and challenged the American people to rethink their patriotism and renew their spirit of volunteerism.

Other questions in this category have the same power to evoke contemplation, but with an expected vocal response. Their goal is not so much to energize and empower others to act as to get them to stop acting.

People manifest aggressive behavior in many ways. Bosses dump work on your desk, employees challenge your authority, co-workers criticize your performance, and customers make unreasonable requests, just to name a few. Challenges like these are not easily surmounted. Stating your feelings directly and expressing your needs directly may add to the conflict. However, the consequences of inaction may be even worse than action, especially if you are identified as a willing candidate for abuse.

A thoughtfully worded question is another matter. It puts the person on notice that you won't simply turn the other cheek. It raises second thoughts in that person's mind about the appropriateness of that approach. It suggests undesirable implications and highlights the issues important to you. It places the aggressor, not you, in the position of explaining herself. Most importantly, it opens the way for you to follow up with a credible and powerful statement that would not have been possible without the disarming done by your question.

Many of the questions in Chapters 3 to 21 are of this variety. As soon as you read the next chapter on how to ask questions, turn to those chapters for the direct help you need to handle those heart-stopping encounters where your mouth goes dry and fear rushes through your being, where you feel cornered and defensive, or where you don't feel that you have the freedom to react as you'd like.

Chapter
2

How to Ask
Magical Questions

The following story comes under the heading, "A little knowledge is a dangerous thing."

Years ago an in-house seminar for first-line production supervisors was conducted. The title of the seminar was "Effective Human Relations," and it incorporated instructional material on communication, coaching, and discipline.

One of the basic themes of the seminar was that effective supervisors praise more than they reprimand and seek opportunities to enhance the self-esteem of their employees. The participants accepted this message wholeheartedly and as a group pledged to apply its wisdom.

On the way out of the seminar the instructor overheard a participant apply this wisdom by praising an overweight employee with the following pearls: "You know, you don't sweat much for a fat person."

Yes, praising is important. But not every message intended as praise is necessarily received as such. Similarly, questions are magic, but not every question posed in an attempt to achieve the eight

11

characteristics discussed in Chapter 1 necessarily achieves those effects.

Unfortunately, many common mistakes are made in asking questions, mistakes that diminish the value, power, and ultimately the magic of questions. If you commit any of these mistakes, your attempt to use questions for purposes of increasing clarity, focus, and resolution may produce just the opposite effect.

Mistake 1

Looking for Something to Say Rather
Than Something to Ask

This mistake may be the most common error we make and is the basic reason we have written this book. We believe that our culture, generally, and our training, specifically, condition us to respond assertively, which for us means statements rather than questions.

We are raised in a culture where strength is defined as acting and not reacting, as asserting and not questioning, and as uttering phrases that end in exclamation points, not question marks. We are taught to stand up and speak our minds. Strength is viewed as "getting it off our chest," "not beating around the bush," and "speaking from the gut." We are not taught that strength exists in probing the other person's assertion or in raising questions that elicit contemplation.

The reason why our mouth goes dry, our hands sweat, and our mind goes blank when confronting a challenging situation is because we are searching for the elusive "magic bullet." We believe that there is a phrase or statement that will unequivocally "kill" our adversary, his request, or his position. We are looking for the one statement, followed by an exclamation point, that will unequivocally make our case and turn our adversary into a whimpering and defeated foe. We search for the elusive phrase that gets us out of frustration, perplexity, or conflict. Our discomfort is nothing more than the natural consequence of not finding that magic bullet.

Once we stop committing this first mistake of interpersonal communication, we stop searching for the magic bullet and, low and behold, our mouth doesn't go dry, our hands stop sweating, and our mind remains clear. We've moved from thinking in terms of exclamation points towards thinking in terms of question marks.

The art of questioning is to come to the realization that questions are neither reactive nor passive, nor a sign of weakness. We achieve our goals with difficult people and in difficult situations by looking for the logical question, not the elusive magic assertion. Rudyard Kipling captured the essence of asking versus stating: "I keep six honest serving men. They taught me all I knew. Their names are what and why and when and how and where and who."

Mistake 2

Asking a Question with Demeaning Tone or Intent

Questions are magic when they solicit another person's honest, spontaneous response, but they are destructive when the person answering feels threatened, manipulated, or psychologically abused. Just as questions can uplift and enhance, they can also demean.

> One of your employees has just informed you about an error he committed. Your immediate response is a question: "How could you *possibly* do something so stupid?" You follow this opening question with a series of equally demeaning queries: "How many times have I told you about this particular problem?" "Did you do that purposely to annoy me and make me look bad?"

> You grew up in a dysfunctional home. Your parents gave you everything except praise, respect, and self-esteem. You remember coming home after being cut from the high school basketball team, hoping to get empathy and support from your father. Instead you got a question: "What's the matter, you weren't good enough to make a lousy high school team?"

All demeaning questions have one thing in common: They are veiled attacks. Rather than asserting our intent to demean another, we camouflage our design in the form of a question.

What are the specific tests of a demeaning question? We believe there are two such tests:

> A question is demeaning if it's drenched in sarcasm. ("Where did you *get* that dress?")

> A question is demeaning if it diminishes the self-esteem of the person to whom it is posed. ("Do you *really* think you're ready

to take on this assignment?") You walk into a chic boutique dressed in T-shirt, cutoffs, and sandals. A salesperson approaches you and in a noblesse oblige tone asks, "Are you sure you're in the right store?"

Yes, demeaning questions will elicit a response. But none of the responses will produce the eight qualities of magical questions discussed in Chapter 1.

We open communication channels by posing questions that treat the other as a mature adult, not an immature child. Magical questions open communication channels; demeaning questions close them.

Mistake 3

Asking the Question in an Attempt to Manipulate, Control or "Play" with the Other Person

In Chapter 1 we said that questions are magic because they have the power to focus thoughts. However, sometimes in an attempt to focus the thoughts of others we consciously or unconsciously manipulate and control. If the respondent feels manipulated, we are not likely to achieve the intended effect. Rather than soliciting a response motivated by an honest desire to explore an issue, we are more likely to solicit a response motivated by a desire to protect, defend, and possibly counterattack.

You're in a discussion with a co-worker regarding vacation schedules. You're torn between two options. Your co-worker asks with raised voice, "I need to know your answer right now. What is it?" Are you likely to feel controlled? Absolutely.

What are the tests for determining if a question manipulates and controls? A question is likely to be perceived as manipulative and controlling if it:

1. limits response options and alternatives,
2. suggests or implies ulterior motives or hidden agenda, or
3. moves you in a direction you would rather not go.

The next time you are cross-examined in a court of law or the next time you observe an attorney questioning a hostile witness, listen carefully to the questions. If the attorney is good, all questions will pass these three tests.

Mistake 3 also indicates that questions may be perceived as game playing. Consider the following hypothetical exchange between Father Murphy and Rabbi Greene.

Murphy: Is it true that Jewish people tend to respond to questions with questions?

Greene: Why do you ask?

Murphy: We got into this discussion one night in my seminary. What do you think?

Greene: What was the consensus of the discussion?

Murphy: That it's a stereotype of Jewish problem solving, but that like all stereotypes it's true for some people some times. What's your opinion?

Greene: Why do you think some stereotypes are true for some people some of the time?

After a few minutes of this dialogue, Murphy should realize that Greene does not intend to answer a question with any response other than a question. Is Murphy likely to feel controlled and manipulated? Possibly, depending on his perceptions of Greene's intent. Is he likely to feel that Greene was playing with him, intending to have some fun at his expense? Probably.

The difference between control or manipulation and game playing is that the former has a bite to it, the latter does not. What they share is the feeling that the questioner is concealing his or her honest intent and is trying to place us in a disadvantaged position.

Mistake 4

Asking the Question and Failing
to Listen to the Answer

The purpose of asking a question is to buy time, to control emotions, to get new information on the table, or to move from a defensive posture to an offensive one. You're trying to turn a gut-wrenching, palm-sweating, heart-pounding situation into one where you regain composure and thought. Yet none of these objectives will be achieved if the other person feels that his response is going unheeded or if you in fact fail to listen.

After you've posed your question stop and devote full attention to the answer. If questioning is the key to unlocking the treasure chest of effective communication, the answer *is* the treasure. That answer will provide you with information you can use to achieve your goal.

When you listen use both your eyes and your ears. What is the person saying and how is she saying it? Focus on the broad range of her nonverbal messages: her facial expressions, gestures, eye contact, posture, and tone of voice.

If you feel that the person is uncomfortable with your question or is having trouble articulating an answer, follow the initial question with probes.

"Could you please explain that?"

"I'm not sure I understand. What do you mean?"

"I sense that you're uncomfortable. Why?"

"Is there something you're not telling me that I need to know?"

Questions are magic because you're able to respond to information you did not have prior to the question. But you can only realize that magic if you listen. Remember this simple three-stage sequence:

Stop looking for what to say;

Ask a question that focuses, clarifies, diffuses, bridges, or delays; and

Listen carefully to the answer.

Finally, listen with your "inner ear." Go beyond the actual *words* the other person is using and listen to the *emotions, inferences, assumptions*, and premises. Magical questions reflect feelings and emotions. They capture the essence of what someone *is* experiencing or what you would like them to experience. You capture this essence when you listen with your inner ear.

Mistake 5

Turning a Question into a Speech

Some people never know when to leave well enough alone. They eat that extra piece of pie even though they're full and then wind up paying for it with an upset stomach. They continue to sell the virtues of the product even after the customer decides to purchase it, casting suspicion both on the sales clerk and on the wisdom of the purchase. They put an extra bag of fertilizer on the lawn believing that if two bags will do the job, three bags will do it that much better, and end up with a burned lawn.

In the same way, some of us begin by asking a simple, direct question and end up with a convoluted message that does little more than confuse. Consider the following example.

> Your boss asks you to stay late to work on an important project. The request comes at 5 P.M. on a Friday, an hour and a half before you and your spouse will be hosting a party for fifteen people.

> You could respond magically by asking, "Exactly when do you need this project, and would it be all right for me to get it done anytime before that deadline, instead of working on it right now?"

> Or, you could turn the question into a speech by saying, "Do you need this done right away, because if you don't, I'd rather hold off starting on it until I'm finished with what I'm doing because I can get this particular job done before the end of the day, whereas if I start yours now it will take me beyond quitting time because it's not the kind of job I can just start and leave without finishing it, and if I stay long enough to finish it that will wreck plans that my husband and I have for this weekend, but of course if it's that important to you, I'll call him, but then I would probably do a better job on it if I waited until Monday morning to begin it, but would that create a problem for you?"

The problem with this speech is that you've given your boss conflicting messages and burdened him with unnecessary details. What exactly are you telling him and what exactly are you asking him? Make it easier on yourself and the other person. Ask simply, directly, and concisely.

There is a story about two seminarians trying to convince the head priest to allow smoking during private meditation. The first seminarian carries on for five minutes, tying together questions ("Why can't we smoke?") and assertions ("I think the policy is silly"). The priest listens patiently and says, "No!" The second seminarian asks a simple direct question: "Father, would you mind if I pray while I smoke?" The priest said, "Of course not, my son. You can pray all the time while you smoke." Focus the issue with a question. Save the speech for the podium.

Mistake 6

Asking Questions That Fail to Elicit
the Information You Need

So often when we're put on the spot, our brain goes dead and the right words escape our tongue. Our options for response seem to disappear or all look equally unattractive (for example, "Do you choose a pay cut or a demotion?"). Your way out of these situations is to ask a question for which the answer increases the quantity and the quality of your options.

The key to such magical questions is determining *why* people believe what they believe. Once you know the *reasons* behind their requests or assertions you're able to suggest mutually agreeable options. Ask questions to find out why insistent people want what they demand of you.

> Your biggest customer calls you and says, "I'm thoroughly disgusted with the way you filled my last order and I'm pulling my business from you." After your stomach bottoms out, you remember the magic words *why* and *what*. "Why do you feel so disgusted, and what can we do to make it right?"

> One of your most important and trusted vendors calls you and says, "We just can't meet your specifications without significantly raising the price." The magic of *why* and *what* save the day. "Why do you feel you can't meet our specifications without raising our prices, and what can we do to help you meet the specs without increased cost?"

> During your semiannual performance review you and your boss are at odds concerning the overall evaluation of your work. He believes you deserve a "Good," which translates into a seven percent raise; you believe you deserve an "Excellent," which would justify a merit increase of at least ten percent. Guess what two words come to the rescue? "Why do you believe I deserve the seven percent and not the ten percent, and what evidence of my performance would it take to change your mind?"

When we probe reasons, values, and needs to learn why people assert what they do, we are asking magical questions. We're obtaining information we can use to broaden our options or to create mutually acceptable options.

Debating the *what* (I said, you said; I believe, you believe; I want, you want) forces you to search for the elusive "right" thing to say, the "magic bullet." Instead of debating positions, probe reasons. When you do, the magical phrases will appear in the form of responses to the answers you've solicited through your questions.

Mistake 7

Thinking in Terms of Win-Lose
Versus Win-Win

Artful questions are those that broaden your options and at the same time are seen as nonmanipulative and noncontrolling by the respondent. They allow you to turn a situation where you feel either cornered or powerless into one where you feel empowered while at the same time making the other person feel that he too has not lost power and control. The key to achieving this goal is to strive for mutual gain rather than believing that there must always be a victor and a vanquished.

There are two techniques for achieving this goal. The first is to use the first person plural pronouns "we" and "us" instead of the singular pronouns "I," "me," and "you." The pronouns used in questions are signals of power, status, ego, and competition. Saying "*I've* got a problem" is significantly different than saying "*we've* got a problem." Saying "*You're* disagreeing with the proposal" is significantly different than saying "*We're* in disagreement."

The second technique is subtly to invite the other person to join you in mutual problem solving. Find a way to have the other person come up with a solution to the problem that he or she is attempting to dump on you. Phrase the question in such a way that the problem is of concern to both of you.

Suppose your boss asks you to work on a project that will overtax an already full calendar. You respond with a question reflecting Mistake 7: "Why do I have to work on it? My calendar is loaded now. Isn't there anyone else you can give it to?"

This line of questioning creates a power struggle: You feel you're going to lose by taking on any more work, and your boss is likely to feel that she's lost because you've questioned her judgment.

Look at the difference when you change the pronoun and reflect a win-win orientation. "We've got a lot to do in the unit right now. Do you have any suggestions on which projects I should table so we can get this out on time?" This question turns a potential conflict into one of mutual gain. It also reflects the strategy of recruiting the other person to help you solve your problem.

Affirming the Art of Asking Questions

This chapter highlighted the most common mistakes that prevent us from constructing magical questions. Let's summarize by recasting the mistakes into affirmations: positive actions to take to make sure your questions broaden your options.

1. Think in terms of question marks, not exclamation points. When you don't know what to say, say nothing. Ask a question instead.

2. Edit your questions for any tone (vocal inflection, sarcasm intonations) that could be demeaning or cause defensiveness.

3. Reject phrases or words that the other person would perceive as manipulative, controlling, or dishonest. Save your playing for the golf course, the game table, and the racquetball court.

4. Listen intently with both your ears and your eyes. Use your "inner ear" to uncover emotion and intent.

5. Pose direct and succinct questions to secure information. Save your speeches for the lectern.

6. Use the magic words *why* and *what* to find out why people believe what they believe.

7. Turn win-lose confrontations into win-win results. Use pronouns reflecting mutual gain ("we," "us," "ours"), and involve the other person in mutual problem solving with your questions.

Chapter

3

Managing Your Workload

In the 1980s American enterprise heeded the cry, "Do more with less." It was a time when we became more aware of the limits of our resources, both natural and financial. It was also a time when the economic aggressiveness of countries from the Pacific Rim, the European community, and elsewhere caused them to emerge as competitors to take seriously.

Management's hope that the 1990s would see a lessening of the demands on time, energy, and resourcefulness has not materialized. Resources continue to dwindle and competition continues to intensify to the point where the present call is, "Do even more with even less." As a result, managers and employees alike are working even harder than before.

The last thing we need in such tough times is to work with and for people who make our lives more complicated and who cause our already full plates to overflow. Here's how to use questions effectively to respond to situations that might otherwise overload you to the breaking point.

3-1

You're Given Too Much Work

There's so much work piled on your desk that you'd have to remove a ceiling panel to make room for another folder, and each job has a deadline attached to it. Then your boss walks in and says, "Please handle this for me. I need it done first thing next week."

? Which of My Current Jobs Should Be Put on the Back Burner While I Finish This?

This question gently reminds the boss of your heavy workload, and it presents you as a worker, not a whiner. Your boss might respond by asking what you're working on. If so, list your ongoing projects, emphasizing the most urgent. Don't take this as a chance to brief your boss on everything you're doing; just give an overview.

You hope your boss will answer the question by telling you what to postpone. If you're strongly opposed to that choice, offer an alternative. Otherwise, just say, "Thanks for the suggestion. That will help."

If your boss insists that you do everything, say that you'll do your best. But as soon as it becomes clear that important deadlines are going to be missed, get back to the boss with that information. Resist the temptation to say, "I told you so."

One way to prevent this sort of thing from happening again is to keep your boss updated on your workload. You also need to assert yourself forcefully, yet tactfully, whenever jobs are assigned to you that should be handled by someone else. On the other hand, consider the possibility that you may not be as overworked as you think, particularly in the boss's eyes.

? To Meet That Deadline, May I Delay Work on Project X? Or, May I Ask Frank to Give Me a Hand?

These are productive and assertive ways to deal with a boss who dumps on you. You're not complaining; merely asking for the go-ahead to meet the boss's needs. If the answer is yes, you're home free. If not, you have at least opened negotiations in a positive tone.

? May I Get This to You on Thursday Morning, First Thing?

You cannot meet the Tuesday deadline the boss has given. You might protest or sheepishly go along with this unreasonable request. Neither strategy is as good as simply asking for an alternative delivery date. The boss might agree! If she doesn't, you haven't lost anything, and you can then proceed to negotiate as suggested above.

3-2

You're Given an Unreasonable Deadline

You learn through your boss that the project you're working on must be brought to a conclusion two days earlier than originally requested. You can't believe that top management could be so short sighted. By insisting on an earlier delivery, they are practically guaranteeing a lower quality product than you know they want.

? Will You Approve the Steps Necessary to Meet That Delivery Date?

Expect to hear something like, "What do you mean?" This type of response opens the way for you to make the point you might not have felt comfortable offering in the first place: "The level of quality we need on this job isn't going to be possible with a shortened deadline."

At some point you hope to hear, "What steps do you suggest?" State them. If you'll be forced by the shorter deadline to deliver less precise goods, reduced quality or quantity, or less formality of presentation, get advanced recognition of these outcomes. If more resources are needed to compress the time before delivery, say so.

You don't want your boss to say, "No. You'll just have to do the best you can." If this is the rule of the road, be certain that the storms you encounter along the way are noted along with delivery of the final product. But *do not* complain about the conditions you faced or apologize for giving it your best effort.

Reflect on these questions for help in dealing with the future. Are you too much of a perfectionist and therefore unable to produce merely satisfactory results when conditions dictate? Do you "cry wolf" often, even though you reliably meet even the shortest of deadlines? Do you take too long on projects?

? May We Negotiate That Delivery Date?

If the answer is no, you can still fall back on the original question. If, instead, you hear "What do you mean?" or "Yes," we hope you have something to offer in trade for a relaxed deadline. That something needs to be of real value to the boss; only you know what that might be.

3-3
You're Asked to Do the Boss's Dirty Work

A disgruntled customer has been trying to get through on the telephone all morning to register a complaint with your boss. Tired of ducking calls, the boss slips into your office seeking refuge with a request: "I can't deal with that customer today. Please see what he wants."

? Can You Help Me See Why It Is Better
for *Me* to Do That?

A boss who would put you out front on tough assignments like this one needs to be put on notice with an assertive question that is not disrespectful. This particular one is likely to elicit, "What do you mean?" This opens the way for you to say, "I believe that this customer would feel much better after the chance to speak to *you*. There are certain problems around here that only you can fix."

If the boss insists ("I want *you* to call that customer") and you've made your point, stop protesting. Handle this assignment as sensitively and as competently as you can. Be certain you're representing the boss's precise intent.

Don't be overly resistive to requests such as these. One of your responsibilities is to help your boss out of tight jams. Furthermore, requests like this make a positive statement about your boss's level of trust in you.

? Wouldn't You Rather Do That Yourself?

Expect to hear, "No; why would I?" This opening is big enough to drive an eighteen-wheeler through. Give the argument you might have hesitated to put forth without such an invitation.

? Don't You Think the Customer Would Rather Hear Directly from the Manager in Charge?

This question is a declarative statement in disguise. It may bring the boss to his or her senses. If not, proceed as above.

? How Do You Want Me to Handle the Situation?

It's no use. *You* are going to be the one who waits on the customer. But you *are* representing the boss. Find out how to do it well. Once in a while this question will frustrate a boss who, rather than tell you how to handle the customer, may actually say, "Oh, I'll do it myself!"

3-4

You're Told to Stop Work on an Important Project

You've put six months of your life and all your energies into a plan that, if successful, will significantly enhance the effectiveness of your department. In fact, you are convinced that the benefits of the plan will go a long way towards assuring the economic future of the company. It's impossible to imagine such a promising project could be a casualty of the recent round of budget cutbacks, but it was. Your boss broke the bad news to you, saying that *no* new initiatives are being continued during the current financial hard times faced by the firm.

? Will You Give Me a Chance to Show You
What This Project Means to the Company?

Without making the boss look stupid or out of touch with reality, this question provides the opening you need to provide information the boss may not have. (Somewhere in that briefing show the boss how your project will enhance either one of the two things he really cares about: the bottom line and personal success.) At the same time, this question enables the boss to straighten you out, if necessary, on the political landscape that supports his demand.

The boss may feel that you've already made your case for continuance and may deny your request. But if you know that compelling benefits of the project are being overlooked, point them out. When you make this presentation be certain to emphasize only those project benefits that top management prizes and only those benefits that are almost certain to materialize.

The outcome of this situation is likely to teach you one of two lessons: Either you need to do a better job of making the value of your projects more apparent to upper management or your priorities are out of step with those of your superiors.

? What Would It Take to Turn This into a
Project That Is Too Important to Cancel?

You may have more luck with this variation than you'll have with the original question. That's because it in no way challenges the decision of your superiors. Instead, it provides them with new options to recast the project in a manner that provides greater benefits to the company. Be prepared, in case the question stumps them, to offer ideas of your own that you know will appeal to them and will keep the project alive.

3-5

You're Reassigned

Just when you've grown comfortable with the people with whom you work, knowledgeable of the customers you serve, and proficient with the tools you use, you've been told that you're needed elsewhere in the company. You move in two weeks and leave your current responsibilities behind.

? Is This Reassignment Negotiable?

There is nothing fancy with this question. If the answer is yes or maybe, start negotiating. Show the boss that it's in the firm's best interest to keep you where you are. Document the benefits of reconsideration, either in terms of *avoidance of pain* (for example, you and your eventual replacement won't have to be trained in new positions) or through *acquisition of pleasure* (for example, you're on the verge of a breakthrough that will fatten the bottom line).

If the answer to your question is no, do the best job you can of getting things in order for your replacement and see that the person you are replacing does the same for you.

? May We Postpone This Assignment Long Enough to Enable Me to Complete This Project?

With this question you're not fighting the original decision, merely asking for a delay that should prove to be in the company's best interest. If the answer is yes, you will be able to save a project that the boss will appreciate. You are also buying some time that may cause the boss to reverse the decision, especially once the quality of work you do on the final project is known. If the answer is no, at least you may have thereby absolved yourself of responsibility for any results that might be botched by your replacement.

3-6

You're Asked to Work Through a Vacation

It's the Friday afternoon before a long-awaited vacation. You've promised yourself and your family a true escape from the rigors of work. To your horror your boss comes into your office, sits down, and burdens you with this tale of woe. "I'm sorry, but I need to ask you to take the operating files with you so that you can fax the budget estimates for next fiscal year to me next week; we need them sooner than I thought."

? What Exactly Is It That You Need from Me Next Week That Cannot Wait Until I Return?

Ask this question as though you're conducting an interview; it may even be appropriate to take notes. Do not show disappointment or antagonism in your tone of voice. Find out precisely what upper management needs. You know your responsibilities far better than your boss does, and chances are excellent that you can figure out how to meet the expressed needs without making the sacrifice the boss assumes is necessary.

It may be that the original request was made in haste out of fear that your departure might leave your boss in a difficult situation. Your question may cause your superiors to think more clearly and to identify exactly what they need from you before you leave. The modified request may be more precise and may likely be easier to fulfill than the original one. And your boss, when pressed, may realize that the need may not be as urgent as first thought.

If you handle this situation with the mutual goals of rescuing both your boss and your vacation, you're both likely to be pleased with the results.

? What If I Can Find Another Way to Meet Your Needs?

You may prefer this opener; it is less confrontive than the original. It also puts a bit more of the burden for a new game plan on you. The dreaded answer is, "There is no other way." Naturally, you are hoping for "That would be fine" or "What do you have in mind?" At this point, make an alternative suggestion that will get the data to your boss without wrecking your vacation. If you cannot think of one on the spot, make certain you understand what the boss needs and then ask for a few moments to collect your thoughts. The smartest strategy here is to come up with a plan that both saves your vacation and gives the boss *even more* than his or her original idea did. ("Boss, I have an idea for getting those budget estimates to you even quicker and with greater accuracy.")

3-7

You Don't Get the Help You Were Promised

You started work on a project with the enthusiastic support of upper management and with a pledge that all the staff needed to complete the project would be available to you as needed. You've held up your end of the bargain; the success of the project is fully meeting expectations. But you're not getting what was promised to you, and what you need, to complete the job. Top management still counts on successful results. You feel betrayed.

? Do You Have Any Suggestions for Keeping the Project Alive?

This question is a recommended alternative to complaining that you have been let down. It should be asked of the person who has commissioned the project and has a stake in its success, and it may jolt that person into making good on the guarantee to commit the resources.

The answer is likely to be, "What do you mean 'keep it alive'?" Your response can be, "Without having the remainder of the previously allocated personnel funds transferred to my budget, I'm afraid I'll be forced to cut back our efforts substantially."

Notice how you could have simply asked for the funds, but without the same impact. You wouldn't have commanded the same undivided attention. Besides, a no would have forced you to say that without the money the project would stop, and that sounds like a nasty threat.

? Are You Aware That Completion of the Project Is in Jeopardy?

Ask this of the superior who may not be aware of what's going on. Otherwise, you should get results similar to what you can expect with the original question.

? Would You Like Me to Stop Working on the Project?

This question is far more confrontational than the original question. Use it only after less antagonistic approaches have failed. The likely answer is, "No, of course not!" or something much stronger and more negative. Be prepared to take your final stand, whatever that may be.

3-8

Your Job Becomes Too Much for You

The word burnout must have been coined for you. You work ten hours a day, six days a week, doing the work of two people. And that's only when there aren't any crises! You don't think you can keep this pace up much longer, and there's no relief in sight. If someone were to ask how your personal life is, you'd have to answer, "What personal life?"

You are thankful to have such a good job, but you're not sure if you're willing to continue paying such a high price for it. You have to figure out a way to talk to your boss about the enormous pressures you are under without appearing to be ungrateful for the opportunities she gives you to take on these important responsibilities.

? May I Have Two Weeks Off?

This is the primary question because it should be your starting point. You need to get away from the job for a while to gain the perspective you need to devise long-term strategies for dealing with its pressures. Besides, people who have intense jobs need intense vacations. Long weekends, or even a week off, may not be sufficiently refreshing and may do little to recharge your mental, emotional, and physical batteries. Two weeks on a beach or, even better, a month, are much more beneficial than a day here and a day there.

While you're gone, make plans for the future: How can you deal more effectively with your workload? What ideas do you have for sharing the work with others who are less pressured than you? Which of the jobs that you now do may not need to be done at all? Should you begin looking for another job? Can you afford early retirement?

If your boss will not give you the time off, either of the last two questions in the previous paragraph may be the most realistic ones to consider.

? May We Discuss the Possibility of a Restructuring?

Use this question if not everyone in the office is working as hard as you are. Your goal is to create a more equitable balance.

Chances are your boss will let you develop this idea further, but be prepared. Base your presentation on a well-documented study of the responsibilities in your department. Show that the current work distribution is unequal. Make recommendations for reassignments, and show how these recommendations benefit the company beyond just making your workload more manageable.

? Are All These Tasks That I Perform Necessary?

Ask this question only after having carefully analyzed the work done within the office. Parkinson's law says that the work in any organization expands to fit the number of people available to do it. The problem comes when the staff size is trimmed, which has been the case in your office, and the work is not trimmed along with it, again the case in your office.

Make a list of all the major tasks you perform, or the entire staff performs, in order of importance. Recommend to your boss that time devoted to some of the lower priority tasks be reduced or that those tasks be eliminated entirely. Help your boss see that what's really important will be done far more effectively if these kinds of decisions are made.

3-9

You Take On More Than You Should

Ever since you were a child you had trouble saying no to your friends. Your desire to be liked and accepted usually meant that you worked yourself to a frazzle. As an adult the only thing that's changed is that the frazzle is beginning to affect your personal and professional lives. You still take on more than you should and you still have trouble saying no. Your committee assignments at the church, your children's school, and your professional association, not to mention the fifty hours you spend on the job each week, are turning you into a nervous wreck.

? What Am I Trying to Prove?

People who take on tasks beyond reasonable limits or volunteer beyond sensible bounds are trying to prove something. Their ultimate motivation is to show others that they are worthy. Unfortunately, this motivation produces one of two consequences: You either meet all demands, thereby exacting a toll on your physical and mental health, or you fail to accomplish everything, thereby disappointing someone.

In either case you lose. Step back and examine your motivation. Stop trying to prove something that has nothing to do with the work you accomplish or the favors you perform. You are worthy.

? What Am I Doing to Cause the Stress and Pressure I Feel?

This question suggests that you may be an enabler: unconsciously reinforcing the behavior you're trying to change. Don't tell yourself that you're feeling abused and overworked in one breath while you take on new assignments in another.

Take a close look at what you're doing to create your own stress. If you're a workaholic, what are you going to do to stop it? Look in the mirror; you may see your own worst enemy.

? What Do I Really Value in Life?

This question is pivotal: Step back and prioritize. What's important to you and why? For example, if you believe that your family is a vital part of your life, what are you doing to live that belief? One primary reason we take on more than we should is because we foolishly think we can do it all without hurting anybody or ourselves. That's a destructive myth. No one can do it all or be all things to all people. Determine who and what's important in your life and make decisions today consistent with that determination.

Chapter

4

Satisfying Bosses

Few of us are in the position to be as direct with our boss as we'd like to be. After all, bosses have more power and authority than we do. When put under pressure or when experiencing distress, we may not be totally honest regarding their behaviors that cause problems for us. In this case, it is especially valuable to have penetrating questions at our disposal, questions that make the point without threatening, angering, or otherwise disappointing the boss. That's what these questions accomplish.

4-1

You're Told That You Don't Supervise Well

You are in the boss's office for your weekly update. She was agitated from the moment you came in and has just revealed why. As the two of you discuss the previous quarter's performance indicators, she says in a frustrated voice that if you would only be more assertive with your employees, you'd get better results. You know this couldn't be further from the truth.

? What Specific Performance Problems Are
Created by the Way I Relate to My People?

Whenever the effectiveness of your leadership style is questioned, it is natural to feel under attack. But a defensive response to your boss is not going to be productive. Stifle your defensiveness. Instead, ask for specifics. Push for evidence that your approach with employees is not in the best interest of organizational quality. If the boss responds with "data" that you consider to be invalid or vague ("It's causing a morale problem"), perhaps you can challenge it respectfully but assertively. If the boss refuses to back up the assertion, yet still sticks to it, you have at least served notice of your refusal to accept opinions about your performance without documentation.

Be prepared for the possibility that the boss will make a good point. Acknowledge it and back down as appropriate.

? How Do You Want Me to Handle Situations
Such As That One in the Future?

If the criticism is of a particular instance that you did not handle as well as the boss would have, this question enables you to push for specific guidance on what you should have done. Make this inquiry even more powerful by replacing "such as that one in the future" with something like "where an employee with Pat's track record and position does what he did with the visible impact on others that it had?" If your response to Pat was a sensible one, you are making it difficult for the boss to claim it wasn't.

4-2

You're Told to Delegate Differently

Your previous boss managed close to the vest and expected his subordinate managers to do the same. To meet his demands for instant updates you needed to be in touch with everything going on. You've had some difficulty getting used to your current boss, who is quite the opposite. She believes in empowering employees by giving them greater ownership for decision making. In the past she has asked you to share more responsibility with your direct reports; now she is demanding it.

? What Responsibilities Would You Like Me to Reassign?

Most managers don't share enough of their responsibilities with employees. Your boss may be correct in asking you to delegate more to them. With this question you'll get the opportunity to discuss just what tasks you should push downward in the hierarchy and perhaps even how to accomplish this transfer. If neither the boss nor you can come up with any workable ideas here, this question may get the boss off your back so you can get on with your work.

? Will You Support My Turning Over the Proofing and Editing of the Newsletter to Rose Marie?

The first step in delegation is to search for untapped talents and unproductive time among your subordinates. The second step is to look for matches between available human resources and tasks that might make sense for you to release. Your analysis tells you that Rose Marie is right for the newsletter, but first you need to confirm your judgment with the person—your boss—who ultimately holds you accountable for the quality of the newsletter.

Should the answer be no, ask whether it's the giving up of the newsletter or the assigning of Rose Marie that is a problem. Negotiate for a solution that meets the needs of both you and the boss.

If the answer is yes, you have accomplished a critical step in delegation: getting the assent of your boss. You may need this later when you're looking for support in dealing with problems surrounding the delegation.

4-3

You're Expected to Act in Conflict with Your Personal Values

You have been steering your customers away from one of your company's products because you don't have much faith in it. Your boss learned about this after reviewing your sales figures. His response was not only to demand that you begin pushing this product again, but to insist that you call on your largest client to extol its virtues. Even though this product is not defective or harmful in any way, the boss's expectations create a serious ethical dilemma for you. This product will not serve the customer as well as other ones you had planned to present.

? Will You Please Help Me to See How
This Request Is Fully Consistent with My
Personal Values?

This statement will need to be stated more specifically in terms of the actual principles being violated. When it is, the boss is put on notice that you have values that are endangered by the request.

You'll hope to get some new information that calms your concern. If not, even though it's obvious that you've made yourself perfectly clear, the time for questioning has passed. Your choices at this point are apparent: (1) Respectfully refuse to comply, (2) agree to comply with the hope that you can buy time to devise another boss-pleasing strategy later, or (3) find yourself another job.

? If I Can Show You That a Different
Approach (other Than Yours) Will
Yield a Higher Profit, Will You
Support It?

Your boss wants to make money. Pushing this hot button may grant you a reprieve. If you've already done your homework, you'll be able to show him how your sales strategy is in fact more profitable in the long run than the one he wants you to pursue. If the product he is promoting is truly not in the customer's best interest, even though it may be more profitable per unit, you ought to be able to argue successfully for its long-run benefits to the bottom line.

If your ethical instincts are correct, regardless of the particular ethical conflict you face in your company, you ought to be able to link your approach with bottom-line victory. If you cannot make the linkage, consider the possibility that your concerns may not be as valid as you think.

4-4

You Receive a Low or Ambiguous Performance Rating

You hate performance reviews, and this one is proving to be no exception. The boss just rattled off a litany of deficiencies to be corrected, but he has not been very clear on what positive actions you can take to correct them. You know he's not satisfied with your work, but you don't know why.

? What Exactly Do I Need to Do More
of and Less of to Convince You That I Am
Meeting Your Requirements?

This is a powerful question. If your performance is indeed substandard, it should yield the information you need to begin fulfilling your boss's expectations in clearer and more specific terms than you have perhaps ever received in the past. (Make certain that the feedback you receive is behavioral and measurable. For example, "Keep me informed weekly on the progress of the XYZ project.") Probe for specifics.

If your alleged deficiencies have no basis in fact, this question will bare that. If your evaluator cannot or will not provide supporting evidence for the low evaluation, you may want to document this unfulfilled request on the performance review form itself or in a memorandum for the record.

? What Strengths Do I Have That You Feel I Can Use to Pull Myself Up in the Ratings?

This question has two purposes. One is to get ideas from the boss for performance improvement actions you can take. The other is to encourage the boss to focus a bit on your positive qualities. You're doing some things well, and you deserve credit for them. You also want to know what current strengths you should show even more of in the future.

? Would This Be an Example of Something I Can Do to Improve My Performance?

Test out several initiatives with the boss. Get a reaction to each of them. Implement the ones that get the most favorable response.

4-5

You're Not Getting Any Feedback on Your Performance

A friend complained to you today at lunch that her boss is overly critical, always finding fault with her work. She asked you what you thought of the feedback you receive from your supervisor. You thought for a moment and then responded, "*What* feedback?" And that's the truth. You know that your company has a performance review form that's supposed to be used once a year along with a coaching meeting. Some of your colleagues claim that their bosses even ask them to do a self-assessment with the form as part of the process. You've worked here for over two years and you haven't even seen the form. You don't know how your boss gets away with not giving you performance evaluations, but he does. You decide to get some action in your next meeting with your boss.

? If I Can Get a Copy of the Company's
Performance Review Form, Would You Be
Willing to Fill One Out on Me?

This request would be difficult for your boss to deny, especially if he is currently in violation of the company's human resource policy. If he agrees, get the form on his desk within twenty-four hours. If he refuses or procrastinates, revert to an alternative question.

? If I Perform a Self-assessment Using
the Company's Performance Review Form,
Would You Be Willing to Look It Over?

Ask this if the original question would make your boss angry or back him into a corner. He's not likely to turn you down. If he does, why are you working for him?

? What Can I Do More of, or What Can I Do
Less of, to Be Certain to Fulfill Your
Requirements on This Project?

You may make it easier for your boss to give you feedback if you ask for it in relation to a certain task you perform. If, in place of a specific question, you were to ask something like, "How am I doing on this project?" you would probably be answered, "Fine" or "No problems that I know of." This response isn't very helpful. You need specifics, and you need them *before* there are problems of which the boss is aware. This question digs for behavioral feedback, which will empower you to make midcourse corrections that get you closer to the performance the boss wants but perhaps hasn't clearly identified up to now.

? Of All the Tasks I Perform, What Do You Like
Best and What Do You Like Least?

This question will work well if you present it along with a listing of, say, twenty tasks you perform. Ask the boss to identify the three tasks he is most satisfied with and to tell you what is good about the job you do on them. Also ask him to identify the three tasks he believes can stand the greatest improvement, and to specify the improvement he desires on each of them.

This approach will be the least threatening for the boss, especially if he adopts this feedback strategy for *every* employee, all of whom are going to have their work criticized in exactly three areas. None will be singled out.

4-6

You're Told You Don't Measure Up to Peers

No one likes to be called on the carpet. It's even worse to be compared negatively to the people who work alongside you. This is exactly what your boss just did. You not only heard about your inadequacies, you were also criticized for not being as effective as one of your peers.

? If Quang Is the Standard Against Which
I Should Be Performing, May I Ask Him to
Share Some Ideas for Success with Me?

Your boss has been as unfair to your peer as to you in making this comparison. Don't be resentful of the wrong person. When you get the go-ahead to consult with this peer, be genuinely interested in the critical success factors he or she has applied in pleasing the boss. Then, make them work for you.

Another goal this question may accomplish is to discourage the boss from making this comparison in the future and instead to begin being more specific with his or her feedback.

? Which Of Quang's Actions Would You
Like Me to Copy?

This question may cause the boss to back down with, "I don't expect you to work the same way Quang does." If you feel sufficiently empowered, respond with, "Then why do you compare me to him?"

If the boss responds with ideas, get specifics. Repeat them back as you hear them. If they are ridiculous, they'll sound that way to the boss as you repeat them. If they are implementable, you can make certain you understand as well as ask questions about them.

4-7

Your Authority Is Circumvented

When you first came to work for your boss, you liked the way she stayed in close touch with the people you supervise and you appreciated her open-door policy. Those you supervise also enjoyed the direct access they had to her.

But over the past few months, it's gone too far. When she wants to announce a change, she often bypasses you and tells them herself. When they have a concern they believe that you can't handle, they take it directly to her. It's now at the point that if they don't agree with something you ask them to do, they go straight to her for an appeal, *and she responds to it.*

? May I Ask for Your Help in Maintaining Authority with My Employees?

It's difficult to imagine any response other than, "Of course you may." This is the opening you want. Now you can say something like, "Great! The next time one of them stops you in the office to inquire about something you and I may or may not have discussed, would you please refer that person to me for an answer? Jan's success in getting approval from you for a fall vacation may encourage his peers to begin going to you for decisions and help that they should bring to me."

? Have You Ever Been in a Leadership Situation Where the Power of Your Position Gradually Eroded Away?

The boss's answer really doesn't matter. This question serves the purpose of turning the momentum of the situation over to you. Say exactly what's happening. Give specific examples. Make certain you have your facts straight. If the boss can refute your claims or if you overstate your position, she may judge you as being paranoid and may replace you with someone who she thinks is not.

In your presentation, document the negative impact the circumvention is having on performance. Don't give her cause to believe that your motive is merely to protect your turf or your ego.

4-8

Your Boss Doesn't Listen to You

A friend once told you she works for a "deaf ear," and now you know what she was talking about. Your boss doesn't pay much attention to ideas from others, particularly those lower in the management hierarchy. For example, you gave him what you felt was a great suggestion two weeks ago, but haven't heard anything back on it. You are convinced that unless you revive the idea, it will remain ignored.

? Were You Able to Make Use
of the Information I Gave You
Two Weeks Ago?

This is one of many ways to jog the memory of a forgetful boss or to jog the conscience of a derelict one. If you elicit a no, ask first if there's any additional information you might provide that would be helpful. If there is none, request permission to carry the idea forth on your own.

? Have You Made a Decision Regarding
the Proposal I Brought to You Two
Weeks Ago?

This is a restatement of the primary question. It may apply more pressure because of the words "decision" and "proposal."

? Can You Suggest a More Effective
Approach for Me to Use in Communicating
Ideas That I Believe Will Improve the Way
We Do Things Around Here?

It's best to say this *immediately* following failure to get response to get one of your suggestions. If you wait until later, expect the boss to say, "What do you mean?" You respond with a description, not an interpretation, of your most recent failed attempt to have your input acknowledged. Listen carefully to the feedback and learn what it will take to get more of your ideas bought. Don't settle for something like, "Give me ideas I can use" without pushing for a description of their qualities.

4-9

You Don't Know What Your Boss Expects, or Your Boss Is a Perfectionist

You have little luck satisfying your boss. It seems as if every time you do something for her she isn't satisfied with the results. When you leave her office with an assignment you *think* you know how she wants it done, but that rarely proves to be the case. She changes her mind between the beginning and the end of an assignment, doesn't tell you exactly what her expectations are at the beginning, or expects far more than is humanly possible to produce. You vow never to accept another assignment from her without being certain what she wants.

? How Will My Efforts on This Assignment
Help You?

It is important that you know *why* you're doing any job for your boss. In this way you are more likely to produce the result he or she desires. Furthermore, you'll be able to make wise decisions along the way when you encounter situations for which the boss's instructions don't prepare you.

? Is This What You're Looking For?

Lay out exactly what you're planning to do, how you will do it, and the type of results you expect. Get the boss's approval. Take notes so that you won't forget the agreement and so you can thrust it in the boss's face later if she switches her desires without notification.

If she appears to be asking for more than you believe you can reasonably deliver, point out the cost of going after it. Don't be negative; you'll be accused of shirking your duties. Get her to see that her unrealistic expectations are not in the best interests of the team or the organization. If, despite your argument, she insists, deliver or resign.

? What Should I Be Most Careful
of in Performing This Assignment?

This is just another way of saying, "What's really important to you?" Repeat the answer you hear to be certain you both share the same mental image of what you'll bring back.

4-10

You're Afraid of Your Boss

You're starting to lose sleep and weight. Your boss intimidates you. It's getting to the point where you look for ways to avoid running into your boss, which is not an easy thing to do considering that his office is adjacent to yours. You seem to be working harder to avoid him than you are in doing your job, and your performance is suffering as a result. After much thinking and with all the courage you can muster, you walk into his office, sit down, and raise the issue.

? What Can You and I Do to Change Our
Relationship So That It's More Mutually
Rewarding and Productive?

Chances are your boss is tuned into your avoidance behavior and is grateful for the opportunity your question provides. He may give you specific feedback concerning why you might be fearing him or why he might be intimidating you.

If he seems surprised by your question, you have learned a very important lesson. Your boss is telling you that he believes the relationship is fine and that it conforms to his expectations.

That's good news and bad news. The good news is that he is not consciously trying to intimidate you. The bad news is that you *are* feeling intimidated. Tell him what you are feeling and why. Don't leave his office until you feel comfortable that he understands you, you understand him, and that your relationship has hope of changing.

? Am I Intimidated by People in Power Generally or Is My Boss the Exception?

This introspective question asks you to consider your self-esteem and self-confidence in general. It's quite possible that you are intimidated by power and not specifically by your boss. If that is the case, you need a course in assertiveness training or a session with a counselor. One of the basic tenets of personal development is that you must feel good about yourself before you start dealing with others.

Don't necessarily attribute the source of intimidation to your boss's intent or behavior. In fact, the reason for your fear lies within you. You can't intimidate someone who refuses to be intimidated.

? Is My Fear of My Boss Hurting My Career?

This question probes the personal costs you may be incurring because of the fear. One of the reasons we might not confront the fear is that we never fully acknowledge the pain it creates or the costs we incur. When you answer this question honestly you should have the motivation you need for confronting and curing your phobia.

4-11

Your Boss Blames You for His Mistake

You make enough of your own mistakes without being blamed for others' mistakes. It's especially discouraging when the boss is the one who is making you look bad. This happened when the CEO called your boss to complain about an expenditure that you were directed to make by the boss. You just learned that the outcome of the conversation was that you took the hit. This isn't the first time you've been smeared when your boss ducked, but you intend for it to be the last. You decide to defend your honor without accusing, threatening, or angering your boss.

? Was I the One Who Authorized the XYZ Purchase?

You fully expect the boss to answer, "No, you didn't have the authority to do so. Why do you ask?" Your response will be, "Because I understand that the CEO is blaming me for it. Will you have the opportunity to straighten her out?"

If he says yes, show shock. Refer to any documentation that refutes his claim. Ask for a complete clarification of your responsibilities to prevent similar misunderstandings.

This question and your responses alert the boss that you are aware of what he has done and that the truth might even get back to the CEO. While it may not get him to retract his story and the blame, it puts him on notice that you will not tolerate his behavior the next time he allows you to be falsely accused.

? Is It True That the CEO Is Blaming Me for the XYZ Purchase?

This is a more direct approach. If the answer is no, provide whatever data you have to the contrary. Ask how you would be faulted for following orders. If the answer is yes, ask why. You may want to use material from the previous question.

? Did I Err in Complying with Your Directive to Make the XYZ Purchase?

This is a powerful question. Your boss has no way out. He will almost certainly say no. Then you will say, "Then why am I being criticized for it?" Perhaps he will respond by accusing you of being too sensitive to pressure, being paranoid, or not being a team player. Responses such as these are cause for discouragement and for re-thinking the wisdom of continuing in your current position.

In the event that he says yes, respond with, "How can that be, since I was only doing what you had requested?" Listen very care-fully to his answer for two reasons. First, there's no predicting what it might be. Second, it may point out some error you made as you thought you were properly complying with your boss's wishes.

4-12

Your Boss Loses Her Temper at You

You'd like to forget today's staff meeting. The boss's strain over delays in her favorite project erupted into a tirade aimed at you. During your report she asked how feasible it would be for you to halve the time you need to finish your portion of the work. You responded that you were already working as hard as you could and that there just aren't enough hours in the day to get everything done. That was the wrong thing to say! She then accused you and everyone else of not being committed enough to stay a little later, forgo coffee breaks, and even take work home to accomplish the work. You were dumbfounded by the outburst, and only later in the day did you summon the courage to confront her. At first you decided just to forgive her, but then you became indignant at her charges. You put in a lot of noncompensated overtime and take more than your share of work home. You are one of her most dedicated and hard-working employees.

? What Can I Do to Help Relieve Some
of the Strain I've Seen in You Lately?

Some would criticize this question as being too kind a response to the awful treatment just received at the boss's hands. Not at all! Yes, it is kind, but it is also cleverly powerful.

Don't ask this of a boss who is likely to say, "Yes, start doing your work!" If you hear yes, you want it to be a genuine request for help. And if you show a desire to help the boss, you're on the right side of one of the most powerful people in your life. You also stand to make a positive contribution to your own sanity on the job.

Even if the boss declines your offer to help, you've accomplished two things. First, you've shown her that you care. Second, you have gently informed her that her actions at the staff meeting have not been forgotten. If she says, "What makes you think I'm strained?" answer that if she were herself, she wouldn't have acted as she did.

? Are You Aware of the Embarrassment I Experienced in This Morning's Staff Meeting?

If this question elicits an apology that sounds sincere, and if the explosion was one of the first you have seen, by all means accept the apology. If, however, the staff meeting was merely a replay of many that have gone before it, you probably won't want to accept the apology. A wiser strategy would be to ask for a commitment that it won't happen again.

If you get no sympathy for your humiliation, this says one of two things: Either your boss is under even more strain than you thought, or you don't want to work for this person much longer.

? Did You Really Mean to Imply That I'm Not Giving 100 Percent to My Job?

If your boss has forgotten the outburst, she may be genuinely puzzled by your question, and you may need to explain the motivation for your question. If she answers that she meant what she said, go on to the next question. If she apologizes, reread the preceding advice.

? What Can I Do to Convince You That I'm Giving My All to This Project?

This is an honest and straightforward request for the data your boss wants as proof that her allegation is false. If she answers with the parameters you want, provide the data on those parameters that will prove your worth. If she presents unreasonable parameters (for example, "Show me that you're taking home four hours of work every night"), tell her why you believe that those are unfair or invalid parameters. If she refuses to cooperate with the question, point out the unfairness of her response, given her accusations in the staff meeting.

4-13

Your Boss Won't Delegate the Authority You Need to Do Your Job

You know what it means to "manage close to the vest." You have a daily example to observe. Your boss expects a lot from you but without giving you everything you need to get things done. You have the people, the equipment, and usually even the money, but you lack something far more important than any of those resources. You lack the *authority* you need to orchestrate the people, the equipment, and the money. An example of this occurred this morning when you had to pass on an unexpected offer from a vendor to provide your company with supplies at a very favorable price, but needed a yes or no within an hour. The boss was out of town and not reachable, but you should have had the authority to accept the offer and save the company money. You've raised the issue with him before, but not as effectively as you plan to when he gets back from his trip.

? How Would You Like for Me to Save Money for the Company?

Expect to hear, "Sounds good. What do you have in mind?" Tell your story about the lost opportunity with the vendor, and describe one or two other plausible scenarios where equal financial advantages could be achieved if you could respond quickly to unexpected opportunities.

? Would You Like Me to Help You Find More Time in Your Day?

If your boss is "micro" managing the operation, he's probably feeling even more pain from his excessive workload than you are. Try to sell the idea of relieving him of some of the tedium that prevents his doing more of the creative thinking that the organization needs from him.

If he answers no to this question, you got three strikes with one swing. If he says yes, be prepared with specific suggestions of tasks for which you can relieve him, including purchase decisions.

? Would You Be Willing to Take a Small Risk with the Potential of a Big Gain?

Your boss may be afraid to trust you with his responsibilities or he may be afraid that he will miss those tasks. This question will lead to a discussion to allay those fears. When he answers yes, describe your proposal replete with the advantages described in the first two questions here. That's the "big gain." The "small risk" is your suggestion that he feel totally free to take back at any time any of the responsibilities that are either giving you trouble or missed by him.

4-14

You've Been Told That Your Operating Budget Will Be Cut Substantially

You may never take another vacation. While at poolside with your family, you answered a telephone page from your boss. She apologized for interrupting your holiday, but she needed to get some information quickly from each of her direct reports. For you the question was, "How would you propose to absorb a 12% funding reduction of your operating plan?" You listen incredulously; just when your unit was beginning to click comes this. You're disillusioned and speechless, but you agree to call her back tomorrow with at least a rough idea of how you'll deal with the reduction.

After regaining your wits, you think of an alternative strategy to merely complying with your boss's request. You plan your call to the boss as a question-and-answer session. You list three questions for her, as well as two that you'll pose in a meeting of your staff as soon as you return from vacation.

? How Does the Cut We're Being Asked to Take Compare with the Cuts Being Taken Elsewhere in the Organization?

Is your area being asked to absorb more or less than its share of whatever paybacks are being extracted from the company's operating units? Put your budget cut into perspective. What does your cut tell you about the relative confidence your boss has in you? For example, if other unit budgets are being reduced by fifteen to twenty percent, you may have just received an unmistakable vote of confidence. Thank your boss for it. But, if you appear to have been singled out for one of the deepest cuts, take notice. Ask why she felt the need to assess you so harshly.

? If I Could Show You That Cutting Our Budget Would Result in a Revenue Loss Greater Than the Budget Savings, Would You Reverse the Decision?

You may not be able to ask this question until you can perform an analysis of the relationship between your budget and your revenues. You may also want to first conduct the meeting where the final two questions of this section are asked and answered. And if you can't stand behind it you certainly should not ask it.

? If I Could Show You That *Increasing* Our Budget Would Generate More Revenue Than the Addition to Our Budget, Would You Approve It?

This is nearly the same as the preceding question. You would ask it of a boss who is more impressed by revenue enhancement than cost containment.

❓ What Can We Do to Save Money? What Can We Do to Make Money?

Convene your employees for a brainstorming session. Tell them of your two goals: to identify waste and inefficiencies that, if corrected, would make any imminent budget cut less severe and might eliminate the need for reductions in force; and to find new ways of generating revenue so that you can show the boss that reduced resources will interfere with the opportunity for increased profit.

Have two large sheets of flip-chart paper mounted in the front of the room. At the top of one write "Save money," and at the top of the other write "Make money." Ask your employees to brainstorm without editorial comment. Get all the ideas out before you or others analyze them for probable impact.

One of the authors actually faced the budget crisis described above. He emerged from a brainstorming session with data that convinced his boss to restore over two thirds of a $175,000 proposed reduction in funding for his department.

Chapter

5

Surviving Plateaus, Layoffs, and Firings

In an earlier, more serene, and more predictable time, competent managers believed that they had control over their careers. Upward mobility was characterized by predictable, if gradual, ascendance in the organizational hierarchy with concomitant increases in power, status, and salary. And in those rare instances where promotion was delayed, thwarted, or denied, managers still knew that things would ultimately work out and that a bit more patience would see them through to eventual career success. They knew that their competence, dedication, and hard work would pay off.

We now live in a different world. Managers must not only be competent, but they must actively negotiate their careers. The chaotic business climate means that managerial success won't necessarily equal career success. Managers must prepare themselves for the possibilities of plateaus, layoffs, and firings as well as the trauma they generate. In this chapter, we present questions to ask when confronting these career shocks.

<u>**5-1**</u>

You Wonder If You're in the Right Job

You've been in your current job for a couple of years and have achieved a degree of success. But you're starting to see your youth pass, along with some drive and enthusiasm. You're concerned because you don't want to look back ten years from now and feel that you've wasted your life. You're seriously concerned that you may be in the wrong job. You recline in your chair and stare up at the ceiling.

? What Could Change in My Job
during the Next Six Months That Would
Make It More Challenging and Rewarding
than It Is Right Now?

This question captures the essence of personal growth on the job. You are projecting into the future and focusing on issues that could reinforce current stagnation or provide the challenge you're seeking.

You can pose this question to yourself or to your boss. Your answer may generate some ideas of what you could do to breathe life back into your job. Your boss's answer may reveal plans she has for you that you have not considered. Posing the question to your boss is also an excellent technique for soliciting career counseling from the one person who currently has the second greatest control over your career.

? How Likely Is It That If I Stay in My Current
Job for Another Ten Years, I Will Look Back
with Regret?

A pundit once observed that the saddest words in the English language are "I wish I had ... " Years hence, when you look back on your job, you'd like to be able to say that you contributed something worthwhile and did so in an energetic, creative way. If you don't think you'll be able to say that about your job, now is the time to change.

Engage in a little imaginary time travel. Move yourself into the future and take a hard look at your job. Examine the time, energy, and creativity you contributed and what you and others got back. Was it worth it?

? In the Past Twelve Months, What Have I
Done on This Job That Made Me Feel
Creative, Energetic, and Important?

If you haven't done anything on your job to feel creative or energetic and the prospects for these intrinsic rewards look grim, you have two options. You can either sit back and hope the job will change, or you can do something to bring about the change.

Hope leaves your fate in the hands of others; proactive behavior makes you the captain of your own ship. Start managing your career today. Set personal development goals for yourself. Learn new skills. Make new relationships. Enrich your job by seeking greater autonomy, by making it more valuable to the customers you serve, and by finding new and better ways to do it.

5-2

You Feel Burned Out

You got the official diagnosis from your physician this morning: "There's nothing wrong with you medically. You're just emotionally and physically worn out." That's the good news. The bad news is that the doctor couldn't prescribe any salve, elixir, or pill. This is something you're going to have to treat on your own. But how? You go back to your office, put your feet on your desk, and ponder your dilemma.

? What Should I Do More of and What Should
I Do Less of to Experience Greater Joy,
Enthusiasm, and Fulfillment in My Life?

When you're experiencing burnout, your body is telling you something important and you should listen. It's telling you that you need to gain control over your life. You need to say yes to those things that are personally and professionally rewarding and no to those that are personally and professionally draining.

This question focuses on the draining and the rewarding facets of your professional and personal life. It tells you that there are things you must do more of (say yes to) and things you must do less of (say no to).

If the answer to this question doesn't come to you while your feet are propped up on your desk, take them off the desk and go to a zoo, beach, bookstore, cathedral, park, or any other place where you can experience solitude and be introspective. As you're walking, repeat the question and listen to your answers.

? How Can I Take Vacations
   without Leaving Town?

Look for ways to take vacations without leaving town. Vacations are therapeutic because they provide a change of scenery and take us away from our daily grind. You can achieve these same objectives without getting on a plane or cruise ship. Seek and you will find therapy in your hometown.

When you do leave work, make sure you *leave* work. Keep your home life separate from your work life. Find an hour for yourself every day. During that hour engage in a true leisure activity. Do something you enjoy. Don't always plan your personal hour in advance; be spontaneous. Vacations can be as much a state of mind as they are an extended physical separation from work.

? What Can I Do to Gain Greater Control
   of My Calendar, My Watch, and My
   Appointment Book?

One of the primary causes of burnout is failure to control your own agenda. Running from crisis to crisis and appointment to appointment is a sure way to end up in an emergency room. Starting today, get control of your calendar and your life. Take a course in time management. Learn how to delegate. Establish your priorities at work and at home. Organize your files and your desk more efficiently. Learn how to say no to those people who would rob you of your time and energy.

? What Can I Do to Help People Less
Fortunate Than I?

Finally, helping others less fortunate than you creates an ironic twist: It may help you more than it helps them. This alternative question has the potential to create significant effects for others, and ultimately for you.

5-3

You Wonder If You're Becoming Obsolete

You've always prided yourself on being aware of what's happening. When you began your career you promised yourself that you would never be one of those "old guys" you saw in the company who realized too late that the parade had passed them by. Lately you've been wondering if there's any chance that's happening to you. Today's the day to find out. You've decided to check where you are in relation to that parade.

? What New Skills or Talents Have I
Developed in the Past Year That Have
Directly Increased the Value I Bring to This
Company?

At some point in your career you must accept the inevitable truth that no one owes you a job. You will be employed only as long as you can return value to the employer who's investing in you. If you can't justify the return, expect to be replaced.

This question clearly defines your current and projected worth to the company. If you haven't learned any new skills or talents to justify your value, you shouldn't be surprised if and when you get laid off.

Get your boss's answer to this question. If you hear a disappointing answer, use the session as an opportunity to secure his commitment to your professional development.

? How Do My Technical Skills Compare
with Those of Recent College Graduates?

We live in a world of constant change. Unfortunately, some managers believe that once they receive their diploma or certificate, their education is complete. These are the managers who are most surprised when their boss taps them on the shoulder and says, "I'm sorry, the world is passing you by."

Other people assume that the certificate or diploma signifies that the journey has simply begun, not ended. They make sure that their knowledge and skills are on the cutting edge of technological advancements.

The answer to this first alternative question provides valuable insights concerning your knowledge and skill.

? Am I Starting to Feel Threatened
by the Skills and Talents and Energy
of People Half or Even a Third My Age?

If you're feeling threatened by recent graduates and employees much younger than you, your internal critic is saying that unless you do something quickly the parade will pass you by. This question is the "litmus test" for determining your obsolescence. Answer it honestly.

? In What Ways Do You Believe I Can Do
a Better Job of Keeping Up with the Latest
Technical Developments and Skill
Requirements in My Field?

Pose this question directly to your boss. Take notes. Go off to devise a preliminary professional development plan. Come back to get his approval and support.

5-4

Your Career Has Plateaued

You've been doing the same job with the same resources under the same working conditions for longer than you care to remember. The only thing that changes is a modest merit increase every year. It's beginning to look like you'll retire in this job if you don't take action to give your career a boost.

? Is There Any Other Job in This Company That I'm Capable of Performing and Would Enjoy Performing?

Ask yourself this question. If the answer is yes, you've got work to do. If the job you want is in another department, you've got to convince your boss and perhaps your boss's boss that a lateral transfer creates a win-win situation for all. You may not get the transfer if your boss believes you need a great deal of on-the-job training. Start learning the skills that you'll need to perform that job now. Convince your boss that you can start off running in the new assignment.

If the answer is no, start looking outside the company. Take a close look at your goals, talents, and abilities. If necessary, seek the services of a qualified career counselor or job placement professional.

? What Can I Do to Expand The Duties and Responsibilities of My Job While Increasing My Value to the Company?

This is another question to ask yourself. One solution for dealing with a plateaued career is to redesign your job. On a sheet of paper carefully analyze what you could do more of to enrich your job. Remain sensitive to the possibility that you may be usurping a coworker's responsibilities. Nevertheless, redesign your job and make a "sales appointment" with your boss. Use your worksheet as the starting point in the negotiation.

5-5

You're a Casualty of Restructuring and Cutbacks

You had a feeling the ax was falling your way and today it was confirmed: You have now joined the ranks of the talented, competent, hard-working unemployed. Your severance package will support you for the next three months. At home that evening you do some planning. After staring into space for a few minutes you write a question at the top of a sheet of paper.

? What Are the Distinct Competencies I Have and Where Are Those Competencies Likely to Have the Greatest Market Value?

When looking for a job, the knee-jerk reaction is to seek out similar work in a similar company in a similar industry. The good news about this strategy is that you are qualified for that kind of job. The bad news is that you were just laid off from that kind of job. Hence, similar jobs in similar companies might be suffering the same fate.

Move beyond your past job title and focus on the competencies that allowed you to perform the job. For example, what analytical, communication, technical, and problem-solving skills did you manifest in your past job? What specific results can you document to support those competencies?

Now do a little research and find out where those specific competencies are in demand today. Move beyond your past job description and you may find a new job.

? What Have Been the Major Themes— both Positive and Negative—in My Last Three Performance Appraisals?

This question provides a quick analysis of what your boss perceived as your strengths and weaknesses over the immediate past. An honest assessment of these trends should provide answers to four important questions: What have you done well? What skills and abilities allowed you to do well? What did you do poorly? What deficiencies accounted for the poor performance?

Also ask yourself these questions: Which projects were the most enjoyable? Which were the least enjoyable? Where did you shine and why? Where did you feel down and why? What does all this tell you about the unique gifts that you have to bring to a vocation?

? Is This the Push I Need to Start That Business I Always Dreamed of Starting?

This question possesses several of the "magical" properties discussed in Chapter 1. It focuses and crystallizes issues and brings forward concerns that you may have previously been reluctant to address or were willing to delay.

Many managers have found that the pink slip and the severance package was the push they needed to start the business they always wanted to start or to get the degree they always wanted to get.

Develop the perspective that traumatic events in your life provide new opportunities. As a casualty of restructuring, your mettle is now being tested and you may want to change the course of your career and your life.

5-6

You're Fired for Cause (Unjustly)

You're shocked. You still can't believe your boss actually carried through with her threat to fire you for something that was not your doing. The more you think about the action, the more angry you become. When you're able to calm down and collect yourself you walk into your boss's office.

? If a Prospective Employer Calls You and Asks about My Performance, What Will You Say?

Being fired from a job does not necessarily label you as an incompetent ne'er-do-well. More than one executive has demonstrated considerable success after a termination (for eample, Lee Iacocca was fired from Ford). But you've got to make sure your ex-employer doesn't blackball you with prospective employers. If possible, get a recommendation that you can show prospective employers in writing before you leave. If she won't write the letter, get a verbal agreement on what she would say.

? What Are Pros and Cons of Filing a Wrongful Discharge Suit?

This is a question to ask yourself. If you believe you've been discharged unfairly, you do have the option of filing a lawsuit. Unfortunately, this decision will result in significant personal and financial cost and is not guaranteed to produce a favorable finding. Depending on the degree of your perceived injustice, you may choose to discuss this question with an attorney or the appropriate human relation commission in your area before you make a decision.

5-7

You're Fired for Cause (and It's Justified)

You've got no one to blame but yourself. Your boss gave you ample warning and ample opportunity to change. But because of your ego and your stubborn streak you continued to buck the system. Today your boss walked into your office and gave you an oral pink slip, with hard copy to follow.

? What Can I Do to Make Sure This Doesn't Happen to Me Again?

Ask yourself this question. Start taking a closer look at what you did to cause the firing. Stop blaming and start learning. If you don't learn from this lesson, you may find yourself in a similar situation the next time.

? How Might This Termination Benefit Me?

Often pain leads to joy, and failure to victory. Sometimes we need a loss to take us out of our doldrums. A good kick in the behind may be just what is needed to wake us up to potentials in ourselves that we've never before explored. What new avenues and career direction options does this firing present to you? Channel your hurt, anger, and frustration towards career-building behavior.

? If a Prospective Employer Calls for a Referral, What Will You Say?

This question for your boss is even more important under conditions of justified termination than it is under conditions of questionable termination. You've been fired for cause. There's a chance that the only things your ex-boss will be willing to tell a prospective employer are your starting date, your termination date, and the reason for termination. Nevertheless, negotiate for the very best referral you can, realizing that it won't be a stellar one. Ask for it in writing.

? Should I Seek Out a Career Counselor?

This self-analysis question may reveal that your firing is a symptom of a deep-seated problem. If that's the case, you need help from a professional. Get the counseling now; you'll be glad you did.

5-8

You're Told to Lay Off Members of Your Staff

You heard the rumors, hoping beyond hope that they were false. You found out today that they were true. Your boss just told you that because of slumping sales you've got to cut staff.

―――――

? Can We Explore Options for Cost Savings
   Other Than Cutting Staff?

Typically, managers believe that the easiest way to cut costs is
through staff reduction. Thus the knee-jerk reaction is to dispense
the pink slip. This question prods your boss into thinking about other
options to achieve the same goals but without incurring the cost of
human trauma.

If he says no, ask him why. Follow up with probes, reinforcing
the pain and trauma reduction will create. If he says yes, start
brainstorming with your staff.

―――――

? Are You Open to a Plan for Increasing
   Revenues to the Point Where We Won't
   Need to Let Anyone Go?

Few bosses would say no to such an offer. To back it up, meet with
your entire staff with news of the impending layoffs. Tell them you
wish to avoid terminations at all costs, and let them know of your
proposed solution. Get their ideas for generating new revenues.
Have a brainstorming session marked by free-wheeling creativity.
The immediacy of the situation will motivate their imagination. You
just might find the solution you seek.

―――――

? What's Going to Happen When Business
   Picks Up and We Have to Look
   for New Staff?

A basic truism of business is that slumps are cyclical. Your company
is now at the bottom of one slump. But when times get better, you
may be understaffed and face an untrained and inexperienced labor
pool. This question begs a discussion of strategic labor planning as
opposed to knee-jerk staffing.

? What Criteria Do You Want Me to Use in Deciding Who Stays and Who Goes?

If you have to make the cuts, at least be certain that you will be as fair and as consistent as the process will allow. Developing a unified plan with your boss is crucial for you, your boss, and all concerned. With this question you are initiating the plan.

5-9

Colleagues Are Being Let Go

You're starting to feel like a rookie on a professional sports team on the day during training camp when the coach announces the cuts. You look around and see your friends getting the hook and wonder if your turn is next. You are determined not to be caught by surprise.

? Are My Days Here Numbered?

You're confronting a situation that requires a direct answer to a direct question. Your pain and uncertainty demand nothing less. In most situations your boss will empathize with your pain and be honest with you, one way or the other.

However, it's possible that your boss cannot disclose the information because of legal or other constraints. If so, solicit as much information as you can without demanding or being overly aggressive.

? Is There Anything I Can Do to Increase My Value to You and to the Company?

With this question you're "asking for the sale." You're determining what else you might do to improve your stock in the company. It's possible that there's nothing you can do; the decision may have already been made. If so, all you've lost is the time taken to ask the question. However, if the decision is still open, you may have asked the question that saves your job.

5-10

Your Boss Is Fired

You weren't surprised. You knew for months that your boss was treading on thin ice. He was coming to work later and later, his lunch hours were getting longer and longer, and his reports were getting sloppier and sloppier. On the day you hear about the decision you make an appointment with your boss's boss to ask a crucial question.

? What, If Anything, Will Change in the Department Because of the Firing?

When a boss is fired upper management may assume he was derelict in supervising his staff. This assumption, however, is likely to lead to the erroneous belief that the staff took advantage of the lax supervision. As a result, upper management may overreact and search for a replacement who will impose unnecessarily close leadership over the staff. With this question you're seeking to determine if your superiors are under such an assumption.

You want the opportunity to point out to upper management that in fact the staff supervised itself successfully despite the lack of direction received. You also want to correct any other misconceptions about the need for change because of the lack of good information they received from your former boss. Be sure, however, that you not be seen as kicking your former boss while he's down.

If your old boss's boss says, "What do you mean?" answer with your concerns about inaccurate assumptions that may be held about the department. Offer to help clear up any misunderstandings or to provide any missing data. And, make sure you leave with a clear understanding of top management's expectation vis-à-vis you and your colleagues during the transition.

? What Can I Learn from This Situation?

There are two ways to learn a lesson: through direct experience or vicariously through the experience of others. Ask yourself this question to make sure you don't make the mistakes your expendable boss did.

5-11

Your Salary Is Frozen

Well, it could have been worse. You could have been laid off as some others were. This morning your boss announced to the remaining staff that because of losses in the last three quarters, all salaries will be frozen for the coming year. Your apparent job security, while a consolation, does not soothe your disappointment. You thought you were in line for a nice raise following your successes of the past year. After a great deal of contemplation and soul-searching, you make an appointment to see your boss to discuss your disappointment.

? Am I Correct in Assuming That Had It Not Been for the Freeze, I Would Have Been in Line for an Above Average Annual Increase?

If the answer is yes, ask what can be done to make up for your loss being greater than other staff. Perhaps your boss will be willing to commit to an even larger increase when the freeze is melted. If you make no headway, move to the next questions.

If the answer is no, find out why your perception of your work is different from your boss's perception. There may be nothing more for you to say about salary, but you do need to learn why the perceptions of your value are so far out of line.

? Will You Consider Nonmonetary Compensation?

When your boss hears this question he'll probably be taken aback and ask you what you mean. This is when you want to be creative and propose options of value to you that are not reflected in salary. Especially attractive to the boss will be suggestions that are easy for him to provide. Possible items include discounts on products or services from vendors, compensatory vacation time, or equipment that you need to perform your job better (for example, a new computer). The more creative you are the more likely you'll find a substitute for salary. Even if you can't find one, your boss may be able to.

? What's Your Best-case and Worst-case Scenario of When Salaries Will Be Unfrozen?

Your expenditures and bills are not likely to stop just because your salary is frozen. You may be willing to accept the freeze, but you'd like to know when it will end. After you've heard his estimates, factor them into your personal plans. Will you stay or seek higher-paying employment?

5-12

The Promotion Is Given to Someone Else

The waiting is over. You no longer have to suffer through sleepless nights or undigested meals. The boss made the announcement today, and for you it was bad news. You won't be getting the promotion. It's going to one of your coworkers.

? What Do You See As My Long-term Prospects in This Company?

You've reached a critical juncture in your career. You've been passed over for a promotion and have thus failed a critical test of upward mobility. This question helps assess whether you should remain with the company.

Your boss should not be surprised by this question. She was probably planning to break the news to you and provide justification for the decision. Your question preempts her agenda and demonstrates your concern and your assertiveness.

If you get a reassuring answer, thank the boss for her time and get back to work, committed to getting the next promotion. If the news is not reassuring, reject the tendency you may have to be defensive and listen objectively.

? What Is One Thing I Should Do More
of and One Thing I Should Do Less
of to Make Sure I Get the Next Promotion?

You need specific constructive feedback and you need it now. Listen to the answer as openly as possible. Even though you may disagree with the shortcomings you hear, accept them as constituting the reality that stands between you and upward ascendancy in this company. Develop an action plan to reverse the judgments before the next position opens up. Thank your boss for her candor and express your commitment to change.

5-13

You Hired Someone Who Is Nice, but Totally Wrong for the Job

When you interviewed the five receptionist candidates sent to you by the personnel office, you were so impressed by one's warmth and amiable personality that you hired her the next day. When she reported for work, you were immediately impressed with her cooperative nature, her willingness to learn, and her loyalty to the company. You were absolutely convinced that her pleasant voice and engaging style would make a stunning impression on those who called or visited your office. But while your judgments were correct, you didn't really understand her job. The stress at the front desk is enormous, the emergencies are never ending, and the workload could bury employees far more efficient than your new hire. After two weeks she had absolutely wilted under the pressure. It was time for you to come to the rescue.

? What Are You Feeling Good About in Your New Job, and What's Giving You Difficulty?

This is an open-ended question that gives the receptionist no clue about your concern that she can't handle the pressure of the job. By giving her the chance to describe her victories and not just her failures, it creates a nonthreatening environment. Reinforce the accomplishments she claims with which you agree. Dig more deeply into the difficulties she acknowledges. Point out those that she doesn't see or is not ready to acknowledge. If you believe she has the ability and motivation to succeed, work with her on a plan for surmounting her greatest challenges. If she needs more training, recommend it. If you don't believe she can handle the job, say so and explain her options. Perhaps you can exploit her strengths elsewhere in the company.

? Is the Job Creating As Much Strain for You As It Appears?

This might be a follow-up probe for the first question, or it can stand alone as a discussion starter. Help her to see the reality of the situation. Engage her in problem solving to overcome her deficits. If she denies feeling the strain you can see on her face and hear in her voice every day, tell her what you see and hear.

? What Can I Do to Help You Deal with the Strain Your Job Appears to Create for You?

Use this question in tandem with the other two or by itself. Since the focus is on your desire to help rather than to place blame, it is best used with employees prone to defensiveness. It is not recommended with employees looking for a scapegoat, those who expect you to solve their problems. When the receptionist suggests something appropriate you can do, agree to assist her. If her request is not reasonable or shows ignorance about what is really going on, set her on the right track.

Chapter
6
Getting Promotions and Raises

In the good old days promotions and raises followed a fairly simple formula: Join the right company, keep your nose clean, perform up to expectations, and you'll get the pot at the end of the corporate rainbow.

The good old days are gone. Companies can no longer promise lifetime employment, clearly defined and unencumbered career paths, or predictable merit increases. The certainty of yesterday has become the uncertainty of today.

Today, methods of promotions and raises are as varied as the managers who negotiate them and the organizations within which they are negotiated. To aid in your personal negotiations, we've focused on eight perplexing scenarios and the questions to pose in them.

6-1

You're Offered a Promotion without a Raise

You're living the classic good news, bad news joke. Your boss says that your performance, education, and experience demand recognition and a promotion. Unfortunately, the corporate cupboard is bare. You grew up believing that promotion and more money went together like hot dogs and mustard. You're now faced with a decision that forces you to challenge that belief.

? What Can We Negotiate As Compensation in Lieu of a Salary Increase to Go Along with My Promotion?

This question turns a good news, bad news scenario into good news, good news. It also shows that you're flexible and cooperative.

If your boss says, "What do you mean?" be prepared to give specific alternatives to salary that you would find attractive. Suggest such inducements as increased profit sharing, increased opportunities for company-paid training and education, a guaranteed bonus paid at the end of a specified period, a company loan at 0% interest, or a promise for more money when profits reach a certain level. Do your homework and be creative.

Also suggest that you'd like time to consider any other options she offers. The message here is clear: You're open to the possibility of promotion without an immediate salary increase if the company is willing to be reasonable.

If your boss says, "No, we can't offer any other form of compensation," ask why. If she says it's because the company has never done that before, say either "I've never been asked to take a promotion without a raise before," or "Given the change in the times, this may be a good opportunity to set that precedent."

? If I Turn Down the Promotion, What Message Will I Be Sending to You and to Upper Management?

With this question you're communicating a very simple, yet powerful message: I don't want to make any decision that will help you now but hurt me later.

Your boss needs to know that yes, you will consider her proposal or promotion without raise if you can be assured of some future gain. You're also telling her that if your decision to reject a noncompensated promotion will raise questions about your loyalty or future in the company, you want to know now. You need to know unequivocally that your decision to forgo the promotion means that you're a loyal employee, not a martyr. Make sure your boss and upper management see the difference.

? If I Take the Promotion Under These Conditions and I Perform As Well As I Have in the Past, When Will I Be Rewarded?

It's possible (and maybe even likely) that your boss won't be able to make any promises about future raises, perks, or bonuses. And, it's better to be promised nothing than it is to be promised something that is later not delivered.

This is a tough question. Your boss may want some time to think about the answer. As a matter of fact, it's a good strategy to suggest that your boss take a day or two to think about your question before she answers it. After all, her answer will have a long-range impact on you and the company.

6-2

A Coworker Is Promoted to Be Your New Boss

No one said the world was fair. Your friend, colleague, and friendly competitor is now your boss. You know that he probably feels as uncomfortable about the situation as you do, but you don't care as much about his feelings as you feel the pain of yours. After all, he got the promotion, you didn't. As soon as you hear the news, you walk into your new boss's office, congratulate him as sincerely as you can, and ask a question.

? What Should I Do More of and What Should I Do Less of to Make Sure That When the Next Promotion Comes Up I Get It?

Even though he has only been your boss for a day, while working beside you he certainly developed an impression of your value. It's important that you start off knowing where he stands. Added value in this question is that it shows you're a good loser and are looking for honest, constructive feedback. It also reinforces your role as a team player who wants to remain loyal and get rewarded for your efforts.

If your boss says, "I can't think of anything right now," ask for a specific time on his calendar when he will be able to give you feedback on your performance. Explain how important his impressions are to you.

If he does answer your question, listen with an open mind. He's not attacking you; he's giving you an honest answer to an honest question. Ask for examples and specific behaviors. Probe until you're reasonably satisfied that you know where you stand with your new boss.

? Where Do You See Me Being Five Years from Now in This Company?

You don't want to be surprised at your next performance appraisal or, even worse, shocked the next time you're passed over for a promotion. This is an indirect yet powerful way of getting an assessment of your strengths, weaknesses, and chances of being promoted.

Chances are this question will probably catch your new boss off guard. Tell him why you're asking (because you want to improve yourself and get the promotion), and give him time to think about the answer.

Your new boss should be in an excellent position to answer your question. First, he saw you on a day-to-day basis in ways that your old boss did not. Second, your new boss was perceived as having the "stuff" for promotion that you did not; and his response is likely to reveal what he believes his unique qualities are. Listen to the answer nondefensively. Use the data you collect to serve him effectively.

? Is There Anything You Would Like Me to Do to Make Our New Relationship Productive and Mutually Rewarding?

Since the answer to this question has serious consequences for you both, he should be given whatever time he needs to muster a response, but remind him later if he has not followed through on his promise. If he opts to answer immediately with a superficial response ("You're doing fine right now, just keep up the good work"), follow up with the concern you have for your future in the company using one of the two previous questions.

6-3

A Coworker Asks How Much of a Raise You Received

You now see why some companies try to limit employee discussions about salary. On the way back from lunch, your best friend asks you how much of a raise you received in your last pay envelope. You're pretty sure you received more than she did.

? If I Told You and It Was More Than You Received, Wouldn't You Be Hurt? If It Was Less than You Received, Wouldn't I Be Hurt?

This is a rhetorical question. You really don't want her to answer; you simply want her to think about the potential damage her question could cause. You hope your question will motivate her to drop the subject and move on to something else.

This question's most powerful quality is that it raises the prospect that you might be the one hurt by the salary disclosure. Many people believe that their efforts are undervalued and, hence, that their coworkers probably receive higher raises than they do. With this question you force the questioner to rethink her assumptions.

If she presses the issue, repeat the question. Affirm your reluctance to discuss something that could cause discomfort for you both.

? If You Were Our Boss, How Much of a Raise Would You Give to You and Me and Why?

This question asks your coworker to step out of her shoes for a moment and step into the shoes of your boss. Right now your coworker is only concerned with her plight; she is not concerned with you or with the larger picture. It's quite possible that your boss finds you to be a more valued contributor than your coworker. Let your coworker ruminate on that possibility.

Empathy is a powerful psychological force. It broadens perspective and takes into account information that can soothe hurt feelings. With this question you'll help your coworker practice a little empathy.

? What Assurances Can You Give Me That
the Answer to Your Question Won't
Jeopardize Our Relationship?

This question focuses even more powerfully on the esteem in which you hold the relationship. Hold out for convincing assurances. If they are not forthcoming, repeat your desire to preserve the relationship, and change the subject.

6-4

Your New Subordinates Used to Be Your Coworkers

You remember a management trainer once saying in a seminar that one of the toughest jobs for a newly promoted supervisor is to supervise former coworkers and, worse yet, friends. Now you wish you had paid more attention to the rest of that seminar. You just accepted the assignment of motivating, coaching, and disciplining the gang you used to work beside and go out with after work. You wonder if taking the promotion was such a good idea. You call a meeting of your new employees to discuss your dilemma.

? If You Were in My Shoes Right Now,
Responsible for the Work of People Who
Once Were Your Coworkers and Remain
Your Friends, What Would Be Going
Through Your Mind?

With this question you invite your new subordinates to experience empathy. Most will feel for you and take pride in one of their own being promoted. Some may even jokingly provide unique twists to the answer.

You're likely to get some lighthearted jabs ("I'd tell them they all had a raise and the day off"). But you're also likely to get a few serious, contemplative answers. Listen to both and probe the latter.

If no one answers this question, answer it yourself. Tell them how you feel about changing from the role of friend and coworker to that of supervisor. Assure them that you intend to be firm and fair in all future dealings with them and that you expect the same treatment from them.

? What Qualities Are You Hoping I'll Display As the New Supervisor?

This question should open the door to a serious discussion of roles, relationships, and expectations. Effective leadership is based on clear communications, which in turn are based on questioning and validating the assumptions we have of one another.

Don't be surprised if your employees stare down at the floor, squirm nervously in their seats, and look to one another to see who will be the first to say something.

If no one answers, repeat the question again. Tell them why you're asking this tough question ("To make sure we begin our new relationship with mutual agreement"). Eventually someone will initiate the discussion that will benefit all.

? If a Supervisor Is Also a Friend, What Does She Do If One of Her People Isn't Performing up to Standard?

This is another tough but important question. One of the most difficult challenges you'll face in your new position is confronting an ex-coworker who is not meeting your expectations. With this question you'll elicit discussion and most likely secure their empathy and understanding. Don't leave the meeting without a consensus on how you will handle the rare need for discipline.

6-5

A Deserving Employee Asks for a Raise and There's None to Give

The best employee you ever had just asked you for a raise. Her timing couldn't be worse. Last week your boss told you that all raises and bonuses would have to be put on the back burner.

? What Other Rewards Would You Find Attractive?

Ask this question after making certain your employee knows you want to reward her and understands why you cannot. It is simple, honest, and direct. It solicits her suggestions for recognizing her valuable contribution to the team.

If she says that money is the only reward she can think of, take out a sheet of paper and list other alternatives: an opportunity to work on new and challenging assignments, company-paid educational seminars, an unconditional promise of a raise as soon as the funds are available, an equity position in personally developed projects or product, and so forth. Ask her to add to the list.

She may insist that money is the only worthwhile compensation ("If I don't get the raise, I'll quit"). If so, question why she would want to leave a company that was creatively searching for ways to retain and reward her? Emphasize the benefits of the nonsalary compensation you can offer.

If she again comes back to money as the only inducement to stay, accept the reality that you've done everything you can to keep a talented employee but that you can't jeopardize the company to keep her. Wish her well in the future.

? Will Your Work Slip If You Remain and Are Not Given the Raise?

When she answers this question, listen with both your ears and your eyes. Focus on her words and on her nonverbal behavior. If you sense discomfort or frustration in her response, chances are her work will slip in the future. Stress that it's important for you both to be honest with one another. Honesty now will prevent heartbreak later. If she says she's not sure, ask what information she needs to commit to an answer.

? What's the Most Persuasive Case We Can Make with Upper Management to Get You the Raise?

This question is appropriate only if upper management is open to negotiation and will make the final decision. Don't seek simply to appease the employee if you really don't believe the raise is an option. If the employee sees your question as a manipulative ploy, you've done nothing but turn a talented and hard-working employee into an angry and bitter one. And, you lose even more credibility when you fail to deliver.

   If you opt for this alternative, be prepared to say "I can't do it" if the case she constructs doesn't appear compelling to you. Don't jeopardize your career by championing a case that doesn't deserve your support.

6-6

You're Asked to Choose Between Staying on the Job at Reduced Pay or Leaving with a Severance Package

Now you know what the phrase "between a rock and a hard place" really means. Your boss just told you that because of decreasing market share and cost-cutting measures, upper management has decided to cut staff. You've been given the option of remaining at 20% reduced pay or leaving with a severance package. What makes the decision even harder is that the severance package option has an immediate window of opportunity. You cannot choose to execute that option later. As you contemplate the situation, you ask yourself a clarifying question.

? Do I Love This Job?

Notice that you are not asking whether you like the job or are satisfied with it. You're asking whether you love it. Since jobs tend to become more attractive as the possibility for losing them increases, it's imperative that you analyze your feelings about this job rationally and independent of its possible loss.

If you're not sure whether you love it, ask close friends and family how *they* think you feel about your job. They'll be able to tell you because you've been telling them. In both actions and words you've shown exactly how you feel about your current employment.

If you love the job, hang in there. If you don't, look for other options.

? How Difficult Would It Be for Me to Find Another Job?

In answering this question consider current labor market conditions, projected labor market forces, and your current market worth. Do not answer this question based solely on intuition or on conversations you've had with neighbors and coworkers. Get valid and reliable information from the library and from experts in the field.

If your research leads you to conclude that your prospects for a new job are slim, stay with the present one.

? Would I Be Able to Remain at Reduced Pay and Not Feel Resentful in the Future?

If you decide to stay, what is your projected morale? Would you be able to hold your head high, put in a solid day's work, and look forward to the camaraderie of coworkers? Or, would you feel so bitter that you'd make yourself sick and alienate your coworkers? Do not remain unless you are convinced that you will find constructive ways for dealing with your frustration and alienation.

6-7

The Mentor-Protégé Relationship Becomes Strained

For some time you've depended on a special relationship you have with a higher-level manager as a source of advice and counsel regarding the progression of your career. When you first started the relationship you both derived personal and professional rewards. You were both open, honest, and objective about the costs and rewards of the mentor-protégé relationship. Now you're feeling a strain. At times you've been disappointed by her response to your requests and you sometimes feel guilty when you don't do exactly as she expects. You sense that she's feeling the same.

? How Do You See Our Relationship Evolving, and What Do You Think We Should Do to Remove Some of the Strain We're Both Feeling?

Mentor-protégé affiliations evolve through several distinct phases. Researchers have labeled one of the later phases in the relationship as "redefinition." During this phase both parties must carefully analyze their respective roles as well as the demands imposed on the other.

With this question you've established the agenda for the discussion. You've also correctly described the strain as a "mutual" feeling. It is neither solely your fault nor hers.

Answers to your questions will usually take one of two directions. The first is to establish a behavioral contract, a statement of specific expectations you have of one another. The second is to agree to terminate the relationship without acrimony. You both derived something from the relationship. Thank each other and move on.

? Are We Imposing Unreasonable Demands on One Another?

Implicit in all mentor-protégé relationships are the demands each places on the other. Sometimes these demands are reasonable, acceptable, and help to foster the relationship. At other times the demands are unreasonable, unacceptable, and detrimental to the relationship. It's crucial that you and your colleague make the implicit explicit. Start talking about your assumptions and expectations. This alternative question can serve as the agenda for that discussion. The discussion may be uncomfortable for both of you, but initiate the discussion anyway. The relationship won't start healing until you start diagnosing.

? Are We Devoting Energy to Maintaining
Our Relationship That Might Be Better Spent
in Other Ways?

If you're devoting too much of your valuable time to repairing a relationship, you may be in a no-win situation. The answer to this question may reveal that, as in many relationships, one or both of you is trying to salvage a dream that is gone.

6-8

You Believe You Deserve a Raise, but Are Afraid to Ask

Your raise is long overdue. You've worked very hard and with good results. Yet the financial rewards that should accompany a record like yours just haven't been forthcoming. You haven't had a meaningful pay increase in over two years, even though the company has been doing fairly well. People have been encouraging you to ask for what you deserve, but you've been putting it off. One reason is that you don't believe you should have to ask for what you have earned. Another is that you are afraid that your boss will say no and see you as pushy because you asked. But now you've gotten up the nerve to do it. First you are careful to time your request with one of your boss's good moods and a personal success that you know he appreciates, and then you pop the right question.

? Are You Aware That My Pay Level Is
Lower than Eighty Percent
of the Employees with My Experience
in This Company?

Consider using this question if: (1) You can quote an impressive statistic showing how the compensation fairy has passed you by, and (2) you're convinced that your boss will see you as more valuable than many of the employees who are paid more than you.

Whether the boss says yes or no, use this opening as an opportunity to plead your case. Plan a sales call that will show the boss why it makes good sense to give you the raise. What's in it for her? Can you think of anything positive that giving you a raise will do for her? Help her see these benefits. Anticipate her likely objections to your request (for example, "There's no money in the budget"), and be prepared to overcome them.

? Are You Aware That I Haven't Had a Raise
in Over Two Years?

If your boss is unaware of how long it's been between your pay hikes, this question alone may be a sufficient stimulus to action. More than likely, however, you'll need to proceed with the sales call recommended above.

? When Will I Receive My Next Raise?

This question is more assertive than the first two. It doesn't ask *whether* you're going to get the raise, only *when*. The boss will either tell you when you can expect it or claim ignorance. If you like the timing she offers, thank her and get on with your work. If you don't like her plan, say why you believe it to be unfair and ask for something sooner (suggest a specific alternative date). If she says that she has no idea when the raise might come, ask her when she will know. If she's not cooperative at this point, you ought to think about working for someone who is.

? May I Have a Raise of Ten Percent Effective Next Month?

If everyone asked for raises with this directness, more people would get raises. More bosses will answer yes than you imagine or will bargain for a little more time or a lower percentage, so ask for a bit more than you expect to get. If you hear a flat no for an answer, ask, "Well, then, what do you feel would be fair given the contribution I have made to the company over the past two years without any financial reward?"

Chapter

7

Dealing with Difficult Employees

In almost every challenge described in this chapter, many managers would not think of opening with a question. It's rather easy and seems natural for bosses to assert their needs to employees with statements in the face of these challenges. Questions may first appear to be a cowardly abdication of responsibility.

However, the questions recommended below actually increase your assertiveness, intensify your power, and magnify employee respect for you by ensuring you won't be engaging in a war of words. They place you in an adult role. They get the employee's attention. They immediately direct the situation to the organizational need to be met. They pave the road to an eventual authoritative statement of the future performance needed from employees.

7-1

Employee Performance Is Unacceptable

You are exasperated. Your new receptionist just reported late for the third time this week. The disruption caused in the operation and the

resentment building on the staff has you fearing a low-level rebel-
lion. Previous talks between the two of you haven't seemed to help.
You vow to give your receptionist one more chance. In a private
meeting in your office, as you engage in eye contact, you ask this
question.

? What's It Going to Take to Keep This from Happening Again?

This question has three important qualities. First, it is assertive, not
aggressive. Second, it places the monkey on the employee's back,
where it belongs. Third, it calls for a solution from the employee that
is likely both to solve the real problem and to be acceptable to both
of you.

If the employee is uncooperative or if you don't like the solution
you hear, impose your own. Specify the two sets of needs—the
company's and the receptionist's—to be met. Establish that company requirements are preeminent should the two sets of needs
appear incompatible.

Once a solution is proposed that you support, secure the
employee's commitment with a question such as, "May I count on
you to do that?" Insist upon a yes in return. Don't accept, "I don't
know," "I guess," or even "I'll try."

Remember that poor performance occurs for one of three reasons: (1) Employees don't know what's expected (communication
problem); (2) employees can't do what's expected (selection, training, or resource problem); or (3) employees don't want to do what's
expected (motivation problem). In your questioning, search for the
cause in this situation.

? What Do You Need from Me to Meet My Expectations for Punctuality?

Who knows? There may be something you are doing or not doing
that is contributing to the problem. In most cases, however, the
employee won't have a useful answer for you. Punctuality is an
example of behavior that the employee, not you, can control. The
most likely result of this question is to focus the responsibility back
on the employee, who may well say, "Nothing, this is a problem only

I can solve." On occasions where you hear an uncooperative answer, such as, "Lower your expectations," respond firmly with, "The expectation stands. It's up to you to meet it."

? What Is Preventing You from Getting to Work on Time?

Your role in the organization and your relationship with this employee may support the direct approach. Depending on the employee's honesty, the answer may enable the two of you to engage in problem solving as a team. Or, you may now be in a position to insist that the employee take the corrective action indicated by his or her answer. If, instead, this person throws up a smoke screen, ask as many follow-up questions as you need to arrive at the truth.

7-2

Your Request or a Directive Is Ignored

You've asked a subordinate to spend less time buried in office paperwork and more time managing by wandering around. You want at least thirty minutes a day spent among employees at their work places. But since you made this specific request one week ago none of this has happened.

? Why Haven't You Been Spending the Time with Your People That We Agreed to Last Week?

Insubordination is difficult to deal with. Some managers react badly to it and threaten perpetrators, thereby exhibiting one of the reasons they get such behavior from subordinates in the first place. Others cower in the face of authority challenges, pretending that they don't really happen. You should neither threaten nor cower.

This question gets right to the point without posing a threat (for example, "Either you start doing as I've told you . . . ") or being accusatory (for example, "Why do you insist on going against my wishes?"). It leads to a dialogue that enables you to find the causes of the resistance, to reassess the appropriateness of your request, and to decide what actions you want to take as a result.

Two typical answers to expect are, "I'm too busy right now" and "I don't feel that spending thirty minutes a day with my employees is a good use of my time." The second answer is more honest than the first. In response to either one, point out that if we make something a high enough priority, we find the time to do it, and that this request has that kind of priority.

Remember that this employee probably feels justified in not going along with your request. Most so-called insubordinates have what they believe are good reasons for not going along with the program. Probe the initial answer you get with more specific questions (for example, "Do you agree with the value of MBWA?") to get to the bottom of noncompliance. If you succeed, you'll know the right thing to do next.

? When Do You Plan to Begin Your Daily Visitations of Employees?

This question is less likely to generate the depth of discussion of the question above. The supervisor may pledge a new starting date in response to which you can state your belated pleasure, while describing your displeasure that the original contract was not fulfilled. Alternatively, you may choose to reject the new pledge in favor of one you prefer. If you get no sign of a positive intent, the preceding question may come in handy or you may choose simply to insist upon compliance ("I want you down there *today*").

7-3
You're Not Being Listened To

The employee in your office is glancing around the room as you speak, occasionally interrupting your instructions with comments that bear little relationship to the points you are explaining. It's pretty clear your ideas are not getting the attention you wish and that necessary information is not being heard.

? What Problems Do You See with What
I'm Suggesting?

An intelligent response to this question tells you the employee really is listening. If, instead, the answer is, "I don't know," you will want to point out the importance of what you're saying and your insistence that it be absorbed.

"Not a thing" in response may be a coverup for nonlistening or it may mean that the employee really sees no problems in what you're saying. Check this by bringing up a potential problem that you see with the task, and find out if the employee has been listening well enough to suggest an informed response.

If you find yourself in this situation with some frequency, examine your communication style for possible causes. Are you too wordy? Do you speak too slowly? Do you cover minute details with agonizing repetition? Do you speak in language that confuses or alienates employees and causes them to tune you out?

? If I Promise to Give You My Undivided
Attention in About Three Minutes, Will You
Do the Same Until Then?

Nothing fancy here. This is simply a polite, yet assertive, way to say, "Shut up."

? Can You Paraphrase What I've Just
Told You?

If the answer is yes, insist on hearing your employee's version of what you said. If the answer is no or if the paraphrase attempt fails, say, "I'm going to repeat myself, and I expect you to listen this time." Be careful with this question. Some people may feel as though they're being treated like a child. Avoid a condescending tone of voice.

? What Do You Think About What
I've Just Said?

This question will tell you whether you're being heard without running the risk of demeaning your employee. If you elicit an intelligent comment, you've probably been heard. Once employees figure out that they can expect to be asked a question like this in your office, they'll begin paying more attention to your words.

7-4
You're Not Kept Informed

Over lunch your boss expresses concern that your allocation in this year's budget is projected to be overspent by five percent and insists that you adopt stringent cost-cutting measures before the situation worsens. You assure your boss that everything is under control and express optimism for the results of your efforts, not admitting that you knew nothing of this problem when you sat down to lunch. Back in your office, you call your financial assistant, who has yet to brief you on the overrun, to join you.

? How Can We Ensure That I Get All
the Information I Need on the Progress
of Our Expenditures?

While this question presumes no blame, your rejection of the status quo is very clear. If the assistant professes ignorance at the motivation for your question, you can explain what's intolerable about the current state of affairs. Ultimately this question will enable the two of you to devise corrective action, with the assistant burdened with the primary responsibility to suggest remedies.

The issue of not knowing something your boss knows about your own operation needs to be raised. But don't position it as an example of your embarrassment, which might make you look like a showboat or might confirm to a devious assistant that the leak had its desired impact. Instead, point out either that it made the *assistant* look bad or that the time that passed before you were notified could have been better spent solving the budget problem.

Ask yourself what role you may be playing in closing off communication from your employees. Are you readily accessible to them? Do you react well to bad news? Do they know what news you need?

? What Can I Do to Guarantee That I Learn of Important Events Directly Through You Rather than Indirectly Through Others?

This question focuses more powerfully on the embarrassment created for you by being broadsided. Otherwise, the results should be similar to the question above.

? Do You Understand Why Bad News Is Just As Important to Me As Good News?

If the reluctant assistant sat on the budget information out of fear, this may be the most effective question. No matter what the answer, your response should make clear your need to hear *all* information—good and bad—the instant it becomes available. Along with your admonition, reassure the employee that you won't kill the bearer of bad tidings.

7-5

Time Off Is Requested at a Bad Time

Business is great, and you barely have enough staff to get everything done. You are in your office wondering how you'll make it through the next week without more assistance when one of your key employees marches in with a request to take a long-overdue vacation next week. Instead of tearing out your hair, you ask this question.

? In Exchange for My Approval, Will You Give
Me a Plan for Satisfactory Coverage
of Your Duties at This Critical Time?

You can easily say no to a request for time off during a busy period,
but should you? What will be the impact on morale of forcing the
employee to work? If the employee can devise a workable plan for
coverage, perhaps you should support it. As it stands, this question
may not be sufficient to enable the employee to create such a plan.
You will want to stipulate conditions the plan will have to fulfill, the
criteria that must be met, and any limits you must place on its
implementation.

The request for vacation generated a problem to be solved. One
nice feature of this question is that it places the responsibility for
solving the problem squarely with the person who created it. Too
many bosses would instead assume responsibility for dealing with
the impact of the request.

Naturally, you won't accept no for an answer. The question
itself makes this clear to all but the most resistive employees. Before
the employee leaves to draft the coverage plan, you'll want to
emphasize that the time off will be approved only when you see a
plan that is acceptable to you and checked out with each other person
whom it affects.

? May I Count on You to Give Me More
Advance Notice in the Future?

Ask this before the employee leaves your office. Demand a commitment to better future planning. Don't accept "I'll try" for an answer.

? Would You Be Willing to Help Us Get
Through Next Week in Exchange
for an Extra Day Next Month?

If you choose not to grant the day off, or if you hope to convince the
employee to change plans before granting the day off, attempt a
compromise or buy-out similar to this one. If it doesn't work, either

turn the employee down, with visible remorse, or request a coverage plan.

? Do You See the Effect of Leaving Us
without Your Services During This Next
Critical Week?

Some employees don't appreciate their importance to your operation; others don't care. Both need to hear your response to their answer to this question.

7-6

Employee Performance Is Overvalued on a Self-evaluation

Your performance review system, like most effective ones, calls for employees to rate themselves prior to receiving your assessment. Unlike the majority of employees who are harsher on themselves than you are, the one sitting in front of you has presented you with ratings consistently higher than anything you can support. You decide to inject reality into her judgment of her performance.

? How Do You Account for the Differences
Between Our Assessments of Your
Performance?

By their nature performance reviews are prone to generate defensiveness in employees. Under this condition, even the most tactful assertions regarding the accuracy of employee self-assessments can be viewed as a threat. This question avoids any hint of attack by putting the employee in charge of resolving differences between your perceptions.

Let the employee go first in arguing for her position. This gives you the advantage of taking the employee's biases into account as you describe the rationale for your ratings.

No matter how the employee responds, you can direct the discussion toward the specific instances and behaviors the two of you are perceiving differently. It opens the way for you to focus back on your expectations for excellence. Finally, this question will position you to describe the specific actions the employee can take to convince you that your performance requirements are being met.

? Where Do You Believe Our Ratings Deviate
the Most?

While the previous question focuses your discussion on the reasons your respective evaluations differ, this one directs the two of you to the evaluations themselves and enables the important part of the discussion to begin. Once the essential differences are identified, you'll use more pointed questions to resolve them (for example, "Do you agree that the slippage on that project is an example of poor time management?").

? What Disappoints You the Most
about the Differences in Our Perception
of Your Performance?

Use this question when your goal is to allow the employee to vent her feelings. Be prepared for anything. Resolve that you will not allow yourself to feel attacked and thereby become defensive. Listen to the employee and you'll profit both from what you learn and from the catharsis your employee experiences.

7-7

An Employee Is Having Personal Problems

You've always known that happiness in an employee's personal life has a direct impact on job performance. If someone is having trouble at home, is engaged in substance abuse, is financially strapped, or is mentally or emotionally disturbed, work is almost certain to suffer.

You suspect one of these problems exists for your assistant, whose effort has recently diminished dramatically.

? What Can I Do to Help Bring Your
Productivity Back to Where It Was
Before This Past Month?

The best way to help troubled employees is to get them to talk. Many times they need little more than a sounding board that will enable them to hear themselves describe their pain, thereby better understanding it, seeing its causes, and revealing their options.

In some cases this question will be all it takes to break the dam. The employee may say something like, "I wish I knew; this problem I'm dealing with at home has really got me down." You can just continue to listen, occasionally paraphrasing or simply repeating what you hear with a question mark tagged onto the end. You'll help heal the wounds with your listening.

In other cases, the employee will be more reticent, possibly denying that any problem exists. Now you'll have to get tough. Document the performance deficiency. Acknowledge that whatever is causing it may be personal and none of your business. But point out that the impact of the problem on your business is your business, and that it must stop immediately.

? What Are You Planning to Do to Bring
Your Productivity Back to Where It Was
a Month Ago?

This question will be useful in bringing the counseling session to closure. After all, performance improvement is the reason for the meeting. Insist upon specifics that you believe will work.

This is also an alternative to the first question whenever you don't feel quite enough personal investment in the employee's success to make an offer of assistance. When used in this way, expect to hear, "What are you talking about?" or even "Nothing." This opens the way for you to get to the point of your concern and ask for the behavior you want.

? What Appears to Be Causing the Recent Decline in Your Productivity?

You might opt for this question when, as with the question above, you don't wish to offer help. It differs from that question in that it focuses the discussion on causes before asking for remedies. Use the one best suited to your situation.

7-8

An Employee Goes Over Your Head

You recently posted the summer vacation schedule. One employee protested about not getting his first choice, which you could not accommodate because of his low seniority and the needs of the work team. You just received a phone call from your boss saying that the employee had been in her office complaining and directing you to keep this sort of unannounced intrusion from happening again.

? What Did You Hope to Accomplish by Taking Your Vacation Request Directly to My Boss?

It would be nice to get a sincere apology in answer to this question, to which you can respond, "Don't ever let that happen again. You work for me, not my boss. It may be appropriate on occasion for you to appeal my decisions, but only after I know you plan to do so."

More than likely the question will evoke, "You weren't listening to me and your decision was an unfair one. I had no other choice." In a nondefensive tone paraphrase the rationale the employee presented to you for the original vacation request to demonstrate that you heard it. Then, slowly and calmly repeat the reasons you already gave for your decision. Finally, state the last two sentences in the preceding paragraph.

Is there any chance that your behavior frustrates employees into going around you? Do you listen to their ideas and to their concerns? Do you give them the rationale for your decisions? Are you flexible enough to change your mind when errant decision making has been pointed out?

? Is It Now Apparent to You That Taking Your Vacation Request to My Boss Was Not the Thing to Do?

Tack this question onto the end of the discussion above. If you don't get a definite yes, state precisely why you will not tolerate a repeat performance.

You may also choose to open the meeting with it. A yes may mean you won't have to go any further, except that it may be a good idea to confirm that the employee is not attributing unsavory motives to your insistence that he honor the chain of command. Use a negative answer to explain completely how and why hierarchy works.

7-9

An Operational Problem Is Brought to Your Attention

An employee comes into your office and says, "We have a problem." It's clear from the way the problem is presented that you, the boss, are expected to wave your magic wand and solve it.

? What Have You Done So Far?

Some employees are afraid to take the actions they should. When something goes wrong, they run to you for answers. This doesn't do much for their development, and it places too much of a troubleshooting burden on your shoulders.

This question works no matter what the reason is for excessive checking in. If in response the employee does indicate prior action, you can evaluate it and suggest next steps, or you can simply say, "Sounds like you're on the right track to handling it yourself."

If the employee hasn't done anything so far, you will, depending on the problem, want to say either, "Good; I'll handle it from here," or "What do you think you *should* have done before bringing it to my attention?" If you hear, "I have no idea how to handle this," respond with, "If you *did* have an idea, what would it be?" These questions alert the employee to think before bringing problems to you in the future.

Why do employees hesitate to take initiative in your absence? Are they insecure, and if so, what can you do about it? Or, do they perceive you as a controlling leader who wants to be in the center of everything?

? What Would You Do to Solve It?

This question goes one step beyond the previous one. Use it with employees who not only ought to take initial steps before coming to you, but should actually solve more problems completely on their own.

? If You Were in Charge, How Would You Respond to an Employee Bringing a Problem to Your Attention in the Way You Just Did?

Here is an alternative way to get employees to become introspective about their behavior. With its implications for performance evaluation, it may also cause them to stop and think before running to you with problems they ought to handle themselves.

7-10

You're Accused of Favoritism

You are conducting a performance review for an employee whose work leaves a great deal to be desired. In the middle of your explanation of a specific deficiency, the employee blurts out, "You always pick on me and others like me. The only ones who please you are your pets."

? What Do You See Me Do That Makes You Feel That Way?

First find out what behaviors the employee is interpreting as favoritism. It is critical that you not ask this question defensively. Get to the bottom of the matter. You might discover that nothing more than a misunderstanding or faulty information is at the root, and it can easily be cleared up.

If you *are* showing favoritism, the answer to this question will help you to see that and you should admit to it. Say something like, "I hear what you're saying, and I can understand why you interpret that as favoritism. You can be certain I'll do what I can from now on to give you no reason to feel that way."

If you are not showing favoritism, the answer will enable you to point out that you are merely responding to high-achieving employees with appropriate recognition and rewards. Do not accept as a definition of favoritism the more positive reactions to employees who perform the best. This is both human nature and good management.

? Can You Think of Any Reasonable Explanations for My Behavior?

Are there valid reasons for responding more positively to some employees than to others? You bet!

You go out of your way for employees who go out of their way for you. You give them the best pay, the available promotions, the finest offices, the most challenging jobs, the bulk of your time, and all the repayment you can for what they give you. Is this favoritism? No, but others may think so.

No matter what the answer, use this question to point out how you treat top performers and what it will take for this specific employee to join that elite. Warning: There is such a thing as favoritism, that is, responding to employees because of personal likes or dislikes. Keep your leadership act spotless in this regard.

? Do You Believe That as a Manager You
Would Respond Identically to Each of Your
Employees?

The employee accusing you of favoritism will probably answer yes
to this question. Disagree assertively, and draw on either of the
discussions presented for the two questions above.

7-11

Two Employees Are Fighting

Not all your subordinates get along as well as you'd like. In particular, two seem to have it in for each other. In fact, they're at it again,
arguing over who said what behind whose back to which other
employees. You'd like to stay out of the conflict, but it's at the point
where it is causing their productivity to decline. You call these two
into your office.

? Would You Each Tell Me in Your Own Words
What You Believe Is Straining in Your Work
Relationship?

This question enables you to set the tone for your role as facilitator
instead of boss or umpire. Listen carefully to what they say, and get
them to do the same. Don't allow them to interrupt each other. Focus
their descriptions of the situation on behavior they have personally
experienced in the relationship. Use as many of the following questions as you can.

? What Do You Hear Each Other Saying?

This question is a useful tool to help these two employees fulfill the
request of the initial question. You may choose to use it at the end of
the dialogue as a summary. Better yet, invoke it each time (before)
one employee responds to the assertions of the other.

Another means to ensure listening is to tell the employees in advance that they are not to respond to anything the other has said until they paraphrase to that person's satisfaction what was said. This is an effective conflict resolver. It eliminates any possibility for misunderstanding between these two.

? What Are the Needs Each of You Has?

Once you have managed to get the employees to listen to each other, you can help them each to define the specific needs they are looking to fulfill vis-à-vis each other. Be certain that you get them to articulate needs to be met and not positions to be taken or demands to be made (for example, "I need to be able to trust you," not "You have to stop stabbing me in the back").

? What Ideas Do You Have for How We Can Meet Both of Your Needs?

Once you've gotten them to listen to each other and to define their combat in terms of mutual needs, you'll be surprised at how much more cooperative these two employees might become. This question focuses them on the common task of simultaneously meeting two sets of needs that may not be as irreconcilable as they once appeared.

? What Do You Want out of Each Other from Now On?

One reason we have trouble getting others to move toward a solution of their quarrel is the tendency for them to dwell on the past injustices that have been dealt to them by others. Get these two employees off this form of destructive behavior by encouraging them to recognize that the only way to successfully resolve conflict is to fix the *future*.

At some point in the discussion you may even want to say that it is out of order to refer to anything in their relationship that happened more than an hour ago. This will force them to focus on solutions (the future) rather than problems (the past).

7-12

You Think an Employee May Have a Substance Abuse Problem

One of your employees hasn't been himself for several months. You've noticed a sharp decline in both his productivity and his cooperation with other employees. These performance deficits have been discussed with him, but with little progress. You're convinced that he has a drinking problem. You haven't caught him drinking at work, but the stories you've heard, the fumes you smell, and the physical signs you see all point to alcoholism. Before confronting him, you call your human resources office for suggestions. They agree that the questions you plan to use are appropriate.

? Are You Aware of All The Benefits of Our Employee Assistance Program?

The employee's answer doesn't matter; *any* response enables you to describe the help your company provides for addiction problems. Remember that you are not an addiction counselor, nor should you delve into the employee's personal affairs. Don't use this question with an employee who is likely to become indignant that you would raise the topic. If the discussion becomes heated, fall back on the bottom line: "My business is your performance on the job. Your business is overcoming whatever has been causing that performance to decline. I'm simply recommending that you look into whether the employee assistance program can give you a solution."

? What Help Are You Getting for Whatever May Be Contributing to Your Performance Declines?

The advantage of this question is that it ties the need for the employee to get help with the need to maintain an acceptable performance level. Whatever the employee's answer, your response should focus on the ultimate reason for asking the question: to make it clear that you will not accept less than a standard level of performance. Don't focus the discussion on alcohol unless the employee is willing to address it with you.

? Is There Anything I Can Do to Help You Get
Back on Track in the Company?

Use this question when you believe the employee would respond favorably to a personal offer of help. This question is not meant to suggest that you can solve the problem. It merely shows that you care. The employee will have one of three answers. If he says, "What do you mean 'get back on track'?" document the performance problems you have observed. Be specific; give examples. If he says, "No, there's nothing you can do," respond by suggesting other sources of help. If he suggests something you can do, decide whether it's an appropriate request. If it is, help. If it isn't, tell him why it isn't and recommend what you believe would be more sensible.

7-13

An Employee Is Doing a Great Job, but Doesn't Fit the Company Mold

You're faced with one of the most difficult leadership situations you could imagine. You have an excellent employee who keeps getting you in trouble. Her performance makes her more valuable to you than any two of her peers, yet her behavior is a problem for both her coworkers and your boss. Here are three examples. She puts in long hours and takes work home, but is not always available in the office from nine to five. She dresses and behaves a little "different" than her peers and is not a member of any office cliques. She is not highly polished or especially tactful in her interactions with upper management. Frankly, you would be willing to wink at her minor blunders if it weren't for the barrage of complaints you have been receiving from both above and below. She's been aware of some negative perceptions of her behavior for some time, but hasn't been very successful in doing much about them. You've put off having this talk with her because you don't want to alienate such a good worker, but you feel that you must now say something.

? How Can I Help You Become a Rising Star in This Company?

No matter which questions you use, be careful of two things. First, be certain the employee knows how happy you are with her every-day performance. Second, do not blame others (boss and coworkers) for the need to have this talk. Help her to see the value both for herself and for the organization of behaving more consistently with their expectations.

To this question she is likely to ask what you mean. Explain the importance of teamwork and how teams tend to develop guidelines or sets of rules to govern its members. Add that while not everyone is always able to follow the guidelines, it's best that all make a genuine effort to do so. Give some specific examples of behavior that you believe would profit both her and the organization. Offer your help in her development of these behaviors.

? How Do You Feel about the Need for Employees to Conform to Certain Standards of Behavior?

Your actual question may replace the words "certain standards of behavior" with a description of the most critical of her indiscretions. Use this as an opening to explain the reason for the rule, guideline, or norm that she is violating. Follow the advice given for the previous question.

? What Will It Take to Get You to Continue to Improve on Meeting Some of the Expectations We Have for Our Employees?

This is the most assertive of the three questions, especially if you replace "meeting some of the expectations we have for our employees" with a description of the goal you have for her behavior. No matter what her answer, reiterate your appreciation of her overall performance, yet insist on greater effort from her to overcome the perception of those who are most affected by the behavior. Be certain she understands that the way others view her is the greatest determinant of her success with them.

Extract a commitment to specific improvement actions from her. Schedule a follow-up meeting in a few weeks to monitor her progress.

Chapter
8
Working Together

Many of us work more closely with our coworkers on a daily basis than with either our superiors or our subordinates. These peers have a profound influence on both our job satisfaction and our job performance. When they cooperate, we succeed; when they undermine our efforts, we may fail.

It's tough to give feedback to colleagues when their behavior puts us on the spot. They do not report to us, and they consider themselves our equals.

Questions are especially valuable for dealing with people at our level in the company hierarchy. They enable us to make important points without appearing to take a superior position. And by opening them up to constructive feedback, questions set the stage for our ideas.

8-1
A Lazy Coworker Asks for Your Help

Many so-called shirkers are absolutely convinced that they have been given too much work and just can't stay on top of it, despite what they believe are Herculean efforts. You work with such a person who asks you to bail him out every time his laziness makes his deadlines scream for help.

? May I First Help You Figure Out What's Preventing You from Staying on Top of Your Workload?

This question is preferable either to saying no (making you look uncooperative) or saying yes (making you this person's dupe). Stated as above, it implies that you might pitch in but only after confronting the reasons for your colleague's lack of productivity. If you wish to make the question more powerful and perhaps off-putting, change "first" to "instead" or follow "of" with "a workload that's no greater than mine." Decide what wording works best for you.

Expect one of two responses. "Never mind!" or something similar means that you've successfully put the person on notice that you're no patsy. A more inquisitive retort ("What makes you so hostile?") may give you the opportunity to say how you feel about the person's behavior and to document the impact it has on you.

? What Prevents You from Doing It Yourself?

This is less cooperative than the original question. You'll want to reserve it for chronic dead weights. After you hear the explanation, there's a slim chance you'll hear a tale of woe that justifies the request. If you do, offer whatever help you choose.

More likely, the answer to this question will allow you to give direct and specific feedback to your coworker on the behavior that you feel causes him to ask you for help. You'll also want to add a few words describing the ferocity of your own workload.

8-2

Coworkers Complain That Your Hard Work Makes Them Look Bad

You enjoy your work, and your productivity shows it. Your job requires long hours and intense concentration. Not all your peers take their responsibilities as seriously as you do. In fact, they some-times tell you to slow down or they accuse you of being a rate buster. It just happened again, and you're prepared with the perfect re-sponse.

? If I Slow Down and the Boss Asks Why My Work's Not Getting Done, May I Say That It Was Your Idea?

The original complaint may be issued in the form of a hint or an apparently good-natured ribbing: "If you turn out any more work around here, the rest of us will be standing in the unemployment line." Just smile or politely tease back, "Not you, Chris. The wheels of progress would grind to a halt without you."

Ask this question when the needling gets less tolerable. It makes your point powerfully. When you use it, be prepared for criticism, perhaps that you take things too seriously. If so, try, "I do take my work seriously. Thanks for recognizing that."

Ask yourself these questions: *Are* you a workaholic? Do you enjoy being the teacher's pet? Are you pleased that your accomplish-ment sometimes causes your colleagues to look bad in comparison?

? Are You Asking Me Not to Do My Job?

Expect to hear, "Of course not!" Respond with, "Good." Say nothing else. If you can turn away or leave without being judged as rude, do so.

? Exactly Which Parts of My Responsibilities Do You Suggest I Ignore?

Expect to hear an agitated, "What do you mean?" Respond with, "Well, I'm only doing my job. If I were to let up as you seem to suggest I should, I'd have to stop doing some part of my job. I just want to know what part you suggest I let slide."

This may shut the other person up, or it may lead to a debate about job dedication and responsibility. Be more prepared than the other person for it.

? Is There Some Particular Reason Why You
Prefer That I Not Do the Job I'm Being Paid
to Do?

The difference between this and the earlier questions is that it will
turn the discussion more quickly to the issues of obligation and
commitment to work. Expect an answer similar to, "What are you
talking about?" Again, be prepared to state your values in a clear
and convincing manner, all the while anticipating what your oppo-
nent is likely to say.

8-3

You Are Made to Look Bad in Front
of Others

This morning's staff meeting didn't go well for you. It all started
when the boss asked why a particular project was behind schedule.
A colleague answered, looking directly at you, "Some of us have
been distracted by personal matters." You and everyone in the room
saw that barb as a reference to recent health problems in your family,
which you have been careful to isolate from your work. In a few
minutes you confront the perpetrator.

? Are You Aware of the Injustice You Caused
in Our Staff Meeting This Morning?

If the answer is a quizzical no, you have created a perfect opening to
give the feedback you are just dying to deliver. If it's something like,
"Are you referring to my comment about personal distractions?" or
if the person denies meaning you or apologizes, deliver the feedback
anyway.

In criticizing this act, follow these four steps. (1) Report on
exactly what was said as well as what you saw or heard in response
to it; in other words, how what was said created a problem. (2)
Document the inaccuracy of the statement as it relates to your work.
(3) State how you feel about what was said. (4) Ask for commitment

to the precise behavior you expect to observe in similar future situations. Throughout be as factual, unemotional, and nonpunishing as possible.

Ask yourself why you think this happened. It will help to be as analytical and objective as possible about your coworker's motives. Is this person frequently punishing, possibly discounted by others, and therefore not worthy of response? Finally, how much truth may there be in what was said?

? What Evidence Do You Have That My Personal Matters Are Delaying the Project?

If the answer is no evidence, ask that a retraction be made to the boss. Even though you are not likely to get one, this notifies the person that you are likely to be alert and instantly protective at repeat performances.

If you receive a denial that the reference in the meeting was about you, indicate your rejection of the denial and insist on more professional behavior in the future. Add your opinion that the unfortunate statement was an equally unflattering reflection on the perpetrator.

Finally, in case your coworker answers with so-called evidence, be prepared to discredit it rationally and calmly. It won't help to become defensive or to counterattack.

? Do You Believe That Coworkers Should Pull Each Other Down in Front of The Boss?

The wisest response would be something such as, "When we see something wrong, we have an obligation to point that out even if it embarrasses the wrongdoer." Agree completely with this statement, but add that there are two times you wouldn't do it. One is when the embarrassment outweighs the value of a public airing of the problem, in which case you would opt for a private disclosure to the boss. The other is when you didn't know what you were talking about. Make it very clear that *this* was the case in the staff meeting this morning.

8-4

A Coworker Consumes Too Much of Your Time

Why does the office "leech" always seem to single you out? That person has just wandered into your office and plopped down in one of your side chairs. You are about to be subjected to a detailed account of what happened during the office party you missed last night. The last thing you can afford to lose is the precious half hour that is about to be snatched away.

? May We Make an Appointment to Get Together Tomorrow?

If the person is already in overdrive, you'll need to break in both assertively and positively with this question. The answer is likely to be, "Sure. Why?" Then you can say, "Because this deadline I'm working on today needs every minute I have." Immediately look at your calendar for a time that you can afford to offer. Chances are good that the person will say something like, "That's okay, don't bother. It's not that important." Smile and say something like, "See you later" in a pleasant voice.

If you wish to be less solicitous, replace the question with a statement about your unrelenting workload and ask for a postponement of the visit.

Whether you ask a question or make a statement, thank the person on the way out.

? May I Finish What I'm Working on Before We Talk?

The implication of this question is that the person may hang around until you finish what you're doing. If agreeable, keep your eyes down on the job without engaging in conversation, and the person will usually leave within a few minutes. If not, you can state after a while, "This is getting a lot more involved than I thought. I'm afraid I'll have to accept a rain check from you."

Alternatively, you may hear, "That's all right. I'll come back later when you're not so busy." Mission accomplished!

If the interrupter objects with something such as, "This is really important" and you give in, you have at least notified your coworker to be brief.

? May I Ask You to Come Back Later When I'm Not As Busy?

More than the previous two questions, this one shoos the person out of your office. Use it when your work comes before any consideration of the other person's needs. Even so, notice that it does leave a crack open for the assertive person to ask for an exception.

8-5

Someone Is Hurt by a "Smart" Remark or Practical Joke

You're having an enjoyable chat with a few coworkers. During a round of humorous stories, the notorious wisecracker in the group makes fun of one of your subordinates who has a learning disability.

? Do You Have Any Idea Why I Didn't Laugh at That Remark?

If the wisecracker says yes and knows the reason for your displeasure, you can simply respond, "You're right," and say nothing more. After three to five seconds of staring in an attempt to solicit an apology, leave the person's presence.

If you get an apology, say, "I wish (person ridiculed) were here to hear it" on your way out of the room. Treat an "I'm sorry" from a sincere person more kindly, perhaps with a simple "I know" minus the departure.

If the answer to your question is defiant, dismissing, or glib, respond with, "Let me tell you why I believe that comment was inappropriate." Then say what is wrong with what was said. Make no comments about the wisecracker's motives or character.

❓ Do You See Anything Wrong with the Comment Just Made?

Expect to hear that it was a good-natured remark meaning no disrespect. You may also be told that a lot worse is said in the office that no one complains about. You may hear that the wisecracker is tired of thin-skinned reactions to good, clean fun. Or, you may be attacked by the practical joker for being a prude or for making something out of nothing.

The answer to your question doesn't really matter. Even if it is an apology (don't hold your breath), use your question as an opening to repeat exactly what you heard and say precisely what damage it inflicts. Don't initiate or be drawn into a discussion of intent. Defend the need for dignity and self-respect to be protected.

❓ How Do You Think It Feels to Be the Object of Public Ridicule?

This question may either stand alone or may serve as a follow-up to the previous ones. If it's your opening shot, expect it to elicit, "What are you talking about?" This opens the way for you to make all the points suggested with the other questions.

8-6

A Coworker Acts Unprofessionally

A friend of yours has been having difficulty in a new leadership role, and things appear to be getting worse. Just now you witnessed him shouting at two of his employees in full view of half of the office staff.

❓ Are You Aware of How the Incident This Morning by the Water Cooler May Be Viewed by the Office Staff?

What do you do when you see coworkers shooting themselves in the foot? Are you a good friend, willing to make them cry a little to learn a lot? Or are you an enemy, only willing to make them laugh with untruthful flattery, false affirmation, or destructive denial?

Once you get attention with this question, the path is clear to report on what you saw and to give your impression of the implications. Be honest, yet gentle, confrontive, yet supportive.

Should you receive justification, denial, or noncaring, give a specific statement on the impact of what you just witnessed.

_____

? What Caused That Exchange Between You and Your Two Employees by the Water Cooler?

If you hear, "Oh, it was nothing," say why you think it was *something*. This question's purpose is to move directly to a discussion of causality. It also gives your friend some objective feedback on the impact of his leadership style. The desired effect is getting him to talk.

_____

? What Can I Do to Help You Avoid Unfortunate Situations Such As the One That Occurred This Morning?

This offer of help is a gentle way to begin. If your offer is refused, you may want to persist with words like, "I think I can help you avoid the damage that I witnessed today. In fact, I have a specific suggestion or two that I'd like to share with you if you're willing."

8-7

A Coworker Checks Up on Your Work

Some people don't know how to mind their own business. One of your peers, in particular, regularly pries into your area of responsibility. You're convinced that queries of how your work is proceeding have nothing to do with concern for your welfare, nor does your progress affect hers in any way. Her most recent intrusion was, "Are you finished with that job yet?"

? Would You Like to Do It for Me?

This question is an indirectly assertive and powerful way of saying, "Stay out of my business." It is preferable to that, especially if stated nonantagonistically, because it is not defensive and puts the other person on notice.

The answer is likely to be a surprised no that you can acknowledge with "Good." You can immediately continue on with what you were doing prior to the intrusion. In the unlikely case that you invoke a yes, be prepared either to subcontract part of your work or to state firmly that although you appreciate the offer, you intend to complete the job yourself.

? Why Do You Ask?

This is another powerful but polite way to say "Buzz off." It immediately focuses on the legitimacy of her inquiry. If she has a good reason to ask about your progress, acknowledge that and give the appropriate status report. If, instead, she's out of line, this question should make her feel that way.

? Do You Think I *Should* Be Finished with It?

This question is likely to surprise and confuse your nosey coworker. If she says yes, you respond, "Well, that shows how little you know about my responsibilities and the quality of results I'm looking for. Perhaps you should keep your mind on your own job."

If she says no, say, "Good. I was worried about you for a minute."

8-8

A Coworker Competes Aggressively with You

It is painfully apparent that a certain coworker has a need to outdo you, vying for the boss's attention, fighting for office resources that can come only at your expense, and quickly snatching credit for accomplishments that might be attributed to either of you. You decide to confront the issue.

? Can We Agree to Replace the Win-lose Parts of Our Relationship with Win-win?

If your boss does not recognize the problem of competitive employees, you have to take matters into your own hands. Expect this question to elicit, "Certainly" or "What do you mean?" Respond by describing the positive behavior you expect in future situations where, in the past, you've been deceptively outdone. Focus on the positive of what you want to see rather than on the negative of what you've been seeing.

If, instead, the answer to the question is something like, "Not if that means you expect me to kiss your feet," you're in trouble. All you can do is get help from other coworkers or from the boss or appeal to the person's desire to avoid declared war with you.

Before you ask *any* questions of the other person, ask these of yourself. Is there any chance that you contribute to a competitive environment in your office? Do you give others reason to feel threatened by you? Do you show off yourself?

? What Benefit Did You Get Out of Leaving My Name off the Annual Report?

Notice how much more powerful this question is than, "Why did you leave my name off the annual report?" It helps keep the focus on the act rather than making it easy for the other person to deflect the issue.

Be prepared to defeat any rationale proposed for the omission. If the person claims an oversight, say, "Then I'm certain you won't mind issuing a notice to that effect to recipients of the report. I'll draft it for your signature."

If the answer is a blunt, "I didn't feel your name deserved to be on it," your only recourse may be to bring the situation to your boss. Take care, however, not to be seen as a whiner. Make a straightforward statement of what happened, what damage you believe was caused, and any remedies you would like the boss to help you pursue.

To make certain that this never happens again, do not trust that others will give you credit for your work.

8-9

A Colleague Asks Your Help in Covering Up Poor Performance

Colleagues and friends ask us for a variety of favors. If the request is reasonable and we are able to comply, we should. But suppose that the request would force you to cover up an intentionally shoddy piece of work and your coworker does not show any true remorse for the poor job.

That's what just happened to you. You've been asked to turn your head the other way.

If you provide the requested cover, you don't believe you'll really be helping your friend. And you will be cheating your company. You decide to turn down your coworker's request with a question.

 ? Will I Be Able To Help You Solve This Problem without Either One of Us Lying?

You achieve two goals with this question. First, you make your value system clear. Second, you make a genuine offer of assistance.

Your coworker's likely reaction to this question is that the only way to solve the problem is to "fudge things just a little." Your friend may add that it happens all the time and try to use guilt as a lever by saying, for example, "If you were really my friend, you'd help me and not lecture me."

Don't be seduced by the guilt. You are helping by listening and working towards a long-run solution. Offer a way out that maintains your values and is least damaging for your friend.

? How Can I Be Sure That This Request Is Not
the First of Many Others?

Again the person will try to assure you that the indiscretion will not
happen again and that your cover story will never be needed again.
His protestations may or may not be true. That's a judgment for you
to make. You don't want your assistance to set a precedent.

? How Are You Changing Your Behavior
to Make Sure We Never Have This
Discussion Again?

You aren't soliciting a commitment to change, you're soliciting
examples. Promises may or may not be kept. Behavioral change
(enrollment in self-help groups, therapy, terminations of relationships) are observable examples that promises are being kept.

One way you can help is to discuss options the person might
consider to help change his behavior. In this way you aren't lying
and you are helping.

8-10

You're Asked by a Coworker for a Loan

It's common practice in your office for people to borrow a few dollars
now and then for lunch or transportation. You've been known to do
this, too. But the request you just received is unreasonable in your
opinion. A member of your team is making a down payment on a
great car deal tomorrow and just asked to borrow $500 until his bank
certificate of deposit (CD) matures in another month. You can afford
the loan, but you don't think it's a good idea.

? Do You Prize Our Friendship?

This is the key question to ask. The biggest reason not to lend money
to friends is that it endangers the health of the relationship. An

unforeseen problem may prevent him from repaying you, thereby introducing unnecessary conflict between the two of you. When you get the certain yes answer to this question, make these points and add that the friendship is too important to you to jeopardize. If he persists, stick with this line of argument. Don't lie by saying you can't afford it, especially if he knows you can.

? What Other Sources Are You Considering to Get the Money You Need?

Chances are good that your friend has not yet fully explored all his funding options. Give him whatever suggestions you can.

? Have You Considered Waiting for Your CD to Expire?

He may answer by saying that the current car deal is too good to pass up. Suggest that he look into the penalty he'd pay by cashing in the CD early. If the car deal is really good, the penalty may be minuscule by comparison.

His real problem may be his inability to accept delayed gratification. He wants the car now, and he's just not going to wait. If you suspect this, ask him, "What is the worst thing that will happen if you have to wait until your CD expires to buy a car?" The thinking he does to answer this question may bring him a little more patience.

8-11

A Coworker Tries to Become Too Involved in Your Personal Life

It's to the point where you do everything you can to avoid one of your coworkers because she meddles in your personal side. She shows an interest in your affairs, is looking for more participation in your personal life than you desire, and has even invited herself to private events outside of work where you did not want her to be. In fact, at this very moment she asked you a question about your family that you feel invades your privacy. You decide to put her on notice.

? Would You Like to Know Why That Question Makes Me Uncomfortable?

Don't wait for an answer to this question. Use it as an opening to say why you feel that her question goes beyond office prattle and violates your right to privacy. You may wish to make some reference to her similar past behavior, but don't punish her. The important thing is to address the current situation and to repeatedly ask this question every time she accosts you for private information.

? Why Do You Need to Know That?

If she answers that she's only making conversation, say, "Then let's talk about something more appropriate." Say why her question wasn't appropriate.

If as her rationale she professes concern for your family, say that you appreciate her concern but that you find it improper to discuss such matters outside of the family circle.

? Do You Ask Other People Questions Like That?

Chances are she will admit that she doesn't. Respond by saying that your family needs the same privacy that others do. If she gives you a reason why your family is different to her, say you are happy about that but not happy about the accompanying curiosity.

8-12

People Seem to Be Avoiding You

The group's going out to lunch, and again they haven't invited you. You're starting to see a trend. You don't seem to be part of the office grapevine and are beginning to feel that you might be the person they're talking about. You're starting to feel paranoid about your appearance and personal hygiene. You go for a walk outside. As you're walking, you consider some questions for yourself and for those who avoid you.

? How Have I Changed, What Am I Doing Differently, or What Have I Done to Hurt My Coworkers?

This question provides two types of behavior to examine: recent changes in your personal style and any pain you may have caused others.

If you honestly cannot think of any changes or any pain you may have caused others, you might pose the question to a trusted colleague. Tell the friend that you're concerned about the cold shoulder you're experiencing at work. Ask for his honest answer to the question.

When he gives it neither defend your actions nor attack what you see as his insensitivity. Simply thank him, go off to analyze his feedback, and try to understand why you are seen the way he reports. Develop a plan to change the current perceptions of your colleagues.

? What's Happening in My Personal Life to Affect My Professional Life and Vice Versa?

When people are avoiding you, you should draw one of two conclusions: either something has changed in their lives or something has changed in yours. If just one or two people seem to be avoiding you, assume that their lives have changed. However, if most of your friends and colleagues are giving you the cold shoulder, assume that you are the one who has changed.

This question should start you towards introspection. Take a long and hard look at yourself. Get outside of your shell and see yourself the way your friends, family, and coworkers do. Once you've taken this penetrating and objective look, you'll know why people are avoiding you.

? Am I Becoming Increasingly
Short-Tempered or Negative?

One reason people might be avoiding you is that you simply aren't fun to be around. You may be blowing up at others, or perhaps you've become excessively cynical. Maybe you get overly defensive at the slightest hint of criticism. You may be looking for the bad in people before giving them a chance to show you the good. Are you exasperating, abrasive, or ill-tempered? Do you need to show more optimism, acceptance, and joy?

8-13

A Personal Relationship
Is No Longer Rewarding

You're not sure exactly what the problem is but you know your relationship with your significant other (spouse, lover, parent, child, friend, coworker) is not what it used to be or what you know it could be. As you mull over what to say to the other person, you remember the wisdom of not saying, but asking.

? What Do You Think Each of Us Is Doing
to Help and to Hurt Our Relationship?

There are two powerful qualities to this question. First, it acknowledges that you are both responsible for the relationship. Your question neither blames the other person nor sets you up as the villain. Second, it solicits examples of destructive and constructive behaviors. You're asking the other person to think about behaviors that are helping the relationship and behaviors that are hurting.

It's crucial that you listen without interrupting. As a matter of fact, simply listening without judging or defending may be the first step toward healing the relationship.

If you hear a litany of your faults, accept the answer as an honest expression of the person's anger and frustration. Then repeat the question emphasizing the words "us" and "our."

? What Ideas Do You Have for Turning This Relationship into One That We Both Want It to Be?

Use this question to force the discussion in the direction of positive actions. Keep the focus on the future ideal that you both want to establish; get it away from the mistakes both of you have made. Push for specifics and suggest some of your own. See whether you can both commit yourselves to healing strategies.

? Do You Think We Should Get Advice from a Counselor?

Acknowledge the potential need for professional help. Many are reluctant to seek outside counsel because they feel such assistance labels them as a failure or as unhealthy. If you sense that the other party feels this way, tell why you think outside help is appropriate for the two of you. Stress the importance of seeking such help as an affirmation of your relationship. You care so much about the relationship that you're looking for guidance to heal it and save it.

? What Are the Costs of Continuing This Relationship?

This question is the litmus test of interpersonal relationships. Regardless of the pain the question elicits, you must engage in honest soul-searching. People change and relationships change. One or both of you may no longer be able to fill the needs of the other, yet you may fill other needs. Redefine and renegotiate the relationship. Let go of what you must; salvage what you can. Be certain that you can distinguish your dreams from what recent history reveals as reality in the relationship.

8-14

You Learn That a Close Friend Just Lost a Loved One

You face perhaps the most difficult circumstance any person could confront. The daughter of a coworker and good friend was killed in an accident twenty-four hours ago. You will be face to face with him in a few minutes, and you're searching for the right thing to say. Naturally, you'll begin by saying how sorry you were to learn of what happened, but that's not enough between close friends. And since everyone will be saying that to him, it sounds hollow to you and probably to him.

You're really in a bind. You don't want to hurt him or say something inappropriate, but you do want to express your support. You know that you're not a trained bereavement counselor, but you do want to be of comfort. You also know that grieving is something to be encouraged, not discouraged. You decide that it's best to get *him* to speak. You ask him a few questions about his daughter, starting with the most concrete and possibly advancing to the more personal over time.

? Where Were You When You Found Out?
   What Were You Doing?

These are ice-breaking questions, intended primarily to set the stage for greater depth in your discussion. They focus your friend on concrete recollections, not immediately related to the death. They may relax him and create a rapport that will encourage him to keep talking. There's no telling where his answer may take him. It may by itself lead to the torrent of feelings you hope your friend can eventually release. A catharsis is one of the important early steps in the grieving process.

? When Did You See Her Last?

If the earlier questions failed to evoke much and you sense a need in your friend to say more, move to this question or one that his state suggests would be more helpful. However, do not be invasive or meddle if he makes it clear that he does not want to continue talking about his loss.

———————

❓ How Will You Remember Her?

You may or may not want to probe this deeply. You certainly won't use this depth of question until you are certain your friend is comfortable with going this far with you.

Be prepared for anything. This question may evoke positive memories or it may bring out unresolved conflict that existed in the relationship. Your friend may even express anger at his daughter for dying, which is a healthy response to the passing of a loved one. Don't discourage it.

At this stage in the interview—that's what you're conducting—you need only to repeat or paraphrase what your friend says to keep him talking, venting, and grieving healthily. You'll also want to empathize with whatever feelings he expresses: "That must have been a difficult time for you" or "It sounds like you were very proud of her."

Chapter

9

Responding
to the Ideas
of Others

One major difference between dynamic and static organizations exists in the number and quality of new ideas generated. Organizations grow on ideas, on suggestions for better ways of doing things, on new solutions to old problems, and on creative strategies for spawning new business.

Organizations that evoke productive thought from employees are organizations where people know how to respond supportively to the ideas of others, even when those ideas may not represent the best possible effort of their creator. In such organizations, there's no such thing as a bad idea; everyone works together to apply their collective intelligence to the common good.

The questions in this chapter show how to respond appropriately to the ideas of others, regardless of their quality.

9-1

Someone Gives You an Awful Idea

If you can't use someone's idea, it probably costs too much, won't be accepted by others, is illogical, or in some fashion violates your work rules. But, if you say, "That costs too much," "We tried that before," or "It won't work," you may discourage a future suggestion that will prove to be a real winner. You recognize this and so let other people uncover for themselves the weaknesses in their ideas.

? What Do You See As the One Greatest Drawback of That Idea?

You may wish to precede this question with a statement of what you like about the idea. If the person cannot imagine any potential problems, give your impression of the most serious possibilities while soliciting the other person's suggestions for overcoming them. The alternate question immediately following is one way to ask for this help.

? If We Use Your Idea, What's Going to Happen When . . . ?

Complete this question with the words that will take others on the journey of discovery you hope they'll learn to make individually before a suggestion is made. Use it to point out a probable or inevitable flaw in what they're proposing. And, this question just may help you uncover a workable idea.

? What Suggestions Do You Have for How to Handle . . . ?

If the person is able to see valid objections to his or her idea, don't say, "Well, then, you see why we can't use that idea." Instead, ask for help in solving the problems it creates. If you have truly received a bad idea, this discussion should make that evident to both of you. On the other hand, you may discover that the idea is more valid than you originally thought.

9-2

You Get Unwanted Advice

One of the most freely given gifts is opinion. Where you work, people are unusually generous. Your coworkers give you their ideas on how they think the work in your area could be improved all the time.

You certainly don't mind new ideas; you're as interested as anyone in finding better ways of doing things. You just wish others would follow your habit of asking people if they'd like to hear your idea before you thrust it on them. But you recognize that any sort of a defensive reaction will label you as close-minded.

? If I Get the Chance to Actually Try Your
Advice, Do I Have Your Permission to Use It?

This question should set back the unwanted adviser, especially if you emphasize the words "actually try." The reaction is likely to be a quizzically emphatic "Of course," to which you respond with a firmly pleasant "Thank you." The message ("Keep your ideas to yourself") may not get through the first time, but it won't take too many repetitions to get the desired results.

Before you use this question, ask yourself why the advice troubles you. Is your colleague truly being overbearing, or are you threatened by and not open to the ideas of others?

? Do I Give You the Impression of Being
Ineffective in My Work?

The answer is almost certain to be a bewildered, "No. Why would you say that?" This gives you the opportunity to say, "Well, all the unsolicited advice I get around here makes me wonder." Then proceed to give some of the most offending examples of unsolicited advice you have been given. If you mix some of what you've received from this person with that from others, this person will not feel singled out for attack.

? How Do You Feel When You Believe That
Other People Are Telling You How to Do
Your Job?

If you hear something such as, "Lousy," say you feel the same about unsolicited advice, especially when you find it to be excessive. If the person doesn't get the message, say, "I even felt a little that way when you . . . "

If you hear, "It doesn't bother me at all," respond with, "It doesn't bother me either. In fact, I welcome it, except when . . . " Complete this sentence with whatever is appropriate to this situation. You might choose to talk about an offensive or condescending tone you hear in the advice, you might comment on the excessive amount of it, or you might describe distasteful behavior on the other person's part when you fail to use the advice.

9-3

A Know-it-all Insists That She's Right

It's one thing when others give you unsolicited advice; it's quite another when they give it as the gospel truth. One of your coworkers has always warned you to check up more on the work of your employees. You've continually responded with your philosophy of empowering employees by giving them greater responsibility for their jobs and greater discretion in how they perform them.

One of your employees was fired today for stealing from the company over the past year. The employee was so devious that no controls could have either prevented the thefts or uncovered them before now. But now the know-it-all coworker is in your office saying, "I told you so!"

? What Was It That You Told Me?

The answer will almost certainly be, "That you weren't keeping a close enough eye on your employees." Here are two suggested responses. First, describe how well all your employees flourish under your leadership style and give specific examples of the productivity you're getting because of the treatment you give them. Second, launch into the following questions.

? Would You Like to Hear the Story of What Really Happened in This Situation?

If the know-it-all doesn't want to hear the explanation, say something like, "Then please leave. I have more important things to do than to provide a forum for your childish gloating."

If the person is willing to listen, share just enough of the situation to emphasize that no amount of practical controls could have prevented the problem. If the theft involves the slightest potential for future legal action, reveal no details beyond your colleague's need to know.

? What Value Do You Find in Saying That to Me?

You hope this question will put the know-it-all in her place. If so, and if she says, "No particular value," respond with, "Then why did you say it?"

If she mumbles something defensively, tell her you disagree and why. Point out that her statement was nothing more than an attempted insult. Add that it does nothing to strengthen your relationship or to improve the ability to work together productively.

9-4

You Are Given an Idea That's Over Your Head

Your boss called you and your colleagues into her office with great excitement this morning. She has an idea for the operation that she wants you to test for feasibility immediately. As you're listening to her description, you realize that you lost her two minutes ago and that the idea is getting more complicated with each sentence she utters. You don't know whether to hide your bewilderment, hoping someone else has this figured out, to show your confusion, hoping your boss will backtrack, or to admit that you're lost. Finally, you decide to ask a clarifying question that doesn't make you or your boss look bad in front of your peers.

? Could You Go Back Over the Part Beginning with . . . ?

Use this question in the middle of your boss's explanation to prevent you from getting hopelessly lost. Ask it as soon as you've lost touch with the explanation.

If you wait too long, this question is not as useful. However, getting the boss to backtrack even a short distance may clue you in to earlier ideas that you had misunderstood.

If your boss is in good humor, you can also use this question light-heartedly to indicate that you are totally lost. Somewhat smiling you say, "Could you go back to the part beginning with 'I have an idea to share with you'?"

? May I Paraphrase That Idea to See If I Understand It Completely?

Don't wait for an answer. Put the idea in your own words, and wait for a confirming or denying response. Do this either at the end of the explanation or when the boss pauses, if you can interject without disturbing her.

? What Are the Exact Benefits You Hope to Obtain from This Idea?

By hearing the benefits you may come to understand more of the details of the initiative your boss just described. Save this question for the end of the explanation.

9-5

The Information You've Been Given Is Useless

You serve on a project team. One of your colleagues has been collecting data for your use in the next step of the project analysis. You waited patiently for the information and received it two days late. You tear open the envelope, eager to begin your part of the project. You've cleared your schedule for the afternoon so you can get a good start today, finish tomorrow, and then take off for a week's vacation.

As you review the information on the sheets, confusion gives way to frustration, which soon gives way to anger. Your project partner blew it; his results are totally worthless. Whether through laziness, incompetence, or misunderstanding, he failed to do his job. You jump up with the mess in your hands and head for his office.

? Are You Aware That This Is Not What We
Need to Complete the Project?

Resist the temptation to replace "what we need to complete the project" with "what I was expecting." The latter is more likely to create personal antagonism. Besides, who cares what you were expecting? The important thing is the project.

If your colleague admits to the inadequacy, whether in an apologetic or contentious manner, describe the impact it has on your workload, and turn the information back to him for correction. You may also need to inform the rest of the team of the delay as well as the cause for it.

If he refuses to acknowledge his failure or, worse, refuses to clean up his mess, inform the team or your supervisors, as appropriate, of the situation.

? Did Something Prevent You from Providing
the Information We Need?

This is a softer way of pointing out the inadequacy of the results you were given. It gives the person an easier opportunity to report what he encountered to you. Otherwise, follow the advice under the previous question.

? What Can I Do to Help You Improve This?

The most likely answer you can expect to this question is, "What do you mean?" This opens the way for you to point out the deficiencies. Remember to do only that; do not ascribe intent or motivation to the effort that yielded the results. Say what you see in the report, show how it falls short, and recommend corrective action, if necessary. Do not allow this question to be misconstrued as an offer to clean up the mess.

9-6

Someone Steals Your Idea

You don't believe what you hear. A colleague you previously considered a friend has infuriated you. She just reported to you how excited the boss was to hear her great idea on how to cut the company's printing expenses by twenty percent while improving the quality of the corporate communications program. At lunch last week you had asked for her comments on this same idea before you would break it to the boss in a meeting scheduled with him the day after tomorrow. You can't let her get away with stealing your idea.

? Where Did You Get That Idea?

The answer to this question will determine how you open your discussion of the "theft," but the ultimate thrust of your censure will be the same no matter what the answer. (Of course, the person may somehow convince you that she developed this idea before you did and that your conversation with her merely convinced her to come forward with it.)

With your response, let her know how you feel about plagiarism, especially when one of your ideas is presented to the boss by someone else claiming credit for it. Before you confront this person, decide exactly what you expect as a remedy, and then demand it.

? Should You or Should I Tell the Boss Where the Idea Came from?

Unless your idea-stealing colleague is willing to negotiate reparations to your satisfaction, this is the ultimate question. Make it clear that you intend to tell the boss exactly what happened with or without her present there. Unless she believes that she has more legitimacy with the boss than you do and is planning to engage in the "big lie" strategy, this should cause her to retreat.

This question is a forceful assertion of your rights, your anger, and your expectation for redress. You're telling the person in unequivocal terms that the boss will be told, either by you or by her.

If you sense that the person is experiencing sincere remorse and is worried about being fired, you have two options. The first is to demand the credit you deserve. Choose this if you think the person is playing you for a sucker or if you believe that the deserved kudos are necessary for your career mobility. The second option is to pull back and allow the person to save face. You might choose this if the person manifests sincere regret or if you believe the joy of victory is not worth the pain of battle.

? Is There Any Reason Why I Should Not Go to the Boss Right Now to Set the Record Straight?

The preceding question conveyed your moral indignation and demanded a remedy. This question implies that you might be convinced otherwise. There are at least two predictable responses to your question. The first is for your coworker to defend her claim to the idea successfully, in which case you'll want to gracefully back down. The second is for your coworker to come clean, apologize, and seek your forgiveness. If you can forgive and forget, do so; you'll prove that you're the bigger person. Holding a grudge can rob you of energy better spent on more productive tasks.

? If You Were in My Shoes Right Now, What Would You Do?

This powerful question solicits empathy and role reversal. Borrowing a coworker's ideas and presenting them as one's own often occurs without thought of repercussions or of the pain it may cause the true originator of the idea. With this question you're implying that there is pain and you want her to describe it.

If she can't empathize or refuses to do so, tell her *exactly* how you are feeling and exactly what you plan to do as a result.

Chapter

10

Selling Your Ideas

One of the greatest challenges at work is to bring other people around to our way of thinking. Whether we are selling ideas to our bosses, employees, coworkers, or customers, success depends on getting a fair share of them accepted.

This chapter shows what to ask in several situations where your suggestions don't get the results you had hoped. The questions enable you to press assertively toward a positive response to your ideas without alienating the other person.

10-1

Your Idea Gets Shot Down

You've got a great idea for improving the service your company gives. After listening to customers' requests and their complaints, you made a suggestion to your supervisors three months ago that will help attract new customers and keep old ones. So far there's been no response. Every day that passes without better attention to customer needs represents a lost opportunity for the firm. You've become impatient, so you've asked your boss for the status of your idea. Her response is, "Sorry, you just didn't convince us that your idea was worth implementing."

? How Can I Turn That into a Great Idea?

The impulse reaction here would be to ask, "Didn't I make a case for how much we need to take better care of our customers?" However, a display of frustration rarely advances your cause with superiors. Jabs are unlikely to get the feedback you need to sell this and future ideas.

This question prevents you from assuming a defensive posture. It asks for a positive recommendation that might enable you to save your most recent idea and certainly to make worthwhile suggestions in the future. Notice how the suggestion is referred to as "that," without emphasizing your ownership of it. This reduces the chance that your boss will view this question merely as a self-serving request.

Hope for an answer that directs you to a new, more successful strategy to get this idea through. If you don't get such help, consider following with a bit of added pressure by testing an alternative strategy or two: "Would it have helped if I had . . . ?"

? What Was the Main Reason My Idea Wasn't Adopted?

Even though this question calls for a negative response, nonetheless it can be effective. Perhaps there was one problem with your idea that killed it more than all other drawbacks combined. Once you learn what that problem is, you are in a position to revise your idea to eliminate the problems.

A more pleasant possibility is that your boss's answer will reveal that your proposal was misunderstood. You may be able to show her how top management's concern really doesn't exist. She may then be willing to resubmit the idea after you make cosmetic changes in the proposal to clear up the misunderstanding.

? How Do You Suggest I Change My
Approach for Giving You Ideas
in the Future to Improve the Way We
Perform Our Mission?

While this question asks for future guidance, it is also powerfully blunt in letting your boss know that you remain convinced of the rejected idea's merit. Use this question as a gateway to a productive discussion with your boss about the priorities of upper management and how you might adjust your ideas to blend more convincingly with those priorities.

10-2

Your Accuracy Is Challenged

You had been in charge of conducting an opinion survey of the office staff. You prepared an organizational climate questionnaire that had been quickly approved by top management, and you supervised its distribution to employees. Once the survey was returned, you analyzed the data so that you could make a presentation to senior staff, which you are now in the boardroom delivering. But things haven't gone as smoothly as you expected. The very first slide you projected on the screen was greeted with skepticism. In fact, one of the vice presidents suggested without being specific, that your data are riddled with faulty assumptions and errors. After listening to the objection, you remain convinced that your data are accurate.

? What Causes You to Believe That
a Problem Exists with the Data?

When your accuser remains vague, use this question to get to the root of the disagreement. Once you isolate his or her precise concerns, you may discover that the two of you don't disagree at all. The most frequent culprit behind an apparent conflict of ideas is communication failure: one person simply not understanding the other. This question creates a venue for fixing communication breakdowns.

Notice that you should not modify the noun "data" with the pronoun "my." Always keep yourself verbally separated from the data you collect. Do this for three reasons. First, it doesn't really belong to you; no one "owns" information. Second, a true professional avoids excessive use of such self-centered identifications. Third, when detractors take shots at the work you have done, you don't want to get caught in the cross-fire.

The purpose of this question is to learn the motives for the attack, which may be political and have little to do with the basis for your presentation. It will help you decide how to meet the needs of the objector. When you respond, do so with verifiable data and not with emotion. Rather than allow yourself to feel attacked, see yourself and the objector as being on a joint quest to uncover the truth. Remember that your kite rises against the wind and not with it.

? Would You Find It Helpful for Me
to Recheck the Data and Get Back to You
Immediately with the Results?

Once it is clear to you that it is your data, not you, that is being challenged, this is the question of choice. If you have even the slightest doubt that the objector may have a point, say no more. If, on the other hand, you are confident of the validity of your findings, you may wish to add that you have already verified the information on your own but that you are pleased to reconfirm the results to give the audience the same degree of confidence that you have.

If the challenger backs down or tells you not to bother to verify the data, don't simply go on with your presentation. The justification for any recommendations you are about to make has been besmirched. In your closing remarks you will need to make at least one final reference to the thoroughness of the report.

10-3

Your Honesty Is Challenged

You believe in keeping your boss informed, and so three months ago you reported an incident between you and a customer that left the customer dissatisfied with the service you had provided. Upon hearing your explanation your boss told you not to worry about the incident. But when the customer filed a formal complaint with the Better Business Bureau, your boss's attitude changed and he accused you of covering up what really happened to protect yourself. Since you had been totally truthful about this incident from the beginning, you are unwilling to accept these claims of duplicity.

? On What Evidence Are You Basing Your Charges of Dishonesty?

Listen carefully to the answer. Taking notes will help you to remember everything and will put the other person on notice to make defensible assertions. Don't respond until you completely hear the person. Think about the situation from your accuser's perspective before becoming defensive. This will help you to clear up any misunderstandings, defuse the situation, and formulate a compelling case for your veracity.

Don't accept vague suppositions or advice to forget it. In most offices, once you are accused of dishonesty you are guilty until proven innocent. And unless you are emphatically cleared of wrongdoing, the recollection that people will have in a few months is that you were connected to some form of sleazy behavior.

If the boss refuses to give you evidence for the accusations, ask that they be formally withdrawn to the knowledge of anyone who may have taken note of them. In extreme cases, you may wish to seek the advice of legal counsel. It is always a good idea to keep your own records throughout these kinds of situations.

? What Would You Have Me Do Differently the Next Time?

If you behaved responsibly, you may be able to say, "That's exactly what I did." If you didn't, you can assure the boss that you will measure up the next time.

If the prescription for next time is impractical or unreasonable, point this out. Demonstrate the problems inherent in the suggestion through a what-if scenario: "If I do as you request and the customer responds by . . . , how should I handle that?" If you can make the folly of the recommendation clear in this way, the boss may come to his or her senses.

? Why Do You Think I Acted As I Did?

Even though you were not practicing deception, your behavior may not have come up to the standard that the boss expects. This question gives you a chance to point out why that standard may not have been possible in this situation.

If the answer is, "I don't know," describe how the circumstance of the situation led you to act as you did. If the answer contains a judgment of devious intent or weak character, correct the boss politely but firmly.

10-4

People Say the Time's Not Right for Your Idea

You've been thinking for a long time about the need for training the administrative staff of your company. Most of the staff has yet to experience any professional development in the time since they were hired. Your manager likes your ideas and asked you to research available training programs. You took the finished proposal to her this morning, but lowered profit reports have changed her attitude toward spending money for employee training now. The bottom line to her response was, "This isn't the time to incur an expense of that magnitude." You swallow your anger and ask these questions in a calm, measured tone.

? When Would the Right Time *Be* to Develop
Our Administrative Staff?

This question is a bit of a jab. It implies that the decision maker doesn't care about the effectiveness of the employees you propose to train. If that's an unfair or imprudent characterization of management, lop off the five words just before the question mark.

Whatever the answer, be prepared to follow with a summary of the rationale for the training. Be certain that your rationale makes postponement look like an unwise decision to management (not only to you) and encourages the immediate adoption of the program.

If nothing else, this question enables you to pinpoint the best time to reintroduce the idea. Following this meeting you may want to put in writing your agreement to postpone your idea until the conditions stipulated by the manager emerge. In this way, it will be difficult for her to renege on the discussion.

? If You Could Change Something
in the Proposal to Make It Right for Current
Conditions, What Would That Change Be?

Don't accept "Nothing" for an answer. If necessary, offer concessions yourself. Listen carefully to the manager's suggestions and concerns and determine how you can change your proposal to overcome the objections to its timing.

? Will You Be Ready to Implement It on (Give
a Date)?

If you cannot convince the boss to reconsider via the first question, pin her down to an alternative date. If she accepts your date, get the agreement in writing if possible. Without hounding her, don't let her forget about her commitment between now and the new date.

If she refuses your date, ask her to name one. Tell her why having a date is important for your plans.

10-5

People Say Your Idea Is Unrealistic

In today's staff meeting, your team brainstormed to improve product quality. In the middle of the process you shouted an idea that was quite creative and surprised even you. As the session proceeded, you became more and more impressed with the workability and probable impact of the idea. However, when the group evaluated the many suggested solutions, yours was one of the lowest rated. While it got a high score for creativity, it was deemed as impractical and unrealistic, and you can't see how they miss its utility.

? What Is There About This Idea That You Find
Most Unrealistic?

Three things are wrong with saying, "Why do you find my idea unrealistic?" First, it sounds like a challenge. Second, the phrase "my idea" establishes your inquiry as a personal battle. Third, the question allows for almost any response.

Instead, this question sounds analytical, calls for an impartial analysis, and cuts directly to the bone. If you can defeat the greatest objection to your idea from the outset, you'll have momentum as you overcome the remaining weaker objections.

Be certain to rely on data as you respond to objections. Don't allow emotions to cloud your judgment.

? What Do You *Like* About the Idea?

This question has two purposes. First, it puts the other person in the position of thinking positively about your idea. Second, the answer may give you a clue about how to assert its practicality in terms that will be important to the objector.

You don't want to hear "Nothing" as an answer, so don't ask this question unless you are sure the other person objects only to the idea's practicality.

? How Might the Idea Be Revised to Make It
More Realistic?

The brilliance of this question is that it enlists the objector to the idea to assist with its improvement. If the person refuses to help or can't suggest improvements, you haven't lost a thing.

10-6

Your Idea Is Labeled As Too Costly

There are very few good, reasonably priced places to eat within walking distance of your office. You've suggested that an old, unused storeroom be turned into a small lunch room that could be furnished with a refrigerator, a microwave oven, and some tables and chairs. You are convinced that the costs of renovation and furnishings will be more than recouped in one year; increased productivity would result from improved employee morale and the time that employees take off for lunch would be reduced. Unfortunately, you just heard that top management finds your idea too expensive.

You have been granted an opportunity to meet with the chief financial officer to appeal the decision. You plan to ask the "right" questions.

? How Do You Define "Too Costly"?

The answer to this question will determine what you're up against. If you hear a specific amount, ask what amount would not be considered too extravagant. Go back to the drawing board to determine what can be done with that amount to furnish the lunch room, even though not at the level you had hoped.

If the answer is something like, "Anything that causes us to go in the hole this year," explain the benefits of the lunch room. Show how, through improved morale and reduction in lost time from work, it will improve the bottom line.

? If I Could Show You That the Idea Will Result in an Improvement in Our Profit Position, Would You Support It?

It's almost impossible for the answer to be anything but, "Of course, but how do you intend to show that?" At this point ask for a day to prepare an analysis that will document the benefits of the lunch room, or reveal an already prepared analysis.

Finance people respond to figures on paper. But be certain that your analysis is persuasive, realistic, and defensible. Organize it in the same way that this person would have. Be cooperative, not cocky, as you explain what you've done.

? What Information Do You Need in Order to Support the Idea?

A promise of profit may not be what it will take to sell this particular person. If you don't know what influences this person, find out with this question and then ask for a day to get back with the information that will win the argument.

10-7

People Complain That They Don't Understand Your Idea

Over the weekend you had a great idea for how to improve the way customer complaints are handled over the telephone. You just spent ten minutes reviewing your plan in detail with your customer service supervisor, explaining the benefits of the plan as well as exactly how you want the customer service representatives to implement it. As you described the process, she asked no questions. But when you finished and asked what she thought of the idea, she said, "Why are we doing this? How is it different from what we're doing now? I don't understand what you're asking us to do."

To avoid responding with an angry criticism of her listening ability or an attack on her intelligence, you calmly ask a question.

? What Exactly Didn't You Understand?

If the person claims not to have understood *anything*, reorganize your presentation and begin again, starting with a summary of the idea that outlines its major advantages and features before explaining it in detail. Along the way, check for understanding by asking or by reading the person's nonverbal cues. Don't make the mistake of speaking louder unless volume was a problem the first time; however, you may need to speak a bit more slowly. Don't speak in a condescending or parental tone.

If the person missed only certain ideas, use this question to find out what they are and to clarify them. Don't be impatient as you go over them. Remember that we are often guilty of internalizing ideas we like to such a degree that we become incapable of explaining them succinctly to others. In other words, the misunderstanding may well have been your doing.

❓ How Much *Did* You Understand?

Actually this is a more reliable way of phrasing the previous question. Your customer service representative might not be a reliable reporter of what she doesn't grasp. But by having her tell you what she believes she understood, you can easily probe a bit to verify that understanding. Now you can go back to repeat those dimensions of the idea that were missed.

❓ Why Do You Think You Had a Hard Time Understanding Me?

Either she wasn't listening well or you weren't presenting well. Beyond the issue of this particular idea, you have a long-term relationship to nurture with her. Don't just clear up this communication collapse. Get to the bottom of the misunderstanding so that future occurrences are less likely. Learn her impression of this breakdown, share your own in a spirit of reconciliation, and take action to fix the future.

❓ Did You Hear Me Say That . . . ?

Complete this question with one of the basic points of your idea. Keep progressing though the concept with more advanced endings to the question until you get to the point where she reports having lost you.

Chapter
11
Pleasing Tough Customers

When the customer's behavior puts you in a tough spot, the need to be tactfully assertive is more critical than it is with employees, coworkers, and perhaps even bosses. The customer is king and must be so treated. On the other hand, when the customer's behavior creates a problem, you must act. The questions in this chapter enable you to make your needs for customer behavior clear without being controlling, punitive, or offensive.

11-1
Making Deceptive Claims

A customer wrongfully claims that you previously quoted a price that is below the amount for which you will sell your product. This may be a deceptive ploy by the customer in hopes you will cave in, or it may be an honest mistake. Choose a question appropriate to your guess of the customer's intent.

? May I Ask for Your Help with Something That Will Enable Me to Give You the Very Best Service?

Be prepared for an answer of either "What is it?" or "Sure!" In either case, you are now positioned to ask for the honesty you need. Avoid putting customers on the spot. Don't accuse unless you are spoiling for an argument and intend to lose this customer.

Describe the specific behavior you need in situations like this one, and say why you need it in terms the customer will understand. Finally, ask for a commitment that the needed behavior is what you'll get in the future.

You might say something like, "I'm concerned that your recollection of my quote could be so far from reality. I'm not sure if it was my inability to communicate clearly or wishful thinking on your part. The help I need is your trust that the price I'm quoting right now is the very best I have ever been authorized to make."

? Did the Price I Quoted Seem Low to You at the Time?

Use this question for customers who you suspect have made an honest mistake. No matter what the answer, respond with, "Well it doesn't appear low to me, it appears ridiculous. And if that's what I told you, I must not have been in my right mind that day. There's also a fifty percent chance that you didn't hear me quite right. Whatever the reason, we'll have to have to stick with the published price."

? In Your Business, Do You Quote Prices That Might Cause You to Lose Money on a Sale?

Here's a question for the deceptive customer. Ask it in a truly curious manner. If the answer is yes, respond by saying, "We do, too," and give examples of those situations where it might in fact make sense to price a product below cost. Then add, "But in transactions like this one, my company must make a reasonable profit. The price you claim I quoted to you makes that impossible and therefore makes that price impossible."

? May I Write Up the Purchase at the Actual Price?

This capstone question should follow any and all the discussions that other questions might have generated in this situation. If the answer is no, respond with, "I'm sorry to hear that. What else can I do for you today?" Respond to a yes with a sincere, but not gushing, "Thank you."

11-2

Payment Doesn't Go Through

A known check bouncer has just handed you a check in payment for a purchase.

? May We Arrange for a Different Means for You to Handle This Payment?

This is a delicate situation. None but the most responsible, knowledgeable, and mature employees should be charged with breaking such news to your clients. You want to minimize the defensiveness or embarrassment that the confronted customer may feel.

Occasionally, the strong hint delivered by this question will be all you need to deflect what is likely a bad check. Nevertheless, be prepared with your comeback to the "Why?" or "What do you mean?" you'll get from less sensitive customers. Be assertive, yet gentle, direct, yet gracious.

Explain the situation in this way: "We would feel a lot better with cash or a credit card this time." If you must be more direct, try, "As you'll remember we incurred considerable difficulty and cost in securing payment from your last check. We're not in a position to do that again."

? Are You Aware That There Is A Problem
With This Check?

This is a more direct way to restate the question above, particularly if you've attempted and have failed to process the payment. No matter what the customer's answer, you will then state precisely what happened when you sought to accept the payment. Do not make any statements about the customer's failings that caused the problem (for example, "You haven't put enough money in your account to cover this check.") Just say what happened. "The bank indicates that the account on which this check is written is overdrawn."

11-3

Not Having the Right Paperwork

A customer is in front of you to be served. You told this person on the telephone yesterday exactly what paperwork would be needed for you to meet his request. He chose not to take your advice seriously.

? When You Are Able to Return with Your
Documentation, Will You Please Ask
for Me?

Like you, customers are busy people; they cannot be expected to treat your needs for completed forms and required documents as seriously as you do. Don't berate them when they fail to comply with your paperwork requirements, and be certain that every requirement is truly necessary. On the other hand, if you're not insistent on compliance with justifiable requests, the fish will manage to wiggle off the hook.

State this question in a helpful and cooperative voice. Make it sound as though you want the customer to return to you personally so that you can be certain that the best possible service is received. This approach takes the focus off of having to go along with your requirements, and it might make the customer feel better about complying.

? What Might I Do to Help You Remember
to Bring It Next Time?

If the paperwork or information is important enough, you shouldn't mind going along with whatever reasonable request is evoked by this question. But chances are the customer will simply say something like, "Oh, there's nothing for you to do. I'll just have to work harder at remembering."

? If I Can Arrange for an Exception to Policy
This One Time, Will You Commit to Bring It
with You on Your Next Visit?

If you plan to serve the customer now even without the paperwork, this represents a nothing-to-lose gesture that may help win loyalty and future cooperation. The only danger is if you fail to persist next time and prove that your threats are empty.

11-4
Taking Up Too Much of Your Time

Some customers have inordinate needs for information about your product or service. They may return several times for information they failed to obtain before. Others hesitate to make a commitment, ask interminable questions, or want to socialize excessively. When other customers are waiting or when you are otherwise squandering precious selling time, you have to be assertive with those who would monopolize your day. The trick is to accomplish the disengagement without alienating the needy customer.

? If I Can Show You That Each of Your
Concerns Is Addressed, Will You Make
a Commitment to the Product?

This is a classic sales-closing question. Once the person says yes and you go back carefully over each of the objectives raised, you should have solved the problem of the time-draining customer. If the person answers no, it is perfectly legitimate for you to say, "Then I don't think we can help you. Please come back when (not 'if') you change your mind."

? May I Write This Up for You?

Once you have completely addressed the customer's concerns, consider this question both as an alternative to the previous one as well as a follow-up. This can be used at any time during your contact with a customer. You'll be surprised how many times this simple question will yield a quick sale.

? What Additional Information Do You Need to Make Up Your Mind?

When you suspect a customer of soaking up product information or, worse yet, being a tire kicker, stay ahead of him with such information. If you're asked one question, assume there's another one lurking not too far behind. The sooner you answer it, the sooner you'll be able to move on to the next (paying) customer.

? May I Ask You to Help Me Serve Other Customers by Continuing Our Discussion After You've Had Some Time to Give More Thought to Your Decision?

This question combines two often effective strategies: asking for help and professing your desire to be helpful. If the customer says no, be patient for one more question and then attempt to close the sale. If you're still not getting anywhere, politely but firmly excuse yourself.

11-5

Failing to Control a Child

Three small children are playing tag in your store. They are running into customers and getting close to causing damage. You locate the parent.

? May I Be of Help in Encouraging the Children Not to Run Through the Aisles?

Parents tend to be defensive of their children, even when you identify a behavior that even troubles them. This question should be sufficiently confrontive, unless the behavior is endangering someone's safety. In that case, you may have to take matters into your own hands without consulting the parent.

Expect to hear, "No, I'll handle it myself," "Yes, please say something to them," or "They're not doing any harm." In response to the last answer, be prepared to state precisely why you are asking for the intervention. Explain the reason for your request; don't merely insist on having things your way.

If you fail to elicit the parent's cooperation, you may have to ask that the children be removed from the store.

? May I Enlist Your Help in Getting the Children to Refrain from Running Through the Aisles?

This a somewhat more confrontive question than the first. Again, the result will be either to activate the parent or to enable you to make a statement of impact that you hope will lead to action.

? Are You Aware That the Children Are Causing a Disturbance in the Store?

This question is likely to generate more immediate defensiveness than either of the first two. (Notice that in all three questions, to minimize the parent's feeling of being criticized, the children are not identified as "your.") Whatever the answer, use it to get the action you need.

11-6

Demanding Special Treatment

Some customers expect to be treated better than others. They make unreasonable demands, they expect you to violate your company's policy for them, and they also skip to the front of the line, as someone has just done to the group of customers waiting for you to serve them.

? Will You Please Help Me Serve You Better
by Waiting Right Here Until I Can Take Care
of Those Already in Line?

Of course, this is a question for which you don't want an answer. Allow the line skipper to remain at your counter until you take care of the people he passed up. Then turn back to take care of him without censure. To do this you need to remain continually vigilant of who is in the queue waiting to be served.

This strategy is in contrast to that of a clerk at a theater refreshment stand who waited on a customer who had bypassed a half dozen others to order popcorn. One of the compliant customers protested when she made her way to the front of the line. The clerk offered this explanation: "Don't worry ma'am. I only pretended to squirt butter on his popcorn. That's my revenge for people who can't wait their turn." She smiled and didn't bother to criticize his strategy, but probably wished he would have used the question instead.

? Did You Miss the Line?

As you ask this question, point to the people properly waiting their turn. This question is usually enough to direct the person back in line. If it isn't, ask the person to wait where he is to be served in turn or to get in line where you'll take care of him at the earliest opportunity.

? Have These Other Customers Given Their
Consent for You to Move to the Front of the
Line?

Recognize that this is an embarrassing question. Use it only with that intent. If the person says no, ask him to wait for his turn. In the unlikely event that he says yes, verify his claim with the other customers before serving him.

? Will You Wait Right There, Please?

When you see that a line jumper has physically moved ahead of others, ask this question pleasantly. In a helpful tone, add, "That will enable me to get to you as soon as it is your turn." Then turn to serve those in line, coming back to him at the point where he would have been had he remained in the queue.

11-7

Challenging the Price

Every customer is conscious of price, but some get carried away. In front of you right now is a perfect example. He says he'd love to buy your product, but the price is too high. He hasn't yet tried to bargain with you, but you figure that's where he's heading.

? Would You Like to Check Our Competitor's Price Before Making a Final Decision?

Use this question when a customer complains that your price is too high and when you know that your price is competitive. Many times this is not a strong objection, but simply a weak attempt to negotiate on price.

"No, never mind; I'll take it" is a frequent answer. If the customer says he'll do just that, say, "Good. I believe that will make you feel better about our price."

? How Much Would You Like to Spend?

This question is indicated when the cost of the product itself, rather than your pricing policy, is the problem. The answer often enables you to match customers with other models that both meet their needs and are affordable.

? Would You Like to Consider a Model Priced
Closer to What You Wish to Pay?

Use this question when customers actually attempt to negotiate a lower price. When you do not have the authorization to bargain price with customers, try to deflect their strategy without putting them off. Occasionally, you will send a message strong enough to discourage bargainers. If not, it will give you the chance to point out that it is as important for you to stick with your price as it is for customers to stick to the product model.

Depending on the importance of this customer, you may want to at least give the impression of making some type of concession: "How about if I do this for you? . . . " That concession may be some personal effort you'll make on the customer's behalf or some other consideration that doesn't cost anything.

11-8

Requesting Something You Don't Provide

You believe your company carries the best brands and models of the products you sell. Occasionally you get customers who ask for a brand you neither stock nor handle as a special order. Whenever this happens use questions to see if you can't convince them to buy one of the brands you trust.

? May I Ask Why You Need That Particular
Brand (Product)?

Successful sellers almost never say no to customers, not when there's a chance they may be able to say yes. To get to yes, use this question to find what specific benefit the customer hopes to gain through the nonavailable product he or she has decided to purchase. Think about how the features of your product might generate that benefit. Then demonstrate how your product provides it. Guaranteed? No. Effective? Yes!

? May I Show You a Brand That We Feel Does
an Even Better Job?

If you have confidence in what you stock, reveal that confidence to
the consumer. All but the most stubborn brand loyalists will give
you a chance to prove the assertion embedded in this question.

Should the customer refuse your offer, begin describing the
benefits of the product, but don't continue to push beyond the flash
point of the customer's patience.

? If I Guarantee Your Satisfaction
with the Brand We Carry, Will You Test It?

This is an even stronger question, especially if you grant the buyer
an unconditional return of the product you are promoting.

11-9

Can't Decide Whether to Buy

You've just made what you thought was one of the best sales
presentations of your career, but the customer doesn't appear any
more ready to buy the services of your company than he did when
you began. You think he likes what he heard, but he doesn't appear
to be able to make a decision. Just then you recall a book on mastering
the art of selling that you once read, where the author suggested that
one of the best ways to close a sale, once you've established a bond
with the customer, is to ask a question. You reread that book in your
mind and think of six questions that might do the trick.

? Are You Ready to Make a Decision Now,
or Do You Need More Information About
Our Services?

Like most effective closing questions, this one doesn't give the
customer the option of answering with a simple and final no. Using

it may tell you that you need to describe more benefits of the service. It may also motivate a procrastinating customer.

? Of the Three Levels of Service I've Described, Which One Do You Feel Would Best Meet Your Needs?

In sales jargon, this is often called an involvement question. It encourages the customer to begin to feel ownership of your service and to visualize vividly what the service will do for him. Once he answers this question, he is a step closer to saying yes.

? Do You Think You'll Be Using This Service Just in Your Own Office, or Might It Be Relevant for Others in the Company As Well?

The possibilities for asking involvement questions are unlimited, and this is another example. In this case, the purpose is for the customer to consider the benefits of your service at an even higher level than he may have up to now. It is difficult for us to phrase an appropriate involvement question for your situation. Much depends on the nature of your service, on the needs of your customer, and on your relationship with him. Practice creating involvement questions of your own.

? If I Can Guarantee to Resolve the Concerns You've Described, Are You Prepared to Sign an Agreement Today?

Customers rarely respond to even the most effective sales presentations by giving you the sale. More typically, they voice some sort of an objection. They may tell you about a feature of your service they don't like, they may need more reassurances about reliability, or they may balk at the price. While no single question can respond to these and dozens of other possible objections, this one has the potential for turning an objection into a sale closing.

If you hear a no, ask what else you would need to resolve to get the sale. Don't give up easily. If you hear yes, you can start counting your commission.

? What Do You See As Your Time Line for Making a Decision?

This question helps to motivate the customer by getting him to think in concrete terms about the timing of a decision. When asked this question, the potential customer of a top seller answered, "Well, I'm trying to think of whether I would want this to come out of my first quarter or my second quarter budget. I guess it would be the first quarter." The seller followed immediately with, "Then that means you'd want to have an answer to me by the middle of next month. Is that possible?" The answer back was yes, and a decision was made.

? What Is It That Makes It Difficult for You to Decide Right Now? Is It . . . ?

Use these questions, with the second one completed, when you have no clue to why the customer won't sign on the dotted line. When you get the answer, ask the immediately preceding question.

Chapter
12

Resolving Conflict

In a sense, this entire book is about resolving conflict between you and the people with whom you work. In Chapter 7, "Dealing With Challenging Employees," we addressed disagreements between your subordinates. In Chapter 8, "Working Together," we explored those times when coworkers compete against you. In Chapter 11, "Pleasing Tough Customers," you were forewarned against clients who would abuse you. Throughout, our focus is on responding to the troublesome behavior of others in the world of work.

For this chapter we have reserved those times of interpersonal strife where the struggle gets particularly ugly, where the other person's behavior is making it very difficult for you to fight fairly, or where a well-stated question is needed to defuse the situation and enable you to gain the upper hand.

12-1

Someone Takes a Position Against You

You advocate a new procedure for your company that you are convinced will improve its profit over time. Actually, the innovation would have been adopted long ago were it not for another employee who has blocked your idea every step of the way. It's clear to you that something under the surface, other than the merits of your proposal, is causing his negative response. You'll not make any more headway until you find out what's really at the root of his opposition.

? What Do You Propose As an Alternative to the Idea?

This question puts your nemesis on the spot. He may answer, "I don't have one. I just know that your idea won't work." At this point ask the question following this one.

If he does have a recommendation, listen to it very carefully. (This will be difficult for you to do, given your negative feelings toward him.) Acknowledge its merits. Objectively consider its strengths relative to your idea. If it isn't as effective, point out why. Ask him to go to the boss with you to present your comparative ideas for a final resolution. If he refuses, say that you will expect his opposition to end.

? What Changes Might Be Made in the Idea That Will Gain Your Support for It?

Notice that this is a superior question to asking, "What don't you like about the idea?" That would engage your adversary in nit-picking instead of problem solving.

If he claims that he can't find one good thing about your plan and you haven't yet used the question above, use it.

? Why Do I Feel That Your Opposition Goes Beyond the Idea Itself?

This question comes the closest to the truth. Don't ask it unless you have documented cases of defiance. Expect to hear, "I have no idea." Provide your evidence of subversion.

12-2

Someone Stabs You in the Back

Reliable word has just reached you of an incident that might harm your career. Someone whom you thought you could trust complained to your boss that you aren't carrying your share of the team's workload and that you are highly paid in relation to your level of responsibility. You decide to confront this person.

? What Evidence Do You Have That
I'm Not Carrying My Share of the Load
Around Here?

Spring this question out of nowhere, when the backstabber would have no reason to anticipate it. Expect incredulity (feigned or otherwise) at the reason for your question. Say, "I understand you've shared your feelings on this subject with others in the office in my absence. I don't find that very professional of you, and I expect it to stop immediately. Is there any reason why you cannot do that?"

Respond this way to a denial: "That denial may be real for you, but it's not real for me. In any case, don't ever let it happen again. Do we have an understanding?"

In case the person stands by his criticism of you, be prepared to provide compelling evidence to the contrary. Add that whatever the truth is, you never again expect it to be used against you behind your back.

Before using this question consider whether it will compromise the witness to the crime by forcing him to come forward, and whether you and the witness want that to happen. This may not be a problem since this question is vague enough to make the person wonder exactly to which of several conversations he has probably had with others you are referring.

? Why Have You Chosen to Slander Me
in Front of Others?

This question comes to the point more quickly. You may even choose to replace the word "others" with "the boss." Otherwise, it should lead the conversation in the same direction as the first question.

? Does It Bother You When People Say
Negative Things About You Behind
Your Back?

In case you hear no, be prepared to say that it bothers most people, including you. It is more likely that you will hear yes, which will open the way for you to reveal your evidence and insist upon no repeat performances.

Note that if the backstabber has lied to the boss, you might insist upon a joint visit to the boss's office for a retraction. While he is highly unlikely to agree to this, you will scare him by suggesting it, and he can be told that you have made an appointment with the boss to clear your name on your own. This appointment should be imminent so that this person doesn't get to the boss first with even more lies.

12-3

Someone Refuses to Speak to You

As a result of a problem with someone on your team, that person no longer speaks to you. You have to deal with her almost daily, and she does so without uttering a word when she can. She communicates to you through intermediaries, and you have been doing the same to deal with her. This situation is ridiculous. It's inconvenient for both of you, a cause of a number of misunderstandings, and time-consuming for other employees who have to deliver messages that should be delivered face to face. How do you ask a question of someone who doesn't intend to answer you?

? When We Need to Conduct the Business
of This Office, Can We Do It in an Adult
Fashion?

This situation calls for a fairly pointed question; otherwise, you may not get any response at all. If you do get a response, document the cost of the inconvenience, misunderstandings, and dependence on others for the company. Create a communication contract between the two of you.

Once you get the person talking, you may even be able to address the friction that exists between you two. If the discussion goes in this direction, steer clear of a prolonged rehash of past wrongs. One way to do this would be for you to admit more responsibility for the existing mess than you think you deserve. Focus on the future of your relationship, that is, what it will take to begin working together more productively.

? Would You Like to Join with Me for a Discussion of This Impasse with the Boss?

This is your trump card if the other person refuses to meet you halfway and continues to give you the silent treatment. If she passes on this invitation, inform her that you intend to go ahead without her. Have the same discussion with your boss you had hoped to have with your coworker, reporting on your failed attempt to get cooperation.

12-4

Someone Needles You Incessantly or Uses You As a Target of Practical Jokes

When you got your recent promotion you were warned to expect a little jealousy from your peers, but for the most part it didn't amount to very much. There were certainly things said behind your back, but you encountered only the most good-natured razzing, with one exception. A certain coworker has been on your case for the past three months. You hear comments like, "Let the new executive do it" and "We mere mortals couldn't possibly handle that as well as you can." You've taken about all you intend to.

? When Is the Wisecracking Going to End?

Get ready for a vigorous counterattack. You may hear feigned remorse in the form of, "I'm only kidding. I hope you don't take my joking seriously." To this you respond, "Psychiatrists have shown that most joking *is* serious, and I think they'd put the fun you've been having at my expense in that category. Why don't you just stop it?"

A more vicious person might respond to the question with, "What's the matter, executive? Can't you take it? Maybe they should have looked for someone with a tougher shell to promote." (The gauntlet has been dropped.) Consider saying, "Whether I can take it is not the question. The question is, why does someone choose to cover up their own insecurity by attacking others? I've asked other people in the office, and no one seems to know."

In using this or any question, remember that this person is a bully, and bullies have been grazing with bullies all their lives. The chances of you winning a duel without a great deal of preparation, are slim.

? Are You Attempting to Be Funny, Vicious, or Foolish?

The teaser will probably want to know what you mean with this question. You might say, "Well, when you jab me about my promotion as you just did, you pretend to be funny, hope to be vicious, but only succeed in looking foolish. I think everyone in the company would be pleased by and benefit from your ability to accept that I got that promotion."

? Why Are You Troubled by My Promotion?

Again, you would expect to hear, "What are you talking about?" You might say, "What else would explain comments like . . . and . . . ? Other people in the office agree with me that your anger about my promotion is at the root of these barbs." After the response, indicate that whatever is going on, you will appreciate an immediate end to the childishness. Even if you don't get it, this opportunity to speak your piece may be just what you need to free yourself from the emotional blackmail of this fool.

12-5

Someone Insults or Belittles You

There's no more horseplay and kidding in your office than in most, but it has been known to get out of hand. A bad example was a recent outbreak that came at your expense. One of the more insensitive employees in the office made a sexist remark, disguised as a joke, in your direction for the second time this week. You let it pass the first time, but now you feel obliged to respond.

? Do You Understand Why That Joke Was Not Funny?

The person will either say no or wonder what you're getting at. This opens the way for you to testify that any joke that comes at another person's expense does more damage than good. Explain the damage and say why you were insulted or belittled by the remark. Insist upon a commitment to greater sensitivity in the future.

? Do You Understand Why I Was Offended by That Joke?

This question is more to the point than the first one. It has the danger, however, of focusing the discussion on you rather than on the joke.

? Has Anyone Told You That Sexist Jokes Are No Longer Cool?

This question has the effect of putting the person down. It is the kind of question to ask if you don't plan on discussing the event but just on reacting to it and walking away. It may be all that will be said on the matter.

12-6

Someone Loses His Temper

You have just been attacked. Someone had an emotional explosion in your midst and you've been peppered with verbal shrapnel. You can't see any justification for the assault, and you don't intend to let it go unanswered.

? What Can We Do to Ensure That We Never Have a Repeat of What Just Happened?

This question says it all: What happened was unacceptable, and it must never happen again. Furthermore, it enlists the help of the exploder to establish those conditions that will prevent a reoccurrence.

If you receive an apology, should you accept it? Yes, if this is the first time this sort of thing has happened; no, if it is a repeat performance. Excuse a chronic exploder and you give him license to do it again. Instead, say, "That apology may be real for you, but after all the times this has happened, it is *not* real for me. What I need instead is to have this never happen again."

? Do You Feel Justified in Speaking to Me That Way?

If you hear no followed by an apology, respond as recommended for the previous question. If the person says yes, strenuously disagree. Make the point that while we all lose our tempers from time to time, verbal abuse is never justified. Give specific feedback on how you believe this particular situation should have been handled, and state your full expectation that it happen that way in the future.

12-7

Someone Misrepresents Your Intent

To retain their credibility with employees, your subordinates who supervise make upper management the villains from time to time.

For example, they may attribute to the company an unpopular policy into which they had input. Generally, this is a useful strategy that should not do any serious damage to your position in the organization, especially if they tell you when they do it. The problem is when one of your subordinates actually lies to employees about the reason behind a position or an action you have taken. This just happened and cannot be tolerated.

? Why Do Your Employees Misunderstand My
Position on This?

Once you ask this question keep pressing until you are convinced that either you were not misrepresented or that the offense will never be repeated. Note that you may not want to insist that a misrepresenting supervisor clear your name with employees at the risk of losing face with them. On the other hand, your subordinate must come away from this conversation resolved to reform.

? Why Did You Feel a Need to Report My
Position As You Did?

It may not be enough simply to catch the person in the act of misrepresenting you and insist that it never happen again. This question seeks to learn why it happened in the first place. Is it because your subordinate harbors ill feelings toward you? Did she use it to compensate for a lack of empowerment with her employees? Is she a person who needs help with her self-esteem? What is the root cause of the behavior, and what can you do to help her eradicate it?

12-8

Someone Is Dishonest with You

You just caught one of your coworkers in another bold-faced lie. For two weeks you've been in trouble because an important customer profile has been missing from your files. You asked everyone in the office if they had seen it. This particular coworker gave you a strenuous denial, going so far as to say he's never gone into your files without your knowledge.

Yesterday, because this employee was sick, the boss asked you to get a report off his desk. As you gathered the report and turned to leave the office you noticed a familiar sheet of paper in an open desk drawer partly covered by a stack of papers. It is your missing customer profile!

Initially you won't say anything to the boss about your find. You plan to confront the thief first when he returns to work. You find a reliable witness to verify that the profile is in the desk.

? Is There *Any* Chance That You Might Have My Customer Profile?

Ask this question when your colleague returns to work. A negative response helps to close any doors this person will try to use when you say that you found the paper in his desk. When you do, take the person to his desk to find where he hid the profile. (If it has been removed, call on your witness.) You'll get any number of feeble excuses or denials at this point. As you fend them off, ask if he wants to join you in the boss's office to explain your find. Assuming he doesn't, say, "Well, that's where we're going the next time anything like this happens" and leave his office.

? After Denying That You Had Seen My Missing Customer Profile, How Do You Explain That It's Sitting in Your Desk Drawer?

This question has the same purpose as the first. Use it if you feel you don't need to close any back doors and you want to get straight to the point.

? Guess Where I Found This?

This strategy has you removing the customer profile when you first discover it in the desk drawer. Again, threaten a meeting with the boss as the price of future dishonesty.

12-9

The Other Person Refuses to Accept Any Responsibility for a Conflict

You've heard that a strategy for breaking a deadlock in a disagreement is to admit the role you're playing in the dispute. You've done this with someone with whom you have been fighting, hoping she'll reciprocate in the same good faith so that the two of you can get beyond this foolish quarrel. Unfortunately, she responded to your admission by saying it was about time you admitted your guilt and by walking away. You catch up with her later to get this matter resolved.

? After Hearing My Admission, What Role Do You Think *You* Have Played in Our Disagreement?

This question will probably jog at least a partial admission out of the person. And, to create a spirit of cooperation, that's really all you want. Don't feel that you have to press for a full confession. That will only anger her.

If you get nothing, move to the two questions that follow.

? Are You Saying That You Have Played No Role in Our Disagreement?

When the other person refuses to respond in the affirmative, this serves as a follow-up to the first question. It may stimulate a concession. If it doesn't work, proceed to the next question.

? If I Offer to End My Irritating Behavior, Will You Do the Same?

This question has two purposes. Once you have both made your admissions of guilt, use it to create a performance contract that will guide your future interactions. Make the first commitment as encouragement for the other person to do the same.

If she has not yet owned up to her role in the conflict, use this question as your last attempt to achieve peace. Again, make the first commitment, and then state the response you need in return. Get her agreement to the contract.

Chapter

13

Running Meetings

You've probably heard the humorous indictments about meetings: "Meetings are places where people take minutes and waste hours," "A committee of three gets things done if two don't show up," and "Had God sent the Israelites a committee instead of Moses, they would still be in Egypt."

Your job as meeting leader is to make certain your members don't feel this way about the group discussions you lead. This means you need to provide the group with guidance in conducting its business efficiently and effectively.

As you lead your meetings you'll find assertive questions to be a powerful tool to keep the meeting on track. As the leader you'll often be expected to make *statements* to execute your leadership obligation, but you don't want to appear to be a tyrant. Questions allow you to provide the direction your group needs and to involve them in problem solving, without being branded an autocrat.

13-1

People Walk in Late

You lead a quality improvement group (QUIG) in your company that meets for one hour on Thursdays at 1 P.M. Rarely does everyone show up on time, and today is no exception. Four of the twelve members of your QUIG arrived after 1:15, and two have yet to show. You've made your expectations for punctuality clear, but they don't appear to have been taken seriously.

? Is There a Better Time to Schedule This Meeting?

The timing of this question is critical. Unless your intent is to embarrass a particular individual, use it several minutes after anyone has arrived and only when more than one person has been tardy. Expect one of three responses.

If the group greets it with silence and blank stares, answer it yourself. Begin with a statement of why the current situation is intolerable, and then ask for ideas on how to get people to the meetings on time. Be prepared for this question to lead to a discussion of the value of the meetings. During it you may want to ask for feedback on how they might be conducted more effectively.

If the consensus of the group is that rescheduling is not the answer, insist that one is found. Devote the rest of the meeting to finding it, pulling specific suggestions out of them for remedies. If the group believes that the schedule is the problem, change it.

? What Will It Take to Get Us All Here on Time?

When you want to help your group solve a problem, it is often best to present an open-ended challenge such as this. You may first want to define the problem more specifically and tell them why punctuality is critical. Then you can lead a brainstorming session of actions that they believe will reduce tardiness.

13-2

The Agenda Is Ignored

The meeting you are leading has gotten way off track. For whatever reason, the discussion has once again digressed from the agenda. You started by evaluating computer hardware vendors, and now you're debating the relative benefits of the newest laptops.

? What Is the Connection Between What
We're Discussing Right Now
and the Current Agenda Item?

As the meeting leader, you have the perfect right to rule any discussion out of order. However, when you do, you risk coming across as a dictator. You will also be embarrassed if the group points out a relationship between the present conversation and the agenda that was not immediately obvious to you.

Little can be said in defense of a meeting that strays from its agenda. This question will jog the group back to its assigned task, unless the agenda has proven to be irrelevant or less important than what is being discussed.

? Can Anyone Tell Me Why We Are
Digressing from the Agenda?

Avoid the temptation to ask, " . . . why are we *always* digressing from the agenda?" Criticisms that include generalizations—often triggered by the word "always"—generate far more than their share of defensiveness.

This question pinpoints why the group is not focusing on its task. It should elicit a discussion of what's really important to the group.

? How Can We Make the Agenda Less Prone
to Digression?

This is a gentle reminder. It will bias the response toward an evaluation of the agenda, rather than toward an evaluation of the group.

13-3

Two People Don't Understand Each Other

A member of your group, Raj, just made a comment that tells you he misunderstood the comment just made by Jennifer. In your role as the group leader you point this out.

? Would You Please Restate Your Last Point
to Be Certain That the Rest of Us
Understand It?

Before you ask this question of Jennifer, indicate that Raj's comment tells you that he may not have understood her. Or to prevent embarrassment to Raj, you may choose to claim that *you* are not certain you understood her.

Once Jennifer restates her point clearly (you may need to ask questions along the way to be certain that she does), state the difference between what you thought was heard the first time and what is now apparent that Jennifer meant. Then, defer back to Raj for any restatement he may now wish to make of his response to Jennifer.

? Can Anyone Restate to Jennifer's
Satisfaction the Point She Just Made?

Again, you'll want to preface this question by saying why you believe the paraphrasing is needed.

This strategy involves group members in working for clarification, instead of making them dependent on you for it. It will also sensitize Jennifer to the possibility that she may not always be as clear as she ought to be.

? Are You Satisfied That Your Last Comment
Was Understood?

If Jennifer says no, indicate that you aren't either, and ask what part of her idea needs to be clarified. Make certain that you understand her restatement. Push for further enlightenment if you need it.

If Jennifer responds in the affirmative, say that you aren't convinced she was understood. Say why and request that she help you and the group by giving it one more try.

13-4

Group Members Argue

You expect disagreement in the meetings you run. It's even healthy because it challenges shoddy thinking and encourages creative problem solving. But the argument between Tyrone and Charlie at this moment has gotten out of hand. They are flaring up and taking rigidly polarized positions. They're talking at the same time with little attempt to understand each other. You intervene before this disagreement turns into a name-calling battle.

? What Do You Hear Each Other Saying?

The first step in conflict resolution is to get the two parties to listen to each other. Get each antagonist to paraphrase to the other's satisfaction what the other person is saying. Once this is accomplished, use the questions below.

? What Do You Hear As Each Other's Needs in This Situation?

Focus combatants away from taking positions. Show them that true conflict resolution results not when their positions are won but when their mutual needs are fulfilled. State your optimism that with a bit of creative thinking the three of you can devise a solution that will meet both sets of needs.

As they respond to this question, be certain that they are indeed expressing *needs*, as opposed to wants, and that their requests are limited to the essential, rather than representing a shopping list of every desire they can imagine.

? What Do You Suggest As a Resolution That
Will Meet Both Sets of Needs?

Once two people in disagreement are listening to each other and
have restated their conflicting positions as competing needs, the time
has arrived for creative problem solving. Join with these two group
members in searching for compatibility in what they are seeking and
commonality in their goals. Assist them in uncovering strategies that
will lead to simultaneous need gratification.

13-5

Someone Is Ignoring the Ideas of Others

Your idea of an effective group discussion is where the majority of
contributions build on the direction in which the group is headed.
That's not often true in the group you lead. For example, Melanie
just described her hesitancy in supporting a decision the group is
about to make. Sandi completely ignored Melanie's concerns to
restate a point she made before in support of one aspect of the
decision. You interrupt Sandi.

? Was Your Comment Intended to Clarify
and Build on the Previous One?

If Sandi says yes, ask for an explanation of the connection you
missed. If you misunderstood Sandi, apologize.

    More than likely, Sandi will admit that her comments do not
carry Melanie's forward. At this point remind the group of the need
not to allow important ideas to be ignored; state that you want to go
back to Melanie's statement. Ask her to repeat it.

? What Do You Think About What Melanie
Said?

Get the group to deal with Melanie's concern. Find a volunteer to
begin. If no one volunteers, respond to her concern yourself and ask
others to follow.

Once this discussion is complete, turn back to Sandi for a restatement of her comment.

13-6

Someone's Comments Are Inappropriate

Someone has just opened up an agenda-related issue that is not appropriate to raise before this group at this time. In this case, the comment is a criticism of a group member who is not present to defend his actions. This is a behavior you have warned your group against. Since no one else appears ready to enforce this rule of the group, you'll do it yourself.

? Do You Think There Might Be a Better Time for You to Express This Concern?

If the critic says no, be prepared to explain why you are about to rule the comments as being out of order.

If you hear, "What are you getting at?" say that what is happening violates an understanding within the group not to criticize group members in their absence.

? Am I the Only One Here Having a Problem with the Direction of This Discussion?

You ask this question in hopes that it will call group members to action in condemning the sneak attack. If no one responds, criticize the group for letting the attack continue unchecked. Ask why no one is willing to speak up. Make clear your future expectations for the group in situations such as this one.

13-7

More Creativity and Originality Are Needed

Sometimes your team gets into a rut. Occasionally they are intimidated by the constraints the company places on them; other times they cannot get out of routine ways of thinking. In any case, the round of brainstorming you just attempted yielded very little fresh thinking. You need to do something to shake them out of their predictable patterns of thought.

? Who Can Come Up with an Idea That Involves Far More Risk Than Anything Yet Proposed?

Aversion to risk is a hallmark of conservatism. When you encourage people to take risk and you provide a safe environment in which to do it, you open the door to creative thought.

When you hear an answer to this question make sure you don't critique it right away. Look for some good in it first. Thank the person who offered it, and solicit reactions from others.

? What Is the Wildest Idea We Have Generated So Far?

As people identify candidates, record them on a flip chart or chalk-board. Put the more conservative ideas out of view. Ask the group to double the size of this list of imaginative ideas.

? Who Can Suggest an Alternative That the Company Would Almost Certainly Reject?

This question gets the team to throw down their shackles of inhibition and self-imposed constraints. It frees them from the censoring they've imposed on their creative juices thus far. They may also be surprised to learn that some of the initiatives they assumed would be verboten are perfectly acceptable to top management.

? If You Were One of Our Customers, What
Suggestion Would You Add to the List We
Have Generated?

Help your group get outside of themselves and shake their constrict-
ing point of view whenever they brainstorm. Have them look at the
problem from positions other than their own. Here we have suggested the customer. You might think of several other roles that you
want group members to play in opening up their minds.

13-8

More Critical Thought Is Needed

In the meetings you lead, decisions are made easily and quickly. You
always thought that was good until you experienced times when the
group's decisions later proved to be poorly thought out. An article
you just read about what the author termed "groupthink" sounded
like she had studied your team. It made you realize that the speed
of your group's deliberations prevented a critical analysis of the
assumptions behind them. There were few challenges of the data
used in making decisions, and there was little consideration of the
ultimate impact those decisions would have on the people who had
to live with them. The article made you determined to get your group
to look at all sides of their decisions.

? Who Is Willing to Play the Role of Devil's
Advocate Today?

The most direct way to combat groupthink is to assign people the
role of challenging the group's decisions. The devil's advocate is told
to think against the group, assume opposing views, and look for
what's wrong with assumptions behind decisions. Call on the devil's
advocate every so often during the meeting. Don't allow other
members to dismiss his or her objections without justification. Rotate

this assignment throughout the group over time so that everyone gets practice in critical thinking.

? What Might Go Wrong with This Plan We're About to Approve?

Follow through on this question by asking each group member to come up with at least one negative aspect of the plan before that plan is actually adopted. Think of the proposed scheme as a beautiful statue that the group has fashioned and placed in the center of the room.

The group's pride in its work may not allow it to see the cracks and imperfections. That's groupthink.

Your job is to place a rock in each person's hand with the order to hurl the rock at the statue. If the statue is still standing and still looking good after the rock throwing, the group has a good plan.

? If You Were One of Our Employees, What Would You Think of This Plan?

Use this question to get people to consider the impact of their decisions on others, especially those whose reaction will determine the final wisdom of those decisions.

? Whom Can We Invite to the Next Meeting to Give Us a Different View?

This question enables you to implement two effective strategies at the same time. One is to hold a second-chance meeting where people have the opportunity to rethink a decision that may have been made in haste. The other is to call in someone from outside the group whose unique viewpoint will add a vital perspective that the group failed to consider.

13-9

The Group Is Silent

Silence is expensive. While the members of your group sit around the table and stare into space, they're collecting their salaries. The last time this happened, you decided to shake them out of their lethargy.

? What Are Your Suggestions for Increasing the Number of People Who Comment At Our Meetings?

This question enlists group members in searching for a solution to the problem of silence. Stand up unexpectedly and move quickly to the flip chart or chalkboard as you pose this question. If no one speaks right away, put one of your own ideas at the top and ask for more. Show lots of energy as you lead the discussion.

? What Is Causing Our Silence Right Now?

This question may not break the silence by itself, so prepare for it to be rhetorical in nature. Offer some possible explanations of your own, adding a few bizarre ones if needed to energize the group. Again, recording the ideas will help to keep the discussion flowing.

? John, What Can You Add to This Discussion from the Perspective of the Marketing Department?

The intent here is not to put John on the spot, but to motivate someone who you know has something to offer to get the conversation going.

? John, Is There Some Reason for Your Silence Today?

This might be the question to ask if you suspect a particular reason for the silence and if you know that John is the person most likely to be willing to expose that reason in front of the group. You hope that if he will be forthcoming, the rest of the group will follow.

13-10

The Group Feels Frustrated or Powerless

You head up a company-wide task force that doesn't have the authority to implement much of what it might recommend in its final report. The members of the group are really stymied by this at the moment. They feel no empowerment and are focused on the limitations of their influence.

? What Is the One Greatest Obstacle Standing in Our Way?

Have the group select the most debilitating constraint without consulting each other, perhaps by writing them down. Then, as you go around the room to hear the choices, allow members to say why the barriers chosen by others are not the most critical in their opinion. The net effect will be to weaken the perceived impact of at least some of the barriers posed. Use the next question to deal with the obstacle that got the most votes.

? What Will It Take to Overcome the One Greatest Obstacle We Face?

It is likely that the obstacle is not as insurmountable as the membership perceives it to be. Give them the benefit of your greater experience and wise counsel on how to minimize the negative effects of the constraints they fear.

? What Power *Do* We Have?

Most people don't give themselves credit for having the power they indeed do have. They tend, rather, to focus on their absence of power.

Prior to stating this question, you might concede that the obstacle they have identified both exists and is as constraining as they claim. Now the task is to get them to identify those aspects of the situation where they are as influential or even more influential than the other side. Show them how they might take advantage of that influence to increase their might.

13-11

You Need to Ensure Follow-through on Decisions Made During the Meeting

You've noticed that by the end of a long meeting some members forget a phone call they've promised to make, data they've agreed to gather, or another job they've agreed to tackle. Sometimes it's the opposite problem where a member performs follow-up that he shouldn't have. You've vowed never to let this kind of communication breakdown thwart your group again. You always check on follow-up commitments as part of the close to your meetings.

? Who Are All the People Responsible for Some Form of Follow-Up After We Adjourn?

Ask all who raise their hands to summarize exactly what they've agreed to do. Correct any misperceptions. Remind those who do not raise their hands of any commitments they may have forgotten.

? Who Agreed to Collect the Customer Profile Statistics?

You may have forgotten, yourself, who volunteered for this assignment, or you may simply want to involve the group in the process of holding members accountable for their follow-up pledges. Always thank those who have agreed to help the group by performing work between meetings. A few days later, in the form of a hand written note, you may wish to gently remind them to complete the promised work.

Chapter
14

Attending Meetings

In Chapter 13 we outlined eleven situations that the meeting leader might control through the use of questions. Clearly the person in charge of the meetings you attend is the one you expect to take action whenever the group's discussion is not running smoothly.

But that won't always happen. The appointed leader doesn't always act at the appropriate time or in a correct manner. In times when legitimate leadership is not forthcoming, you or one of your colleagues need to take the chair long enough to get maximum value out of the meeting.

Because you'll want to intervene without threatening the sanctioned leader or arousing resentment from other group members, it is prudent to limit your comments and present them in the form of questions.

14-1
Having a Meeting Is a Waste of Time

Your boss just returned from "charm school" (the term your colleagues give to the company's executive development program).

Ever since then he has been on a participative management kick. It's great that he has been consulting you more than before on decisions affecting you, but he's gotten a bit carried away with democracy. Today, for example, you are at a meeting he called to make a decision that you and your fellow attendees believe he should make on his own. As the meeting begins, the others are looking to you, the boss's direct assistant, to say something.

? Isn't This the Kind of Decision That Is Best
for You to Make on Your Own?

You may wish to add the words, "after brief consultation with those of us who are most affected by it" to the end of the question. You may also wish to preface it with a statement of appreciation on behalf of your colleagues that the boss wants to incorporate all your ideas into the decision.

You hope that the boss will see his error and adjourn the meeting, but that's not likely to happen. He is more likely to affirm his desire to have the meeting. At this point you can say why you raised the question. Validate your position in one or more of three ways: Say why you believe this decision falls within the domain of executive privilege, attest to the brutish deadlines facing your colleagues, and confirm that the rest of the group feels as you do.

? Can We Help You with This Decision
without Us All Attending This Meeting?

If the answer is no, respond as suggested above for the previous question. If the answer is yes, help the boss to determine person by person who needs to remain for the meeting. If your argument is well documented and presented, you just might talk him into canceling the entire meeting.

? Who Do You Feel Are the Most Essential
People to Remain Through This Entire
Meeting?

Be prepared for this question to evoke a "Why do you ask?" response. Explain your concern from the perspective that the meeting may be more costly than its value justifies. Do not comment on the motive your boss may have had for calling the meeting in the first place.

14-2

You Don't Believe You Should Be at the Meeting

Last week a counterpart of your boss asked that you be sent as your area's representative to staff a task force she is chairing. Halfway through the first meeting it becomes clear to you that you are not needed on this task force and that to attend its weekly scheduled meetings over the next six months would be a horrible waste of time. You consider not saying anything during the meeting and talking to the chairperson afterwards, but realize that speaking up now is probably the best thing to do.

? How Do You See Me Contributing to These Meetings?

This is a safe starting question to get you out of these meetings. Anything more direct risks the chance of you looking foolish if someone reveals a compelling need for your presence.

Listen closely to the answer. If it makes a persuasive case for your continued involvement, put the group's meeting dates on your calendar. If it confirms your suspicion that you won't be needed, make that case tactfully and forcefully. Base your argument on the needs of the organization and not on your own convenience. Report your intervention back to your boss before the chairperson does.

? What Impact Do You Think It Would Have If I Were Unable to Attend These Meetings?

This inquiry is somewhat abrupt and leaves you less room to squirm if your prejudgment is off. Otherwise, it should lead to the same result as the first question.

? May I Suggest a Better Way for Our
Department's Needs to Be Reflected
in the Final Report of This Task Force?

Make certain you know what's going on before you ask this and that
you have a good idea with which to back up your assertion. This
question might be used in tandem with either of the two previous
ones.

? If It Turns Out That I Cannot Attend These
Meetings on a Regular Basis, What Should I
Look for When Selecting a Replacement?

You may not want to propose your resignation to this group, yet
want to put them on notice that you won't always be in attendance.
The answer will also help you decide whom to send in your place,
and it may even help you to make a case that no one from your
department, you included, fills the bill.

14-3

You Want to Challenge an Assumption

You can't believe your ears! The group is about to make a decision
based on a theory that is wholly inaccurate. You have to stop them
before they make a horrible mistake. You don't want to offend
anyone, especially the advocate of the theory, but you've got to speak
up.

? What If Our Assumption Doesn't Hold?

Expect to hear, "What do you mean?" Begin your response with,
"What if . . . ?" Describe the worst-case scenarios that you believe
will happen as though they might happen.

You will probably awaken a few others whose enthusiasm for
the group's direction blinded them to seeing the disaster the group
is inviting with its current line of thinking. If you cannot enlist any

allies in your cause, push a little harder by saying that you believe the worst-case scenarios are likely to be realized.

If the group still will not heed your warning, ask for a second-chance meeting. This means the group agrees not to take final action on the decision unless they still approve the proposed action when they meet again several days later.

? Can We Spend Some Time Discussing Anything That Might Possibly Go Wrong with Our Decision?

The group is likely to agree to this strategy, which gets at the faulty assumption through the proposed decision on which it is based. Suggest that everyone be asked to volunteer one possible drawback to the group's conclusion.

? May I Play the Role of Devil's Advocate for a Few Minutes?

The group may be so tied to the decision or so unwilling to confront each other on issues that they cannot perform the critical analysis suggested by the previous questions. Hope that they grant you permission to do it yourself.

Before you play devil's advocate, make it clear that you do not necessarily stand behind any of the concerns you raise, but that you are intentionally taking a contrary position to everything the group champions to minimize the chances of oversight. Make your points as persuasively but as dispassionately as possible. You want them to counterattack your ideas, not you.

14-4

The Group Is Making Too Little Progress

This is typical of your group. The meeting is getting nowhere. Everyone has something to say, but little is getting done. There's no way the agenda will be covered in the time left. The group leader is not going to speak up, so it looks like you'll have to.

? Is Anyone Else Feeling As Frustrated As I Am?

Since you're not in charge of the meeting, it might not be wise to criticize the group's progress. This question initially draws attention away from the group and onto your feelings about what is happening. It may also relieve you by stimulating someone else to decry what's going on before you have to.

If you are asked what you're aiming at, describe the source of your frustration. Be sure to limit your comments to what you've observed. Do not name names, do not guess at motives, do not speak in critical tones.

? Am I Mistaken in Believing That We Have Gotten off the Track?

This question gets to the point quicker than the first one. It is a great water tester; if the consensus is that you are mistaken, you can easily retract your question. If you generate a ground swell of agreement with you, the problem has been solved.

? Isn't This Discussion Getting Us Far Afield with Respect to the Agenda?

This is an even more direct question. If others agree, you'll get results quickly. If they don't, you'll be put down quickly.

14-5

The Group Is Not Making Good Use of Its Members

This is one of the most dysfunctional groups you've ever been in. They are a group in name but not in spirit. Pareto's law suggests that twenty percent of group members make eighty percent of the contributions to a meeting. This group has an even worse record; it's more like ten percent make ninety percent of the remarks. You're suffering through another such meeting where people who could be very helpful to the group aren't speaking up. You decide to.

? Shouldn't We Be Making Better Use of the People Here?

You're likely to be asked what you mean by this question. When you respond, steer clear of opinion or interpretation. Give specific examples of discussions where you knew people could have contributed but didn't.

You will almost certainly have to name names. Bring as many people as you can into your description of the problem so that no one will feel singled out. Implicate yourself as appropriate. Don't criticize members for not contributing; criticize the group for not drawing them out.

Be prepared for disagreement with your position. Defend it with data, not emotion.

? Do Others Agree That We Waste the Time of Many People in These Meetings?

The group leader and others may get defensive at this question, and they may ask what you mean by it. It is a stronger way to generate the discussion described under the first question. Use it only if you believe that you need to shake people up.

? How Can We Call Ourselves a Group?

You'll get their attention quickly with this question. Continue with the direction suggested under the first question.

14-6

You're Not Being Heard

Twenty minutes ago the group leader began going around the table for solutions to the problem at hand. As group members offered their ideas, she asked others to comment on each proposed solution. You and several others had given your ideas, with yours generating little comment. Near the end of the line, one of your colleagues made a suggestion that received rave reviews from nearly everyone sitting around the table. You liked it, too; it was essentially the same idea you proposed ten minutes earlier. This isn't the first instance of your ideas not being heard in this group. You need to get to the bottom of this.

? Can Anyone Tell Me How What Was Just Proposed Differs from What I Said Ten Minutes Ago?

This question deals directly with the specific instance of nonlistening that you attribute to the group. You may wish to follow it with a restatement of the proposal they just embraced and a restatement of yours. Make every attempt to ask it without any trace of resentment.

The feedback you receive should prove helpful. They may not see the similarity you do, which indicates that you didn't outline your proposal as thoroughly as you thought. It may have been a matter of timing; perhaps they weren't ready for your idea when it was revealed. You may not have presented the idea as assertively or as persuasively as the last person did. Or you might have failed in a dozen other ways to paint a clear and compelling picture.

? What Did (Name The Person Whose Idea Was Applauded) Do That Caused You to Respond More Positively to His Recommendation Than You Did to Mine?

This asks the group to focus on the matter of style. Answers to it will tell you what type of communication this particular group appreciates. It may also point to some barriers that you may throw up when you present to them.

? Does Anyone Have a Suggestion for What I Might Do to Become More "Listenable"?

This could be an alternative question to the first one. As it stands, it addresses the generic issue of you not being listened to, with the present frustration being one example. This question might also serve as a follow-up to the first question. In this role, it is a call for suggested remedies.

14-7

You Don't Understand What's Being Discussed

The group is discussing an issue that left you at the starting gate. Your main problem is that you didn't understand the person who raised it a few minutes ago. You should have said something then, but you hoped things would crystallize after you heard a few more comments. You're in a greater quagmire now than you were then, so you decide to confess your ignorance.

? Are You Saying That . . . ?

You may understand enough of what is being said to use this question. Reflect back what you think you're hearing for verification. If you're incorrect, the person will modify your statement to bring it more in line with what was said and thereby bring you on board.

? Could Someone Please Summarize the Essence of This Idea to Be Sure I'm Following It?

Use this question if you're totally lost.

? How Would This Idea Help Us to Achieve Our Goals?

By getting advocates to explain the advantages of their idea, you should come to understand it. This question has the simultaneous benefit of directing the conversation toward the meat of the issue, which is the merit of the proposed solution.

14-8

The Leader Is Too Dominant

"Why are we having this meeting?" You've been asking yourself this question ever since you sat down, and not because the agenda is unclear. Your question is incited by the group leader's totally domineering behavior. If she plans to achieve this agenda according to her specifications, why does she have others in the room with her? She is wasting your time as well as everyone else's. How do you confront a meeting dictator except with a question?

? What Can We Do to Be More Helpful to You with This Agenda?

This is another question to which you expect an answer of "What are you getting at?" Your subtle jab of a response should be, "Well, we don't appear to be much help to you. You're having to do all the work so far and make all the decisions. Very few of our ideas sound good to you. If we can't do better than this, the company would be better off with us back in our offices."

? Are You Finding Us to Be Helpful at This Meeting?

This alternative question should move the discussion in the same direction as the previous one, but it could elicit more interesting initial answers. The meeting leader may say she is not happy with the way the meeting is going and may even become introspective about her behavior. However, she is equally likely to attribute the meeting's nonproductiveness to the rest of the group.

? Would You Like Some Feedback on How the Meeting Appears to Be Progressing?

This high-risk question is intended to pave the way for you to discuss the meeting leader's behavior. If she invites your comments, deliver them as diplomatically but as honestly as you can. Your feedback may come out something like this: "I think we're allowing ourselves to be intimidated by your enthusiasm for this topic. Your preferences are clear to us, so we assume you won't listen to arguments to the contrary. And when you respond with such vigor as you just did to Paul's idea, we clam up. Unless we can all figure out a way to make us feel less dominated by you, it may be better for you to make these decisions by yourself and merely announce them to us. And I don't believe that any of us want to see that happen."

If she doesn't get the message, she may say, "What are you saying?" This is a crucial decision point for you. If you have the courage and if she can take strong medicine, your response might be, "Perhaps you could do a little more listening and a little less talking."

Chapter
15
Negotiating

You negotiate when you meet to resolve conflict with someone whose goals are incompatible with yours. Examples of the negotiation situations you may confront include resolving a vacation dispute with a coworker, working out a supply agreement with a vendor, creating with your employee the conditions of a new responsibility, and establishing your salary in a job you have just been offered.

In these encounters we are searching for a win-win outcome. In other words, you want both you and the other party to walk away winners. This result is much preferable to one where what one person wins the other must lose.

Unfortunately, the goal of win-win resolution is easier said than done. Through lack of training, lack of experience, or lack of self-confidence, too many potentially constructive outcomes are sacrificed at the altar of unilateral demands and self-interest.

In Chapter 1 you saw that questions can be magic. There is perhaps no greater illustration of this principle than in this chapter. Here you will see how the correctly phrased question can turn destructive disagreement into constructive consensus.

15-1

Someone Poses a Take It or Leave It Ultimatum

You're starting to feel pressured into accepting a proposal you would rather not accept. You also sense that the other party is as frustrated with the negotiation as you are. Even though you're upset, you continue the discussion to get more issues on the table. Unfortunately, the other party makes a final offer and says, "Take it or leave it."

? If We Can Come Up with an Alternative, More Attractive to You Than the One Just Proposed, Would You Still Want Me to Take It or Leave It?

With this question you raise the prospect that further discussion can lead to increased benefits for both of you. You're also telling him that the current offer may be less attractive than the one that has yet to be discussed.

The other party may find your question intriguing and respond with a door opener ("What do you mean?"). Your task then is to focus on mutual equity and to generate creative solutions to your common needs. Focus your energy and thoughts on *why* you want what you want, not *what* you want.

If he refuses to open the door and merely repeats his either-or proposition, do a quick cost-benefit analysis to determine whether the proposal fills your needs and allows you to walk away with dignity. If so, accept; if not, reject.

? Do You Want Me to Take It or Leave It *Now*, or May I Have Time to Think More About Taking It?

This question enables you to stall for time. You don't want to feel pressured to make a decision you might later regret. You also want to make sure that you and the other party have exhausted all options. You want to create the impression that any gains in bringing the negotiations to an early close are not as great as the costs of over-looking an option that is currently not on the table.

? Are You Feeling Pressured to Bring
the Discussion to a Close?

This alternative is designed to stall for time without labeling the motives of the other party. He may or may not be using the take it or leave it gambit as a pressuring tactic. You don't know. What you do know is that you're feeling pressure and you don't like it. Don't alienate the other party by attributing motives to his ultimatum. Find out what pressure he is under and help alleviate it if you can.

15-2

You're Pressed to Respond
to an Unreasonable Deadline

"You've got until five tonight to make your decision." This statement sends shivers up your spine and causes a knot in your stomach. You need much more time to think about the options, and you hate being pressured.

? Why Can't We Negotiate the Deadline?

His statement is an assertion, a statement of what he wants. Since you're in the process of negotiating, any statement of wants is subject to revision. Your question labels his deadline as negotiable.

If he gives you a reason for the stated deadline that seems rational and is acceptable to you, then work within it. If you don't accept the reason, tell him why.

If he refuses to give you a reason, tell him that his refusal creates unnecessary pressure in the negotiation. Add that this pressure will only serve to produce an outcome less satisfactory than would have been created without the pressure. Tell him that deadlines should be mutually agreeable unless there are external constraints.

? If You're Under Pressure to Meet This
Deadline, What Can I Do to Help Remove
Some of the Pressure?

Negotiators often represent the interest of others rather than themselves (for example, purchasing agents representing the manufacturing department or a recruiter representing the human resource department). In these situations, deadlines are imposed by others and simply communicated by the negotiator. Find out if this is the case. Tell the person that you'll be happy to ease the pressure on both of you by developing reasons why the deadline should be set back and by communicating those reasons directly to the parties who imposed the deadline.

If the other party set the deadline, ask him to consider alternative times. Get him to see how selecting an alternative time will bring about a more favorable outcome for both of you.

? What's Magical About Five Tonight? Why
Not Eight Tomorrow Morning?

With this alternative question you're asking for a rationale. The qualifying adjective "magical" is a tongue in cheek suggestion that you see the deadline as arbitrary. But if not, you're willing to hear why.

15-3

The Other Party Plays "High Ball" (Unreasonably High Demands) or "Low Ball" (Unreasonably Low Offers)

You know that negotiations typically involve some form of game playing, but you honestly believe the other party has broken the rules. You've just been insulted; you've been made an offer far below what you think is reasonable and fair. You control your anger long enough to ask a question.

? What's Your Reasoning Behind This Offer?

The natural and expected response to a ridiculously high demand or a ridiculously low offer is to get angry and accuse the other party of deceit and dishonesty. With this question you give the party the benefit of the doubt and move from the what to the why.

If you can't elicit a reason other than "Because that's what I'm offering," follow with a genuine counteroffer and the reasons behind it. Let him know that there are valid and justifiable reasons why you believe your counteroffer is reasonable. Don't label the initial offer as insulting. Rather, stress the fairness of your offer, based on the reasons you provide.

If he is able to provide support for his position, listen very carefully. When he's finished talking, respond to each of his reasons in turn. Question the assumptions and premises of his reasons. Where you find fault, indicate why.

? What Do You Think I See As a Fair Offer?

With this question, you're getting the other party to engage in empathy and to focus on mutually equitable solutions. High ball/low ball, whether motivated by chicanery or not, puts pressure on you and unless challenged produces a solution that will ultimately return to haunt you both.

If the other party can't engage in empathy or seems to stick with his initial offer, tell him why it's in his interest to have you walk away a winner, too. If he looks dumbfounded at your suggestion, tell him why he wins when you win. Tell him:

- You'll walk away thinking better of him.
- You'll look forward to helping him out in the future.
- You'll realize that he also had your interests at heart and because of that you will look out for his interests in the future.
- Others who may hear about this equitable outcome will think more of him and thereby make relationships with him more beneficial in the future.

? What Criteria Do You Think the Final
Resolution Should Meet?

This question forces the other party to move from *what* he wants to *why* he wants it. It's possible that when you hear his reasons you may no longer see his position as a high ball or low ball. In any event, this alternative question gives you another opportunity to focus on mutual equity. Stress that the lack of mutual equity hurts both of you in the long run.

15-4

You Reach an Impasse

You've been at it for almost six straight hours. Your team is exhausted, their team is exhausted. You've haggled over the major issues and the minor issues. But you're still at odds regarding the final solution, and neither side appears ready to budge. Just as frustration is about to turn into despair you get an idea.

? What Else Can Either of Us Bring
to the Table to Close the Gap
Between Our Positions?

Again, you are looking for strategies to create win-win outcomes. Even though you may both believe you're deadlocked, always view deadlocks as only temporary, never permanent. This question may bring the one bargaining chip to the table that you have both overlooked and that could break the deadlock.

Welcome anything the other party brings. Ask the other party for the same receptivity to your suggestions.

If you're willing to concede one point, do so. Don't let your pride and ego get the best of you. Right now all you have is impasse and frustration. If you make a concession or split the difference, you may have a win-win outcome.

? What Concession Do You Need to Close the Deal Right Now?

An impasse may be nothing more than a natural state of exhaustion and frustration. When this occurs you need a zinger, a question that smashes through the mental blocks. This question is designed to end the stalemate and get the mental juices flowing once again.

It's quite possible that a final concession will close the negotiation and remove the frustration for both of you. If you can grant one that will cost you less than the value of the final agreement, you'll be glad you did.

? If It Were Now Six Weeks into the Future and We Were Looking Back at This Negotiation, What Might We Wish We Had Brought to the Table?

With this question you're forcing a change in perspective. You're saying let's look at it in retrospect, as if it were completed and we're now in the future. Let's take off our mental blinders and look at our problems in a new and fresh way. If you're looking for creative problem solving, set the example yourself. Take off your perceptual blinders and start generating as many fresh alternatives as you can.

Anything that will change perspective will serve as the catalyst. Sometimes simply calling for a break will work. If you opt for this strategy, your break should last longer than one hour but less than twenty-four hours.

15-5

The Other Party Is Torn Between Accepting or Rejecting Your Proposal

You've offered everything you can possibly offer. You sense that the other party is receptive to your proposal but is still reluctant to make a final decision. You're worried that she may decide to seek a better offer elsewhere. Rather than pressure her with a take it or leave it ultimatum, you take a different approach.

? What's Your Best Alternative to Accepting
This Proposal Now?

This question is designed to crystallize the pivotal choices: accepting what is currently on the table, hoping to get a better offer from someone else, or maintaining the status quo.

After you've posed the question, listen intently to the answer. Help the person articulate the consequences of not accepting your proposal. If she has trouble answering your question use follow-up probes: What other current offers do you have? Are they better than mine? If you accept the best offer, will you come out better than you would if you accepted mine?

The answer may create either of two scenarios. The first is an opportunity to make a final offer equal to or better than the alternative offer currently considered, and the second is to move the person off dead center, thereby bringing closure to the negotiation, even if that decision is to reject your offer. Once you realize that a decision based on remorse will ultimately prove unwise, you can still define a rejection of your offer as winning.

? If You Reject My Offer, What Will Take Its
Place That's Any Better Than What You Are
Assured of Receiving from Me?

This person is torn because of indecision. This question is designed to provide a nudge.

Get her to do a quick cost-benefit analysis. She knows exactly what you're presenting. What is available from another party who might be competing with you in the negotiation? Comparing the two offers might highlight the attractiveness of your offer. If not, find ways of outshining the competing offer or find selling points in your current offer that she may have overlooked.

If there is no other offer, the decision is between the status quo and what you propose. Sometimes the security of knowing what you have is strong enough to compensate for the insecurity of not knowing the future, even if the future promises increased benefits. That's why many people reject attractive job offers or fail to switch to new vendors: They are simply comfortable and secure with the old. Your questions should force the other party to challenge the security of the status quo and to recognize the benefits of your offer.

? How Can You Be Sure That You Will Get a Better Deal Elsewhere?

Sometimes the other party might be playing you against another bidder. If this is the case, probe to determine if the other bidder really will deliver what is promised. This question also provides you an opportunity to match an offer if you believe it's in your best interest to do so.

15-6

You're Asked If Your Offer Is the Same As That Quoted to Others

You're trying to recruit a college graduate to fill a vacancy in your department. At the conclusion of two days of on-site interviews you make him an offer. He thinks about it for a few minutes. After what you feel is a deafening silence he asks, "Has any applicant for this job been offered more money?" You respond to his question with your own.

? What Do You See As a Fair Offer, and Do You Think We're Making One to You?

The purpose of the question is to get the other party to focus on the merits of this offer independent of negotiations into which you may have entered with other parties. If the person says that it's not a fair offer, find out what he would need to make it so and negotiate from there. If he says it is fair, he then must simply make his final decision.

If he says that he can only judge what's fair once he knows what others have received, tell him that individual offers are made on the basis of individual applicants. If someone has received more or less, it's because you saw that person as more or less qualified. But the real issue is whether or not he believes your offer is fair based on what he needs and what he thinks he's worth, not what someone else is receiving.

Stress that it's in both of your interests to treat him fairly, regardless of what anyone else gets. Make it clear that you don't want to bring anyone on board who will ultimately be unhappy with his or her salary.

? Do You Think I Believe It's in My Long-term Best Interest to Treat You Unfairly Now?

There is a natural tendency for negotiators to question the fairness of your offer relative to offers they think others may have received. This questioning will increase as the other party's paranoia or distrust of you increases.

With this question you minimize the paranoia and distrust. Your strategy is to get the other party to recognize that your intent is not to win at all costs but to create a win-win solution. You're emphasizing that you have not won if the other party feels as if he or she has lost. This question is a powerful cue to discuss your long-term relationship. Often this discussion is the push needed to decide.

? Do You Believe That People Can Be Treated Differently and Still Be Treated Fairly?

Get the other party to accept the reality that no two people are exactly alike, no two situations are exactly alike, and hence no two negotiations will be exactly alike. Different people can be treated differently and still be treated equally. Expand upon this important point.

Stress the criteria you are using to make your offer. Get him to focus on the criteria, not the offer itself. If he thinks the criteria are unfair, ask how he would make the decision. Remember, you want to focus on why he wants what he wants. Reasons are more supportive of win-win than demands.

15-7

You're Feeling Pressured, Controlled, or Manipulated

You feel like you just walked onto a used-car lot. What started out as a relaxed negotiation between two parties interested in securing a mutually agreeable solution has turned into a situation where you're feeling pressured and manipulated, and you don't like the feeling.

? Isn't It in Our Mutual Interest for Both of Us to Walk Away from This Negotiation Feeling Satisfied?

This is a pointed question that solicits a specific answer. And the answer you're likely to get is yes.

Follow that answer with a statement indicating that you feel extremely frustrated and anxious and don't see how you can walk away from the negotiation with the goal the other party has already agreed to, that is, mutual satisfaction.

Don't ascribe motive or intent. Simply describe what the other party is doing—or, better yet, what is happening—and how that makes you feel.

? How Would You Feel If the Roles Were Reversed and You Had to Respond to the Pressures I'm Currently Experiencing?

This question focuses on the pressure you're experiencing without attributing motive or intent. You're not exactly sure why the other party is pressuring you, but you are willing to give her the benefit of the doubt. Be certain to emphasize the word "feel" and not the word "you" in either of its two locations in the sentence.

One of the most powerful techniques for diffusing the pressure is empathy. Get the other party to look at the situation through your eyes. This technique is sometimes enough to encourage her to remove any pressure she may have exerted on the negotiations.

Tell her in specific terms what you mean by pressure. Say what you're feeling and experiencing. Describe *what* she's doing to make you feel this way, but do *not* ascribe intent to her behavior.

? Are You Experiencing Outside Pressures
to Conclude These Negotiations?

Put yourself in her shoes. By asking if there are outside pressures you're acknowledging the difficulties she may be facing. This thoughtfulness may make her more thoughtful of you. If you sense that there might be pressure she is reluctant to disclose, follow with probing questions.

15-8

A Peer Is Fighting Turf Battles with You or Is Trying to Get a Bigger Piece of the Pie at Your Expense

It's been a tough year and your boss has asked all department heads to pare their budgets as much as possible. Because of this you're knocking heads with the manager of another department. When the two of you sat down to negotiate your budgets, you weren't prepared for outright war. This person won't budge an inch and is making you fight for everything. You look him straight in the eye.

? How Do You See Our Department Helping
Your Department to Achieve Its Goals?

The surprise element embedded in this question may succeed in side-tracking an empire builder. Its ultimate purpose is to move him from viewing the negotiation as win-lose to win-win. You want him to realize that helping your department is ultimately in his best interest. And if you're both working for the same employer, it is.

If the other person is hedging and can't seem think of how you help him, take out a sheet of paper and list all the ways your department helps his department. Get him to focus on the bridges that exist between the two departments, not on the moats.

You might feel like you're pulling teeth to get him to acknowledge the bridges and interdependence, but pull anyway. Once you've established that your department helps his department and vice versa, you're in a better position to develop a mutually equitable budget.

? If Our Department Didn't Provide
the Services We Do, Where Would You Get
Them and How Much Do You Think They'd
Cost?

The first question is designed to reinforce the value of your department. One reality of organizational and family life is that we tend to take one another for granted. We usually don't realize how much a person or thing means to us until we no longer have it or until we have to replace it. Encourage your colleague to think about how much he would have to pay for your department's services if he had to purchase them on the open market.

It's also in your best interest to consider the value of your colleague's department. If you expect him to consider your value, you should engage in the same empathy. In so doing, you may realize that his share of the corporate pie should be increased and that you both win when it is.

? How Do You Want Our Negotiations Today
to Set the Stage for Negotiations a Year
from Now?

Here you're moving the focus from the present to the future. Colleagues who try to secure organizational resources at your expense often fail to consider that the acrimony and bitterness created today will show up in future negotiations.

Chapter

16

Being Interviewed for a Job

One popular myth about the job interview is that the interviewer has the easy job of asking questions and the applicant has the tough job of answering them. This is a misconception for two reasons. First, asking the right questions, listening to the answers, and following up to get the precise information needed is much more difficult than it appears. Second, a good applicant, one who sincerely wants the job and has prepared for the interview, does more than answer questions. He or she is also challenged to ask revealing questions, questions that help to determine if he or she is suited for the company and vice versa.

In this chapter, you will learn how, as the job applicant, you can use questions to gain control over the interview process.

16-1

You Want to Learn How Much Power Your Prospective Boss Wields

Keeping your nose on the grindstone and keeping it clean when it's not on the grindstone are two strategies for getting ahead. A third strategy is to work for someone who has clout in the company, someone with the power to support your efforts. When you feel the time is right to broach the subject of your prospective boss's power, ask a penetrating question.

**? How Would You Characterize My
Prospective Boss's Influence
with Colleagues in Other Departments
and with Her Boss?**

If the interviewer is recruiting you for a specific assignment in a specific department, he should be able to answer this question with a specific referent. Follow the answer with probes soliciting examples and illustrations (for example, "Why is she seen that way by colleagues and superiors?" "What is the basis of her influence?" "Where does she appear to have the least influence?")

If the person interviewing you will be your prospective boss, pose this question: "How successful has the department been in garnering support from other departments [marketing, finance, human resources] and from top management?" If this person is politically astute, she should have no trouble answering the question. After all, her astuteness has sensitized her to issues of power and influence. Listen carefully to the answer. You want to make sure your boss is a powerful team player, not strictly out for personal gain.

**? How Has This Department Fared in the Last
Few Budget Allocations?**

One important test of a boss's power is the size of the budgetary pie she can negotiate. If you sense that your boss and her department are getting crumbs, you may want to look elsewhere. Conversely, if you sense that your boss gloats over the share she gets at the expense of other department heads, be forewarned, you may be working for an empire builder who is not well respected by her colleagues.

? Where Do You See the Department
(or Yourself) Being in Three Years?

This is the turnabout of the classic question recruiters typically ask applicants. When you hear the answer you will know something about your boss's promotability, ambition, and personal goals. You may also learn how long she plans to stick around. Listen and probe if necessary.

16-2

You Want to Know What the Corporate Culture Is Really Like

You've read all the literature about the company you could. You're starting to get a feel for the strengths and weaknesses of the company, but you're still not sure what it's really like to work there. You now set out to learn the unwritten rules, policies, and norms of the company.

? Based on Your Experiences
in the Company, What Have You Seen
or Heard That Best Symbolizes the Basic
Values of This Company?

Corporate culture is reflected in rites, rituals, ceremonies, heroes, and heroines. Your question is designed to solicit information concerning these corporate culture "markers."

If the interviewer says he doesn't understand the reason for your question, say that you believe corporate culture is reflected in events signifying values. You want to understand the culture by hearing about some of those events.

You may hear the standard company mission statement or a prepared formal statement of company values ("We believe that people are our most important resource"). Tell the person you want to hear about incidents that don't appear on any brochure or in any formal policy statement. You're interested in stories that reflect these values. If the interviewer can't share any with you, determine whether that's because he isn't plugged into the culture or because he doesn't appreciate the importance of assessing culture.

? If I Were to Ask Family Members of Current
Employees What It's Like to Work Here,
What Would Those Family Members Say?

Corporate culture is always experienced by family members of employees, even if those relatives aren't on the payroll. Family members hear the gripes, complaints, praise, and compliments, the good news and the bad news. Family members are also the ones whose personal plans may have to change because of demands and pressures at work.

Most likely, the interviewer has never heard this question. That's great. You'll stand out in his mind. What's not great is that he may have trouble answering it. Listen carefully to the answer. You'll learn a lot.

? When the Company Has Had to Lay Off
People, How Did It Go About It?

Human resource policies are tested not during prosperous times but during lean times. With this question you're measuring the human resource values of the company. What you're hoping to hear is that the layoffs and terminations were conducted with as much compassion as possible. You also want to determine whether or not it created anguish for those managers who had to execute the plan.

Expect to have to push for specifics, details, and examples. Remember to ask this and all questions with a flat, nonaccusatory tone. You don't want to be perceived as a prosecuting attorney, but rather as someone who honestly needs to determine what the corporate culture is really like.

16-3

You Believe That You're Being Asked Inappropriate Questions

You know the law and you know your rights. You're not going to be asked a question that in any way might be used to discriminate unfairly against you, but luck is not on your side today. You were just asked a question about your religious preference. You don't want to sound like a defense attorney for putting the questioner in his place, but you also don't intend to answer it. You respond with your own question.

? May I Ask Why That Question Is Important?

Don't attribute motives to the questioner. Rather than making a conscious decision to pressure you by violating your rights, the questioner may be doing nothing more than making ill-advised small talk. In this situation, err on the side of being too forgiving rather than too challenging.

With this question you're simply asking the interviewer to provide a rationale. If the rationale makes sense to you and you feel you can answer the question without jeopardizing the chances for the job or subjugating your rights, answer it.

If the rationale doesn't make sense to you or if you feel that an honest answer might hurt your chances for employment, answer with another question: "Do you really want me to answer this question and waive my protection under the law not to answer it?" If this gets you off the hook, thank the interviewer for his sensitivity. If it doesn't, walk out of the interview.

? How Does That Question Relate to the Requirements of the Job?

This question focuses on the job description and job requirements. Politely, tactfully, yet assertively indicate that the information an answer would provide seems far removed from the job description.

Again, give the interviewer the benefit of the doubt for being stupid and insensitive rather than malicious and prejudiced.

If you agree with the rationale for the question, answer it as best you can. If you disagree, say so and indicate why. Be assertive but not abrasive or strident. You don't want to win the battle (prove your point) but lose the war (forfeit the job).

? Are You Aware That This Question Violates
My Rights As a Job Applicant?

Although we'd like to believe that recruiters have been schooled in the protocol of questioning, it's safe to assume that not all recruiters have received or retained such training. With this question you confront the issue of due process directly, but not abrasively.

Most recruiters will probably beg ignorance, retract the question, and apologize. If they do, drop the issue, or if you feel magnanimous and safe, answer it anyway.

Should the interviewer insist on an answer, get up and leave without further comment. Consider exercising your rights through your state enforcement agency.

16-4

You Want to Know What Steps the Company Is Taking to Ensure Its Competitive Stance in the Marketplace

No company can guarantee you a job for life. But job security increases as the prospects for the company's long-term survival increase. You have a need and a right to know what the company intends to do about long-term competitive survival.

? What Is the Company Doing to Maintain
or Expand Its Competitive Position?

You are not likely to get a detailed strategic plan or any information that might be seen as proprietary. After all, you're only an applicant, not an employee. But the interviewer should have sufficient information on hand with which to answer your question. Probe gently yet assertively for a complete response.

A corollary form of this question is to introduce information about a new technology or product you found in your research (for example, "The latest issue of . . . said that you'll be introducing a new product. How do you expect that to affect your competitive position?")

If you don't get a satisfactory answer to this question, be prepared to pass on this company. You don't want to bet your career on one of the late, great industrial giants of the nineteenth century.

? How Is This Company Changing to Become More Competitive?

This is a leading question, based on a simple premise: To remain competitive companies must change. In a simpler time when competitive forces were predictable and economic forces were less harsh, this question would probably label you as a troublemaker. You would probably get the perfunctory rejection letter and the company would never contact you again. In today's world, however, the question signifies something totally different: You're an astute observer who needs information to make an informed choice. Listen carefully to the answer and follow with clarifying probes.

? What Will This Company Look Like Three Years from Today?

With this question you're tapping into strategic plans, long-term visions, new product developments, and organizational restructuring. This open-ended question provides the recruiter with considerable latitude and freedom to structure a response any way he pleases.

This question might initiate a five- to ten-minute discussion. Probes are crucial. Explore as many avenues as the recruiter's response provides.

16-5

You Want to Know the Company's Commitment to Your Professional Development

You're smart enough to know that unless you receive periodic training and development, you're bound to become obsolete. You also know that unless you are given formal training from the company, you are not likely to get it on your own. You decide to learn the degree and extent of the company's commitment to your development.

? What Will the Company Do to Ensure That My State-of-the-art Skills Today Will Also Be State of the Art Three Years from Today?

Committed as you might be to your personal development, the company must be even more so. It's in their best interest to assist you in developing an action plan that incorporates periodic training and development programs. If this plan exists, the recruiter should happily elaborate on it. As a matter of fact, he is likely to do so with considerable pride. After all, this plan could be the selling feature that brings you on board.

If the plan doesn't exist or if the recruiter says that it is negotiable, be prepared to negotiate. Don't accept the job without a written commitment from your boss that you will receive continuing education. At a minimum you should attend one training seminar each year, with the topic to be negotiated with your boss.

? What Kinds of Training and Development Opportunities Have You Had in the Past One or Two Years?

The answer to this question should indicate the kind of opportunities you are likely to have. It's possible the interviewer may not have had any opportunities because of a hectic schedule or because he chose not to avail himself. Probe to determine whether or not opportunities were provided, what kinds of opportunities they were, and how often they were provided. And if he turned them down, why?

16-6

You Want to Know How Your Performance Will Be Evaluated

Getting the job is one thing. Getting promotions and raises is another. Clear expectations prevent later frustration and conflict. You have a need and a right to know the criteria that will be used to determine your advancement in the company.

? May I See a Copy of the Evaluation Form That Will Be Used for My Performance Evaluation?

Probably the most informative response to this question is showing you the actual form that will be used to evaluate your performance. This form presents the categories, questions, and relative weights used to arrive at an overall assessment.

Typically, employee evaluation forms are not confidential. What's personal and confidential are the responses to the form, not the form itself; hence, it ought to be available to you. If the interviewer says he can't show you the form, ask why, and be prepared to challenge the answer. There really is no good justification for withholding it from you.

Even if you're permitted to inspect the performance review form, it may not be immediately available. Interviewers seldom keep them handy, and interviewees seldom ask to see them. If you encounter one who does, or who stops the interview to get one for you, give that company ten bonus points. If, instead, the interviewer offers, without being asked, to share it with you, give that company 100 bonus points. When you get it, study it carefully and ask any questions you might have.

? How Are Internal Pay Levels Determined?

With this question you're trying to get a sense of internal equity issues. Of course, you're concerned with the absolute levels themselves, but you should also be concerned with how the levels are computed. If the answer is that the information is secret or there is no formal method, you should probe further.

Pay systems that are confusing to employees, unknown to employees, or determined capriciously are fraught with problems. If you don't like what you ultimately learn through this question, find your life's work elsewhere.

It's possible the recruiter may need more time to secure the information. That's understandable. But make sure you do get an answer.

? What Options Are Open to Me If I Disagree
with a Performance Evaluation?

This question does not label you a troublemaker, just a realist. Human beings can and do have honest differences in opinions. You need to know what you can do if you find yourself in that situation vis-à-vis your boss.

Most companies will allow you to attach a written rebuttal to your evaluation, and some will not. Find out what kind of company this is.

? Will I Have an Opportunity to Do
a Self-assessment of My Performance?

The best performance review systems call for employees to do a self-evaluation prior to receiving one from the boss. If this company does not include this provision in its system, consider negotiating this privately with your new boss. It will motivate him or her to exercise greater responsibility in rating your performance.

? Will I Have an Opportunity to Evaluate My
Boss's Leadership of Me at the Same Time
My Performance Is Being Assessed?

The *very* best performance review systems ask employees to provide feedback to the boss regarding the leadership they receive. Even though there is little chance that this company has one of them, the value of asking this question is in alerting the interviewer that you expect to receive competent leadership on the job.

Chapter
17

Interviewing Job Applicants

It would seem that conducting an interview should be one of the easiest tasks a manager faces. After all, you simply have to determine what information you need, develop the questions to elicit that information, ask the questions, and then listen.

Unlike most tasks in life, however, what seems easy to the untrained or naive is extremely complex. Managers work in an era where certain questions are illegal, where certain applicants are deceitful in their answers, and where perceptual biases and stereotypes run rampant.

Rather than being simple and intuitively obvious, asking the right questions at the right times in an interview requires training and skill. In this chapter, we summarize the most frustrating interview situations and the questions needed to resolve that frustration.

17-1

Breaking the Ice and Putting an Applicant at Ease

You realize that the applicant in front of you is intensely concerned about projecting the most favorable image possible. She appeared nervous as she shook your hand and sat down. You want to calm her nerves as quickly as possible so that you can get to the meat of the interview.

? What Questions Do You Have About How This Interview Will Be Conducted?

There are two advantages to this question. The first is that you've removed the burden and pressure from the applicant's shoulders and placed them on your own. You're taking it upon yourself to answer the first question. The second advantage of this question is that most worthy applicants are concerned about how the interview will be conducted and what the next stage in the selection process is likely to be. The questions you get will assist you in gauging sharpness and will reveal something about how the candidate thinks.

When the applicant asks you an initial question, answer it as candidly as you can. If she says, "I have no questions about this interview," provide a summary of the ground rules and expectations anyway.

? What Motivated You to Interview Us?

When you want to put an applicant at ease, ask open-ended, familiar, nonthreatening questions. This question meets these three criteria. The applicant has undoubtedly thought about this question and prepared an answer. Even if she hasn't, she should be able to give you a response with a minimum of fear and anxiety.

? What Was It Like Growing Up in (Name of Applicant's Hometown)?

The value of this question is that it is not threatening, does not solicit specific information regarding qualifications, and is likely to trigger calming recollections and attitudes. The applicant will often use the opening response as a transition into job-related attitudes or qualifications (for example, "I grew up in a town where your company had a subsidiary, and I always dreamed of one day working for you").

If the applicant doesn't provide a transition, use her response to develop your own (for example, "You say you grew up in a small town. How did that shape your values?").

17-2

Learning What Motivates a Candidate

The applicant's résumé and application tell you what she has accomplished, where she accomplished it, and when it was accomplished. You want to find out what the résumé and application form don't reveal: what makes this person tick. You want to be certain to hire someone who will be motivated to perform well in the organizational climate of your company.

? Of All the Projects and Assignments You've Worked on, What Was the Most Personally Rewarding and Satisfying for You, and What Was the Least Rewarding and Satisfying?

The answer to this question gives you comparative data. You'll be able to compare the characteristics of assignments that motivated the applicant to those that did not.

Make sure she focuses on specific assignments, not hypothetical ones. You don't want to know what projects *would* or *would not* energize her; you want to know what projects *have* or *have not* energized her. You also want to hear about her actions in *recent* situations. Her values may have changed since an assignment she took on three years ago.

The answer to this question is crucial to making your selection decision. Follow the applicant's answer with probes: "What exactly was your responsibility in that situation? How much freedom did you have? Why did you respond the way you did?"

? Under What Conditions Do You Find
Yourself Going the Extra Mile or Putting
Forth Extra Effort?

Every employee has control over discretionary effort, the effort that
goes beyond the job description and is the difference between performance that's good enough and a performance that's great. With
this question you can find out what motivates this applicant to excel.

As with the previous question, it's imperative that you probe.
Find out exactly what characteristics of the job—working conditions,
supervision, incentives, and so on—excite this applicant. Determining an applicant's drive is essential to your selection decision. Don't
assume; probe and validate.

? Under What Conditions Do You Find
Yourself Pulling Back from a Job,
Decreasing Your Effort?

This question puts a spin on the previous one. You're soliciting the
same information except you're doing it with a negative scenario
("What turns you off?") instead of a positive scenario ("What turns
you on?").

In an attempt to project the most favorable image possible, the
applicant may give you the socially acceptable response to this
question: "I always work at peak level and never pull back on effort."

Make it easy and safe for the applicant to be more honest. Say,
"At some time or another we all get burned out or frustrated and
pull back, me included. I'm just trying to get a sense of when you do.
Only a robot works at full efficiency all the time." It might help for
you to describe the working conditions that turn you off.

17-3

Finding Out What Minimum Salary Will Attract a Candidate

You've always found that salary offers represent one of the trickiest
decisions to make in the employee selection process. You don't want

to offer more than needed to attract someone; neither do you want to lose a good prospect for a few dollars or have to engage in heavy negotiations at the outset of a relationship with a new employee. To make just the right offer you have a set of favorite questions you ask.

? What Is Your Current Salary? Do You Consider That to Be a Fair Compensation Level?

The candidate's degree of satisfaction with her current pay will tell you something about how high you'll need to go to attract her.

? What Minimum Increase Over Your Current Salary Would Compensate You Fairly If You Came to Work for Us?

This question gets directly to the point. Ask it before the candidate develops confidence in her chances to be offered the job.

? If We Were to Offer You This Job at (Give Dollar Amount), Would You Take It?

If you decide to use this question, ask it very early in the interview, once the candidate fully understands the duties, but before the candidate may realize that you are interested in her and feels she can bid the amount up. For a dollar figure use the amount you are hoping to pay the person you hire, tempered of course by this particular candidate's experience and salary history.

If the candidate says yes, you now know that your price will land her if you're ultimately interested. If she says no, you have three choices. You can drop the subject, knowing that a job offer will have to include at least a slightly higher starting salary, you can keep probing until you learn what her minimum requirements are, or you can thank her for coming for the interview and move to the next candidate.

17-4

Finding Out How Determined a Candidate Is to Do a Good Job for You

You've just read the most impressive set of credentials you've seen in a long time. The candidate you are about to interview appears in his résumé and application to be ideal for the position, but reading between the lines leaves you a bit uncertain about his desire to work hard and to commit himself to the goals of your unit. Before he comes in your office, you give some thought to questions that might reveal his motivational level.

? If I Were to Ask Your Last Boss Which Three of Your Qualities She Appreciated the Most, What Would She Say?

It is far more reliable to ask a job candidate what he has done than what he plans to do. And while admittedly a fishing expedition, this question may yield insights as to where this person shined brightest on his last job. With appropriate rewording, this is also a good question to ask his previous boss on the telephone.

? What Do You Have to Offer This Job That Would Make Me Glad That I Hired You?

Does he take greater pride in his potential or in his performance? Does the candidate's response dwell on his credentials or on his commitment, on his education or on his energy, on his knowledge or on his know-how?

? Which of My Expectations Are You Happiest to Find on the List I Just Handed to You?

Present all job candidates you interview with a list of your expectations for how they will perform their duties and request the same from them: a list of the expectations they have of the company, of you, and of their career progression.

This question asks for a response to your list. What does his choice tell you about his attitude toward hard work and accomplishment?

His list should be even more revealing. What does it tell you about the willingness of this candidate to give you his very best?

? If in Making the Final Selection Decision for This Job, I Am Considering Two Finalists—an Exceptionally Hard Worker with Reasonably Good Skills and a Reasonably Hard Worker with Exceptional Skills—Which One Would You Advise Me to Hire, and Why?

The candidate's selection and explanation will reveal a great deal about his work ethic.

17-5

Determining the Applicant's Leadership Style

You've already determined the applicant's professional image and style. Personal appearance, composure, speaking ability, and social graces have provided that information. What you still don't know and what you haven't seen in the interview is the applicant's leadership style: how he can be expected to relate to his employees.

? How Did You Resolve a Recent Performance Problem of One of Your Employees?

The test of a person's leadership style is not what is done when things are going smoothly and all employees are performing up to expectations; rather, the test of a leader's style is what he does when performance is not meeting expectations.

Again make sure that the applicant does not tell you what he *would* do in a hypothetical situation. You want to hear about a *specific intervention* to solve a specific performance problem.

If the applicant cannot think of a specific problem or says, "All my employees met my expectations and performed up to standard," follow with the affirmative corollary to the question: "Which of your leadership behaviors do you believe had the most to do with securing that outcome?"

Probe for behaviors. Leadership is reflected in what people do, not in what they think. Don't settle for answers such as, "I was fair," I followed the golden rule," or "I just used common sense."

? What Do You Do to Make Your
Subordinates Tell You Both the Good News
and the Bad News, the Things They Think
You Want to Hear and the Things You Need
to Hear?

Another litmus test of leadership is how one solicits open, candid communication from the people reporting to him. You do not want to hire anyone whose style intimidates subordinates or who is inaccessible to them.

A neophyte to the management ranks may not have given this issue much thought. Nevertheless, this interview is the time to challenge the applicant to give you his best thinking. What would he do? Why does he think he'd do what he recommends? What would he do if it didn't work?

From a seasoned manager solicit specific examples documenting what he did in previous jobs to foster open communication from subordinates. Probe and listen.

? What Experience Have You Had Managing
People with Diverse Backgrounds, Values,
and Demographics?

The work force is quickly changing from Tom, Dick, and Harry to Juan, Ravi, and Mary. Determine this applicant's comfort level with people different from himself as well as his ability to manage those who have a different skin color, religion, or first language.

Since this question potentially touches on prejudices and stereotypes, the applicant is likely to project the most tolerant image possible ("I like everybody and everybody likes me," "I'm color blind," or "I don't have a prejudiced bone in my body"). Your task is to move beyond the socially acceptable responses and determine what this person really believes and what he would really do.

Ask for recent examples or incidents that demonstrate his ability to manage diversity. Never make hiring decisions on the basis of platitudes or promises. You need to know what the applicant did and why. You need to know what the applicant would do and why. Listen and probe.

When you listen use your eyes and your ears. Body language, eye contact, gestures, and tone of voice are powerful indicators of the applicant's true feelings regarding this highly sensitive topic.

In the event that the candidate has no leadership experience with people different from her, ask this follow-up question: "It's a year from now, and looking back you have experienced one major problem leading people who aren't like you [you may wish to insert a particular group here]. What was that problem?" This is a retrospective question that, while not as reliable as one that probes recent behavior, is superior to the speculative question that asks, "How do you think you'll handle . . . ?"

17-6

Learning If the Candidate Will Fit in with Your Team

The marketplace is strewn with technically qualified people who were let go because the chemistry wasn't right. To find out if this applicant across from you will fit in, look him straight in the eye and ask the right questions.

? How Do You Feel About What We Do, How We Do It, and the People You'll Be Doing It With?

Fitting in means that values, norms, and attitudes are shared. It means more than possessing the technical competence to perform the assigned work. Technical competence is easy to assess; beliefs and norms are not.

The most powerful quality of this question is that it's open-ended. The applicant is free to address the three elements of your question (goals, processes, people) or anything related to them. Because this question will reflect values and beliefs, it's crucial that you probe: "Why do you feel that way?" "What specifically do you like about the people?" "Please explain."

Finally, you may want to consider having team members sit in on interviews where you're trying to determine if the applicant will fit. The best answer to this question is often provided by the team members who will work alongside the person. Their gut feelings will tell you whether or not the applicant has the right chemistry.

? Aside from Talent and Technical Skills, What Qualities Do You Think a Person Needs to Fit into This Company?

You may also want potential coworkers to sit in on this part of the interview. Opening the interview to people who may be the applicant's coworkers communicates the importance of the question and sends the unequivocal message that coworkers' preferences will be considered.

As with the primary question, you are looking for values, attitudes, assumptions, and expectations. The most insightful answer is one that reflects a degree of self-assessment (for example, "I know that I'm the kind of person who requires freedom and autonomy and I could fit into any company culture that expects that from employees"). If you don't hear an answer based on self-assessment, ask a corollary question to obtain it: "What are you looking for in a working environment that would fulfill your personal needs and values?"

17-7

Predicting If the Candidate Will Be a Team Player

You're tired of hiring loners, employees who do good individual work, but who do little to contribute to the success of their peers and to the good of the whole. You've been told that the best way to get team players is to hire them, and you believe it. You're determined to find out in job interviews whether a team player is staring you in the face.

? Do You Work Better by Yourself or in a Team Environment?

The first answer to this question will not be as revealing as what she says when you ask her to explain it. Does she enjoy working together with others? Will she fit in with your existing team? Will she pull her share of the load?

? If You Get the Job, Should You Be Evaluated More on Your Personal Excellence or on Your Ability to Contribute to the Excellence of a Team?

It's pretty hard for the candidate to tell what you're looking for here, so you're likely to get an honest response. Does the response say that she is looking forward to contributing to a team effort?

? What Are Some of the Problems That Arise When People Are Assigned to Work in Teams?

The answer to this question will reveal her optimism about teamwork, especially if you probe her statements for more detailed explanations.

17-8

Knowing How Much Freedom and Autonomy the Candidate Needs or Expects

A primary reason candidates don't perform as well on the job as they did in the interview is that expectations were never fully tested or confirmed. One of the most important expectations concerns autonomy: how much the organization provides versus how much the applicant expects and needs. It's possible to test and confirm these expectations through interview questions.

? Can You Give Me Examples in Previous
Jobs Where You Thought You Were Given
Too Much Autonomy and Examples Where
You Thought You Were Given Too Little?

As with previous questions in this chapter, push for examples of actual incidents, not hypothetical scenarios.

The beauty of this question is that once answered, you should have considerable insight concerning the applicant's desire for autonomy. And because you have not asked "How much autonomy are you expecting in this job?" you don't have the problem of flushing out truth from what the applicant believes you want to hear.

As the applicant provides examples, listen carefully and follow with probes. Why did the candidate feel that autonomy was or was not sufficient? What were the specific features of the job, the boss, and the organization that made the applicant feel as he did regarding the autonomy?

If the applicant says, "I've always had enough autonomy," follow with probes. Does this say something about the jobs he selected, his ability to negotiate autonomy, or his low expectations?

? With What Kinds of Management Controls
Do You Feel Most Comfortable and Why?

Expectations concerning freedom and autonomy are reflected in the types of controls the applicant sees as appropriate. With this question you solicit that important information.

There are myriad controls present in any organization and any management system. Chief among these are written reports, performance appraisals, meetings, period feedback sessions, and informal walking around. What is the applicant most comfortable with and why?

Finally, find out how the applicant feels about control as received (executed from above) or control as given (control executed downward). It's possible that the applicant may expect more freedom than he is willing to delegate. Find out.

? When Do You Think Management Controls
Are Necessary?

Find out from the applicant his perceptions of the conditions under which managers should exert control. Follow with probes: "Why do you feel that way?" "Have you always felt that way?" "If not, what specific incident prompted this conclusion?" "Did you learn from personal experience?" "Are there any mitigating circumstances that should be taken into account?"

17-9

Uncovering the Real Story Behind a Botched Assignment or Other Blemish on the Applicant's Work History

You're really troubled. You like the applicant, but you're concerned that he did not leave his last employer under the best of circumstances. The résumé listed personality differences as the reason for quitting. You're determined to find out what this means.

? If Your Former Boss and Coworkers Were
Sitting in This Room and I Asked Them
to Detail the Reasons for Your Leaving,
What Would They Tell Me?

It's safe to assume that the applicant has prepared a canned explanation for why he left his last job. That answer probably places the applicant in a more favorable light than the former boss.

The beauty of this question is that you're likely to catch the applicant off guard. You're asking him to put himself in his former boss's and coworkers' place. What does he think they would say?

The most favorable answer (from your perspective and that of the applicant's) is, "I know exactly what they'd say because we've talked about it. They'd say . . . " An applicant who unabashedly tells you the truth (self-serving or not) and bases it on conversations with the former boss is one who deserves your careful consideration.

An applicant who says, "I have no idea what they would say" or "Their answer would be a highly biased one" may require further investigation.

? How Do I Know That If I Were to Hire You, There Wouldn't Be Personality Differences Again?

Explore thoroughly every blemish on a work record. You have to be convinced that this particular one is either an aberration or is inconsequential.

This question is likely to elicit one of two responses: The applicant may explain his side of the story, thereby putting a self-serving spin on the events. Recognize the potential bias and follow with probes. You might also ask, "How do I know I'm not hearing a biased interpretation?" If this question generates defensiveness, you may just have learned something important about the root causes of the conflict that led to this candidate's demise. The other common response is to guarantee that the blemish was an aberration and will never happen again. Your acceptance of this answer is ultimately based on your total impression of the applicant. Ask what is different now that would prevent a reoccurrence.

? If You Were in My Shoes Trying to Make a Decision About You, What Would Be Going Through Your Mind About the Conditions Under Which You Left Your Last Job?

This question is designed to reverse the roles. You're inviting the applicant to step out of his skin and into yours. First, you're looking to see if he has enough flexibility and empathy to do it. Second, you hope to hear an objective recognition of the risk that the applicant represents. This response might sound something like, "If I were in your shoes, I would be concerned about this problem in my last job."

The least comforting response is one that demonstrates no empathy at all, such as, "I would not be at all concerned."

17-10

Choosing from Among Equally Qualified Candidates

Your search has produced three equally attractive applicants. Their backgrounds, abilities, skills, styles, and accomplishments are uncannily similar. You've decided to conduct a second interview with each of them as the final screening. At the end of each of the interviews you ask what may prove to be the deciding question.

? What Can You Tell Me to Convince Me
That You're the Right Person for the Job?

This is the "sell me" question, the last opportunity the applicant has to convince you that you would be making a mistake by not hiring her.

When you listen to the answer use both your ears and your eyes. An applicant who passionately wants a job will respond with passion. Listen for a voice that is credible and emphatic. Look for body language that reinforces the message.

You are likely to hear answers falling in one or a combination of three categories: past accomplishments ("Hire me because I've proven myself"), commitment ("Hire me because I'll work harder than the other applicants"), or values ("Hire me because I represent what your company stands for").

Regardless of the answer, probe and listen. Don't accept generalizations without supporting evidence.

? What Do You Think Sets Our Company
Apart from Its Competition?

The answer to this question will tell you how much homework the candidate has devoted to this interview. It will also provide significant insight concerning her understanding of the competitive strengths and weaknesses of your company.

Applicants who deserve the job will go beyond the typical self-analysis of personal strengths and weaknesses. They will also dig into published reports and data banks to find out as much as they can about the company and its respective industry.

If you ask a set of equally qualified applicants this question, you will have data to differentiate how well they match the management needs of your company.

? What Have Any Recent Major Setbacks or Defeats in Your Life Taught You About Yourself?

Any qualified applicant should be able to catalogue her major accomplishments and setbacks. However, the special candidate is able to tell you what she learned about herself in coping with defeat. This person is introspective and learns from her experiences, just the person every organization needs.

It's highly unlikely that the candidate will not be able to recall a defeat or setback. However, in the event that you have that rare person in front of you, ask the corollary question: "To what do you attribute being immune from defeats and setbacks?"

Chapter
18

Presenting
on the Podium

It's here; we are in the information age. Managers of today and tomorrow will be judged by how well they analyze, synthesize, and communicate information. One of the most important means for disseminating information and persuading others is the formal presentation.

Not only is the podium a vital forum for presenting information, it is also one of the most valuable tools for upward mobility. Managers who can command attention with the spoken word, think on their feet, respond to challenging questions, and who can handle hecklers are managers who find themselves destined for greater opportunities and advancement in their organizations.

Unfortunately, for too many managers public speaking represents more of a threat than an opportunity. Moreover, the trepidation they feel when stepping up to the podium is further increased when confronting certain taxing speaking challenges. In this chapter, we highlight nine challenges and the magic questions that will resolve them. Study each situation and the questions recommended carefully, and use them to your advantage.

18-1

Preparing a Speech for Someone Else

It's tough enough to write your own speech. It's even tougher when your boss or your boss's boss says, "I'm going to be in Atlanta next week to speak to our 300 sales reps. Write me a speech that will blow them away." You want your boss to look good—thereby making you look good—so you ask questions that will increase the probability of her success.

? In One Sentence, What Do You Want Them
to Do or to Know When They Walk Out
of That Room

The answer to this question provides the focal point of the speech. Everything you write is an elaboration of this single sentence. When you have an answer to this question, you have the bottom line of the speech.

If your boss can't give you a single sentence, she might give you two or three key ideas. Use these as a basis for constructing the speech.

If she says, "I don't know, that's why I'm asking you to write the speech," analyze the situation through her eyes. What is the single most important issue those sales reps need to know right now? When you think you've found the answer, confirm it with your boss before you construct the speech.

? How Do You Want to Split the Allotted Time
Between Presentation and Questions
and Answers (Q&A)?

This will give you a sense of the format within which your boss feels most comfortable. She might opt for a five-minute speech followed by a thirty-minute Q & A or vice versa. She may feel greater control when delivering prepared comments as opposed to responding to questions. Find out where her comfort zone is and work within it.

? Would You Feel More Comfortable
with a Topical Outline or with a Written
Manuscript?

This is another question designed to assess your boss's preferred speaking format. If she's not sure, prepare both and let her choose. Remind her that the topical outline will best support a spontaneous and exciting delivery, while the written manuscript will give her more precision and control over what she says.

? When Is the Earliest You Could Set Up
a Time for a Rehearsal?

Make sure your boss answers this last question. It's imperative that you hear the speaker before the audience does. A run-through will give you a chance to edit and adapt the notes to the specific strengths and weaknesses of your boss's speaking style. It will enable you to give the boss feedback on the strength of her introduction and conclusion and will reveal weaknesses in the argument. It will also indicate the need for any audiovisual material such as slides, flip charts, or handouts. If she says that a rehearsal is not necessary, sell her on its importance.

18-2

An Audience Member Contradicts, Challenges, or Disagrees

You did it! You got through the speech looking good and sounding good. Some people actually laughed at your jokes and seemed genuinely interested in what you had to say. Your spirits are buoyed as you offer, "I'll be happy to answer any questions." The first question you hear brings you quickly back to earth. The questioner refutes your basic position and claims that his view is more accurate. You have just heard the most dreaded question you could imagine, which, although not really a question, is a challenge you'll not be able to ignore.

? Could You Please Tell Me Exactly Which of My Conclusions You Believe Is Wrong?

This question moves the inquisitor from his agenda back to your agenda. It reasserts your control and shows that you're not going to slug it out with him.

If the questioner merely reiterates his assertion, politely interject and ask him to again focus more specifically on your evidence and conclusions. Remember, this speech is your forum, not his. Tactfully and assertively draw the questioner to the data.

If you follow this strategy, many times you will discover that the two of you, in fact, are not really taking different positions. That's because most conflict stems not from actual disagreement but from simple misunderstanding. Chances are excellent that after he identifies where you two disagree you will be able to show that you don't disagree at all. Perhaps you are saying the same thing but in different ways or are addressing different problems. If, however, the two of you are truly at odds, acknowledge that, restate your research, and offer to discuss it one-on-one following the Q & A.

If the person appears to present evidence that raises legitimate questions about your assertions, ask for the sources of his data. Move from the defense to the offense. Before you ask for his sources, list your sources. If the inquisitor begins to pick at your evidence say, "I'll be happy to continue this discussion with you privately after the break." Turn your attention to other audience members and ask, "Are there any other questions?"

? If We Were to Ask a Random Sample of 100 People to Judge the Merits of My Position and Seventy-five Were to Agree with Me, How Would You Explain Their Conclusion?

Whenever you're confronted by a questioner challenging, debating, or trying to score points at your expense you must regain control tactfully and assertively. The audience is witnessing a debate that you dare not lose.

One strategy for winning the debate is force the questioner to step back and look at the problem through the eyes of others. If he says that seventy-five people would not agree with you, put him on the defensive by asking him to support that conclusion with data. It may also be time to agree to disagree with your challenger.

? Do You See Any Merit at All in My Position?

This question is designed for a compromise. Most likely, the questioner is willing to grant some degree of reasonableness and validity to your position. If he does, thank him and move on. If he does not, thank him for his question and move on.

18-3

You're Asked an Irrelevant Question During the Question-and-Answer Session

The Q & A is going much easier than you anticipated. You're moving through it as deftly as Fred Astaire moved across a dance floor. Then you are asked a totally irrelevant question, a question coming from someone who obviously was not paying attention during your speech.

? Would You Please Restate Your Question, Being Even More Specific About How It Relates to This Talk?

This question gets both you and the questioner off the hook. You aren't labeling the question as stupid or irrelevant (thereby demeaning the questioner) and you aren't answering it (thereby giving it credence).

If the person simply restates the original question, recast it yourself before answering so that it does relate to your thesis. Do this by listening to key words and underlying premises. Preface your interpretation with phrases such as, "I think you're asking me . . . " or "Perhaps another way of asking your question is . . . "

If the person wants to use your forum for personal purposes, tactfully but assertively stop it immediately. Don't be brought into debates beyond the scope of your presentation or into areas you have not fully researched.

？ Could You Please Clarify Your Question?

When someone asks us an irrelevant question during the Q & A we are likely to respond with one of two emotions: annoyance or pity. You get annoyed because this person has listened to what you believe was a clear, intelligent speech and at the end asks an unrelated question. Fight the temptation to get annoyed. If the audience senses your annoyance, they will side with the questioner, not with you.

You feel pity if you conclude that this person must be incompetent to ask you such a silly, irrelevant question. Do not respond with a condescending or placating tone. Again, your audience will sense it and side with the questioner.

A more sensible strategy is to help the questioner phrase a question that relates to your speech and that you can answer to the audience's benefit. This question places no value judgment on the quality of the question you received. Unlike the first question it does not request an improved restatement. The burden is yours to help the questioner clarify the question.

？ What Specific Points in My Speech Do You Not Understand?

Ask the person to focus on the points of the speech that were confusing. In a sense, this strategy puts you in the role of helping the questioner articulate clearly and specifically the reasons for the misunderstanding.

18-4

Your Boss Hands You a Manuscript and Says, "Give This Speech"

You're sitting alone in your office feeling proud because your in box and out box are nearly empty. You're in control of your job and all is well with the world. Just as you lean back in your chair, your boss rushes in, drops a ten-page manuscript and a stack of 15 slides on your desk and says, "Give this speech in Chicago next week."

? Do You Want Me to Give This Speech Exactly As Written or Do I Have Some Freedom to Edit?

You want to feel comfortable with the material so that you'll appear credibile and enthusiastic. Knowing how much freedom you have to edit will help you add your personal tone or signature to the speech.

If your boss says, "Give this speech exactly as written," follow with concerns you might have if the speech contains phrases, examples, or supporting material you might not be able to clarify or defend if questioned during a Q & A.

If your boss says, "What do you want to edit?" tell her you'll get back to her within twenty-four hours with any specific editing. Assure her that the editing will retain the purpose and scope of the speech; you're simply concerned with style and supporting material.

? Is There Anything in This Speech That My Experience or Knowledge Has Not Prepared Me to Defend or Define During a Q & A Session?

A speech that you've not written but must give is a ticking time bomb; it can explode at any minute. It may contain words and phrases you don't understand and can't pronounce or statistical summaries that you don't understand, can't explain, or can't defend.

If she says, "Don't worry, you can handle it," respond asseritively. Tell her you'd rather be safe than sorry and studying the speech carefully will protect both of you.

? What Do You Think Are the Three Toughest Questions I'll Have to Answer?

Ask your boss to play devil's advocate. If you isolate your weakest, most vulnerable position you'll be better able to mount a defense. Do not give the speech unless this question is answered to your satisfaction. Without the answer you're approaching the lectern unprepared.

18-5

You're Asked to Say a Few Words
without Benefit of Preparation

You're enjoying your dessert at the year-end company dinner while your boss is on the podium droning on about the previous year's success. Just as you finish the last mouthful of cake, you hear your name mentioned. Your boss says, "I know [insert your name] is not expecting to be called up, but I think we should hear from [you]. Since you played such a vital role in what we celebrate tonight, I think you should come on up to the microphone and say a few words." You walk slowly to the dais, flattered by the praise, encouraged by the flutter of applause, but having left part of your stomach back at the table. You shake your boss's hand, step up to the microphone, look out over the audience, and pose a question in a voice that you hope won't reveal your jitters.

? What Is the Most Important Thing I Can Share with You?

The value of this question is that it provides you two options. The first is to simply thank everyone for making this a successful year and then elaborate on what they did to make it so. You've introduced the praise by saying it's the *most important thing* you could share with them. The other option is to recollect your favorite quote or personal philosophy of management. Why do you believe that people and businesses are successful? If you don't have a favorite quote or personal philosophy, stick with option one.

? What's Our Past? Our Present? Our Future?

A quick and easy way out of delivering an impromptu presentation is to rely on the rule of three. Think of exactly three ideas you can share on the topic and then elaborate on these three ideas. In this case, you have chosen to present where you've been, where you are, and where you're going. You could just as easily have said, "What were the three greatest challenges we faced in making this past year what it was?" or "Of all our achievements this past year, what were the three most satisfying?"

This framework provides both freedom to be creative and structure for organizing your thoughts. Provide your unique perspective on the organization as you see it evolving. As you progress in your career you should have a dozen stock speeches you can deliver at a moment's notice. The rule of three will provide the structure for those speeches.

? What's the Question on Most of Your Minds Right Now, and What's the Best Answer to It?

An extremely powerful and memorable impromptu speech is one that answers the most pressing question confronting the audience at that time. There are two ways to determine the question. One method is empathize with the audience: If you were a typical audience member, what would *you* want to know? Pose that question and answer it. The second method is to actually solicit questions from the audience. Listen to the questions, paraphrase the common themes, pose a specific question, and answer it.

Remember, in Chapter 1 we said that questions are magic because they focus thoughts. There is probably no greater illustration of this principle than the focusing questions for an impromptu speech. Whenever you don't know what to say, don't say anything. Ask a question and then answer it.

18-6

A Person of High Power and Status Monopolizes the Question-and-answer Session

You see him out of the corner of your eye during the entire speech. You're more concerned with his response than anyone else's. Your speech ends and you ask if there are any questions, hoping he'll sit there quietly. But that is not the case, and not only does he ask you difficult questions, he monopolizes the entire Q & A. Others are afraid to ask questions and he's reluctant to relinquish his power as the major inquisitor.

? What Do Other Members of the Audience Feel Is Most Significant About the Last Question and the Answer I Gave to It?

This question provides you two escape hatches. First, it specifically solicits an answer from the rest of the group. You are asking someone other than that person to say something, without alienating him. Second, it gives you an opportunity to move off details and back to general themes. Chances are you'll hear someone say it dealt with issues of service, value, reliability, integrity, or cost. Each of these issues gives you another chance to gain control and talk about the benefits of your proposal.

If no one answers your question, answer it yourself. "The question dealt with the basic issue of value. Let me take a minute and reinforce how we intend to provide it." With this intervention you can end the Q & A or move it onto another track that may generate more involvement from other members of the audience.

? Who Else Has a Question You'd Like to Ask?

This scenario is indeed tense. You're trying to make the most favorable impression you can and this person is making your life miserable. You want to maintain control and be assertive, but not at the cost of alienating someone who will make decisions about your career.

By soliciting contributions from other audience members this question provides a strategy for walking the fine line between control and appeasement. Establish eye contact with other members of the audience as you ask this question.

18-7

A Speaker Freezes

One of your employees is making his first speech before a large audience. You've coached him thoroughly and have confidence that he will impress the audience with his findings. Unfortunately, he doesn't share that confidence. He got off to a shaky start and a few minutes later stands behind the lectern, paralyzed with fear. You rush to the rescue with a relaxing question.

? What Are the Three or Four Main Points of Your Presentation?

Have the speaker simply read off his main points, and engage him in a brief dialogue about each of them. Then tell him to continue with an elaboration of the main points. In this way, he'll get on with the speech.

? What Is the One Most Important Conclusion You Want Us to Take Away from Your Presentation?

Once the speaker states his conclusion, with your help if necessary, you can ask him to explain how he came to that conclusion; in other words, he can give the speech. If he remains shaky, continue to ask questions you know he can handle.

? Would You Like to Take Some Time Before Continuing?

If the speaker is frozen solid, this question will get him off the podium with the least amount of damage. Move to the microphone yourself with a different topic and with no reference to the speaker.

? Would You Please Talk About What You're Experiencing Right Now?

Preface this question with an acknowledgment that podium anxiety has been documented to be one of the greatest fears in people's lives and that many people in the audience undoubtedly share this fear. Mention the times you experience it yourself. Say that you feel everyone there could learn something by having the speaker talk about his fears as he's experiencing them. If he responds to the question, he'll almost certainly be able to continue with the speech itself afterwards.

18-8

You're Assigned to Introduce Another Speaker

You've always wondered where people who introduce speakers get their material, and you're about to find out. Your company has invited a distinguished CEO from out of town to address the annual sales meeting, and guess who's going to introduce her? Inexperienced in this area, you ask around and learn to your surprise that the best way to assemble a worthy and appealing introduction is to go beyond the speaker's name, title, and other demographics by interviewing her before the date of the talk. So, you call the CEO armed with your questions.

? In One Sentence, What Is Your Philosophy of Management?

The answer to this question will help the audience put the speaker's remarks in a context that will aid their understanding. However, confirm with the speaker that there is no chance that your reporting of her answer will take anything from the actual presentation.

? What Single Event in Your Life Has Had the Most Profound Impact on Your Career?

The answer to this and all the other questions will help the speaker build instant rapport with the audience. It shares something of the person beyond the mere role that she represents.

? What Single Person Has Shaped Your Life the Most?

You may get a surprising, and therefore attention-getting, answer to this question. Don't ask this question, however, unless you absolutely plan to use it. You cannot ask the speaker to divulge such personally revealing information and then unilaterally choose to withhold it.

? What Lifelong Ambition Have You Yet to Achieve?

The answer to this question shows audience members that this speaker is not perfect and may have the same unrealized dreams that they do.

? As You Were Working Your Way to the Top, What Is One Thing Looking Back Now That You Would Have Done Differently?

This is perhaps the most revealing question of all. Use it only when rapport building is an especially prominent goal of your introduction.

? Is There Anything in Particular You Would Like Me to Say, or Not to Say, About You?

End your interview with this question. It gives the speaker the opportunity to recant something she may have revealed to you without thinking, and it may jog her mind for one more choice tidbit of information.

18-9

You're Told to Make All Necessary Preparations for Another Speaker

You have been asked to handle all the arrangements for a distinguished CEO coming to town to address your annual sales meeting. You want to make a good impression on him and on your boss. You also want to help him make a good impression on the group of 200 salespeople who will hear him. You call to find out how you can help him be a success.

? What Are Your Audiovisual Requirements?

Find out exactly what he needs in the way of flip charts, markers, projectors, screen, video playback, audio playback, and slide or sign preparation. Learn where he wants these located in the room. Find out exactly how he plans to use the materials so that you can make good decisions before his arrival.

? How Much Time Do You Need?

Learn how much time he'll need for the presentation and the Q & A. Add time for your introduction. Build in an extra ten minutes for slippage and verbosity. Advertise the results to the audience.

? How Would You Like the Room to Be Arranged?

Does he want a lectern? If so, what kind and where located? Is any one seating arrangement preferred? Will he be walking into the audience as he speaks?

? What Type of Microphone Do You Prefer?

Offer whatever choices are available: fixed on the lectern, movable handheld or lavaliere, with or without wire.

? Are There Any Handouts You Would Like Us to Prepare for You?

Preparing handouts for the speaker is a nice courtesy that relieves him of having to carry them along. Ask him to send you camera-ready copy of his materials with instructions. Promise to provide the very best copy quality available.

? What Help Will You Need in Setting Up?

This question could prevent a disaster the day of the speech. Many speakers don't anticipate the set-up time and help they need to prepare for their presentation. Offer to be on hand one hour before the speech with an engineer, custodian, or audiovisual specialist for all advance preparations.

? Can You Think of Anything Else We Can Do to Make Your Presentation a Success?

If he can't think of anything more, ask him to call if he does. Call him yourself a few days prior to the presentation for a quick review of the questions above.

Chapter
19

Resolving Ethical Dilemmas

We all know how we *should* act. Who except for the most cynical and hardened person would deny the wisdom of the golden rule, the ten commandments, and other equally moral guides to human existence? We all know what we should do, but we also know how easy it is to be seduced into behavior that violates these tested principles.

The temptation to breach what we know to be the proper course of action is heightened in today's business world. Pressure to produce greater profits with fewer resources places many managers in weakened positions from which to resist unethical entrapments. Moreover, when corporate and societal norms appear to give only lip service to ethical behavior, the pressure to act expediently rather than morally may be overwhelming.

19-1

Your Boss Asks You to Falsify a Report or Otherwise Misrepresent the Facts

It's 4:30 on a Friday afternoon. Your boss comes in your office, plops down in a chair, and in a tone of desperation says, "We've got a problem." She proceeds to describe the test results on the product you both hoped would be the corporate winner. The results aren't horrendous but they aren't great. She asks you to write a report for immediate release that washes over the negative data and highlights the positive results.

? If I Write This Report and the Product Sells Like Hot Cakes, Might the Two of Us Later Regret What You Have Asked Me to Do?

With this question you challenge your boss to contemplate the consequences of her request. You raise the prospect that the short-term gain could result in long-term sorrow.

If your boss says, "I won't regret it," follow with probing questions: "What assumptions are you making and why?" "What do you see as the most likely scenarios and why?" Play the role of devil's advocate, forcing your boss to move from short-term thinking to long-term thinking. Raise the possibility of a public relations disaster should the test results be revealed to the public eventually.

If your boss still asks you to falsify the report, respond with another question: "Why don't we put our heads together to write a report that incorporates all the information while highlighting the positive features of the product?"

? What Are the Consequences If I Decide Not to Write the Report?

This question puts you on record as saying that you would rather not fudge the numbers and that you want to know the consequences of your refusal. If she says you may be fired, you then have a gut-wrenching decision to make. However, if your boss is ethical, she may respond to your question by withdrawing the request.

Make sure that you probe any resistance. Ask your boss to consider the implications for releasing a falsified report and placing you in such a burdensome position.

If you decide to comply with her directive, you might first put your concerns in a memo to her. Your copy of the memo may prove helpful later if her strategy backfires.

? Will You Assume Full Responsibility
for the Consequences of Falsifying
the Report?

This question places the blame for falsification where it should fall. Remember, the buck stops at the top of the hierarchy, not at the bottom. Remind your boss of this important principle. Tell her that the press, the public, and maybe the courts understand that accountability is at the top, not the bottom, of the chain of command. But don't threaten to report her unless you have every intention of doing so.

? What Are We Saying About Ourselves
and Our Company If We Falsify the Report?

This question is designed to get your boss to think about the long-term implications of her request. After you pose the question, offer a twenty-four-hour break to consider it. Sometimes a day of contemplation is enough to convince a wayward boss to change direction.

19-2
You're Tempted to Act Unethically

This has been an unusually tough month. In a three-week period you had to repair your car's transmission a month after the warranty expired, your water heater had to be replaced after leaking in the middle of the night, and you felt obliged to buy an expensive wedding present for your best friend. All these bills came at about the time that a vendor asked if he could see his competitors' estimates before he submitted his own. He assured you that no one would ever find out about it and that "he'd make it worth your while."

? What Other Options Do I Have to Get Out
of This Bind Other Than the Unethical One?

This self-imposed question serves two purposes. First, it focuses on your options to solve your temporary financial problem. Moral dilemmas are created when we believe that we have no options, limited options, or equally unattractive options. Second, it labels the tempting option for what it is: unethical. When we talk to ourselves in this way about temptations, it's imperative that we be honest and not engage in euphemistic excuses (it's just a loan) or conscience-soothing rationalizations (they would do the best job anyway).

? If I Succumbed to Temptation, Would I Be
Able to Look My Spouse (Best Friend, Child,
Parent) in the Eye and Say What I Did?

We take the moral high road the moment we honestly look at ourselves and honestly label the options before us. By labeling the option as unethical you're not playing semantic games. You're not searching for euphemisms to rationalize behavior you know is wrong. This question is designed to prepare you for that intensive self-analysis.

If after posing this question you are still torn between the low and high roads, do one other thing before you make your decision. Seek out a friend or colleague whose opinion you respect. Pose the options and listen to the recommendation.

If you're reluctant to seek out a trusted colleague for fear of embarrassing yourself, you already have the answer: Deep down you know it's unethical. Don't do it!

19-3

An Employee or Coworker Accuses You of Being Unfair

You're in your favorite chair in the company cafeteria, enjoying your second cup of coffee of the day. Mary asks if she can join you and talk about something that's troubling her. As you slowly sip your drink she says, "We've got to talk. Last week you put Sam on a project that should have been mine. I was more qualified and deserved the chance to reap the rewards. I think you're being unfair."

? Why Do You Think I Made the Decision I Made?

When people accuse you of being unfair all they see is the decision you've made and how it affects them. They are not concerned with your reasons.

This question forces Mary to put herself in your place. She may search for your perspective and your reasons. If she honestly seems to search for your reasoning and state of mind at the time you made the decision but has trouble doing so, help her. Provide clarification and elaboration.

If she can't engage in empathy, tell her why you made the decision. What was going through your mind at the time? What factors did you take into account? In as honest and straightforward a manner as possible tell her why you did what you did.

If you cannot justify your action easily, accept the possibility that you might have been unfair. Apologize if there's a chance that you were, thank her for the courage it took to confront you, and search for a mutually agreeable solution.

? If You Were in My Position Faced with the Decision I Had to Make at the Time I Had to Make It, What Would You Have Done and Why?

The power of this question is that it sets the stage for role reversal and empathy. Looking at the situation from your viewpoint at the time you did may bring a perspective your accuser had never considered. If she has trouble developing the perspective, help her with directed questions: "What information did I have at the time?" or "What pressure was I under?" Listen carefully to how she reconstructs the scenario. If necessary, tactfully correct her.

? Are You Attributing My Decision to Malice, Insensitivity, or Ignorance?

Her attributions of your intent are assumptions on her part, and these assumptions must be validated. With this question you force her to confront and label her attributions. You also suggest that there may be reasons for your behavior other than malice, which was her initial accusation.

If she responds with what you believe is an incorrect interpretation, fight the temptation to label her as silly, stupid, or emotional. Instead, empathize with her by professing, "If I were in your shoes, I might feel the same way. Now let me tell you what really happened and why."

19-4

Someone Misrepresents You

You just found out that one of your coworkers attributed false information to you. He said that you supported the project when in fact you distinctly told him that you did not. You suspect he did it to use your good name as a leverage to overcome resistance from others to his pet project. You're seething.

? What Are Your Plans for Retracting the Statement You Falsely Attributed to Me?

If he denies the misrepresentation, follow with specific irrefutable evidence. If you don't have the evidence, don't waste your time confronting him.

If he refuses to take any action, tell him that you will be happy to have the issue resolved further up the organization. While your preference is for the two of you to resolve the problem, make it clear that you are quite prepared to bring in the boss.

If he proposes a remedy, be prepared to allow him to save face. Remember, pressure to perform is everywhere, and you don't want his hide. You simply want to set the record straight.

? What Do You Think Will Happen to Our Future Working Relationship If the Record Is Not Set Straight?

This question implies that if there is to be a productive relationship in the future, the wrongdoer must repair the damage caused by the lie. If not, the future will be one of controlled hostility. Trust is one of the keys to productive, satisfying relationships. This question is telling the person that he has violated that trust and severely wounded the relationship.

But you're also telling him that the damage may not be irreparable. If he is willing to be honorable, the relationship can be salvaged.

? How Will We Ever Be Able to Trust One
Another If We Don't Solve This Now?

This question raises the same issue of future working relationships but specifically incorporates the word "trust." With it you're forcing your coworker to realize that trust has been violated and that he must act to save the relationship.

19-5

You Suspect Someone Is Deceiving You

You know something isn't right. You have enough background information to raise serious doubts about what you're hearing, and you're quite sure it's not simply that the other person is misinformed. You think this person's trying to pull a fast one on you.

? Do You Realize That I Have Serious Doubts
About the Truth of What I'm Hearing,
and That I'm Convinced You're Digging
Yourself into a Deep Hole?

You're assertive, focused, and unequivocal with this veiled statement. You're offering the person the choice of coming clean or continuing a course that you've stated she will later regret.

If the person asks you about your doubts, tell her what they are and reveal the evidence on which you base them. Ask her to describe how her statements jibe with your information.

If she asks about your implied threat ("digging yourself into a deep hole"), tell her that deception will create an extraordinary strain on your relationship. Emphasize that once lost, credibility is very difficult to regain.

? Is There Something I Need to Know That You're Not Telling Me That Will Remove the Doubts I Have?

This question underscores your concern without labeling the person a liar. You're offering her a way to clarify her remarks without having to defend herself. You're simply seeking information to reduce uncertainty; you're not calling her a liar. Your goal is to secure information, not mount an attack.

It's quite possible that your assumptions and information are incorrect. With this question you explore that possibility. This question also allows the person to save face and extricate herself from a potentially embarrassing (if not litigious) situation.

? If I Take You at Your Word, Will You Have to Come Back Later and Make Excuses for What You're Now Telling Me?

This question raises the prospect that her current behavior may return to haunt her. You're telling her that you have doubts about her truthfulness and that these doubts should be cleared up now. Apologizing or clarifying in the future won't have the same impact as coming clean now. As she answers this question, focus intently on nonverbal cues: eye contact, gestures, facial expressions, and posture. If you sense that she's uncomfortable, she's telling you nonverbally that your suspicion is probably justified.

19-6

You're Being Sexually Harassed

It's happening again. Your boss just approached you in the corridor outside your office, touched you on the shoulder, and made a sexually suggestive remark about your appearance. The last time he did this you told yourself that the next time your boss made you feel uncomfortable with sexual innuendo or inappropriate touching, you were going to say something.

? Why Are You Doing That?

The value of this question is to create immediate discomfort for the harasser without shouting, swearing, or otherwise becoming emotional. If the boss says, "What do you mean?" respond with, "Why are you touching my shoulder and making suggestive, sexual remarks?"

You have specifically labeled the behavior, which must now be defended. At this point in the conversation, the boss may become flustered, embarrassed, or apologetic and may even physically pull back.

If instead you get insistence that you're misinterpreting the behavior, say that the behavior is causing the perception and the way to stop the perception is to stop the behavior. Affirm that a mutually professional and rewarding relationship is possible only in the absence of what you just experienced. If this affirmation doesn't sink in, promise to report the behavior to upper management or to other appropriate officials.

? Why Would You Want to Jeopardize Your Career?

This question makes it clear that there will be repercussions if this behavior continues. Make certain the person understands that your remarks are not a hollow threat and that you are prepared to follow through. Convince the boss of this by being very specific as to what the repercussions might be. Say who you will contact, what evidence you will present, and what your testimony will be. Express concern that your report would be career threatening. Communicate your message in a slow, controlled, emphatic tone. Don't shout or scream. Do sufficient homework so that you can make your protection under the law very clear to this person.

? Have You Ever Been in a Situation Where
You Felt Demeaned, Manipulated,
and Victimized?

Asking this question reveals exactly how you're feeling and in a subtle way invites empathy. Most harassers either distort in their minds the effect they are having on their victims or never fully understand the effect. In unequivocal terms, explain how the boss's behavior is demeaning, makes you feel like an impersonal object, and turns you into a victim. If you evoke an apology, say, "I want more than an apology. I insist upon a commitment that you will never do anything like this again."

19-7

You Are Accused of Discrimination

This can't be happening to you. Throughout your management career you have prided yourself on the equal opportunity you have afforded to all your employees. But now that's all blown. Two employees are in front of you right now and are threatening to expose your racial bias to upper management and to the news media. You can't believe your ears. You feel attacked, insulted, and defensive, yet you still hope to resolve their complaints in a rational manner. You decide to ask questions and listen to the answers.

? What Is the Most Recent Example You Can
Give of a Time When I Showed Prejudice?

You may be able to use these four questions in sequence. This first one pins down the exact situations that concern the two people accusing you of bigotry. Push for specifics and probe for details. Listen without rebutting. When they have finished recounting the example, firmly indicate your agreement or disagreement with the incident depicted.

? Can You Think of Any Reasons Other Than Prejudice That Would Explain Why I Behaved the Way I Did?

You may agree to some extent with the descriptions given in answer to the first question; however, you probably disagree with the intent of discrimination attributed to your action. The two accusers will probably not be able to ascribe anything other than evil motives to your action, but you can. Tell them what organizational needs you were meeting with the behavior they observed.

? How Would You Have Handled the Situation You Are Concerned About Differently Than I Did?

Once you have clearly stated the needs met through your actions, get them to agree that these were valid organizational priorities for someone in your position. This question asks what different methods they would have chosen to meet those needs. If they can offer none, your point has been made and the accusation should be defused. If they recommend unrealistic alternatives, tell them why their suggestions would not have worked. If they come up with ideas you didn't think of, say so honestly and pledge to use their ideas in the future.

? In the Situations We'll Be Facing Around Here Over the Next Few Months, What Behavior on My Part Would Be Evidence to You That I Handle Them Fairly?

This question serves three purposes. First, it brings the discussion to a close and gives you a chance to summarize what was agreed. Second, it presents your accusers an opportunity to say anything that may not have come out to this point. Third, it may give you some good ideas of how to avoid repeats of this situation in the future.

19-8

You Observe a Coworker Stealing from the Company

You are faced with one of the most troubling dilemmas the workplace has to offer. About thirty minutes before quitting time you saw someone with whom you work closely pack a small piece of valuable electric gear into her briefcase as she looked around nervously. Your first reaction was shock that someone you work with would do what you just observed. You were relieved that she didn't see you, because your second reaction was to look the other way and pretend you didn't see anything. After all, you reason, what she did is the company's business, not yours. You don't want to earn a reputation as a tattler, and you don't want to alienate a member of your team. A handful of strategies flash before you. One is to make an anonymous tip to your boss, but after thinking about this for a few minutes, you change your mind, and decide to confront her before she leaves for the parking lot. You make up your mind not to accuse or anger her, but rather to get her to leave the equipment behind and maybe even to see the error of her ways. (Note: Before implementing any of the advice below become familiar with the laws in your state and the policies within your company regarding employee theft. It may be that you are liable for criminal prosecution or termination from your job by not reporting what you saw immediately.)

? May I Ask You to Help Me Out?

The answer to this question is not important. Ask it simply as a nonthreatening way to bring up the topic of what's tucked in her briefcase. Following her response, state that you have been put in a very difficult position that only she can get you out of. Tell her what you observed, and ask her to help you by putting the equipment back or by showing you that it's not there. Point out that by not reporting a suspected case of stealing, you can be implicated as an accessory to the crime and that you must protect yourself.

If she pulls the equipment out of her briefcase, thank her. Ask her if she'd like to talk about what just happened. Remember, though, that you are not a counselor, a psychiatrist, or her boss. Once you've helped as much as you can by listening and it's apparent she needs more, refer her to someone who knows where she can find help.

? Taking Work Home Tonight?

This question represents a totally different and less kind approach. Its primary goal is to let her know that you know. If she says no, respond with, "Then why are you taking that [name the stolen item] home?" If she says yes, this is your cue to ask, "Will you be using that [name the stolen item]?"

Don't proceed any further along this line of questioning. You are bordering on an accusation, and you don't want to overstep your bounds. If she leaves with the equipment, you have little choice but to tell the boss what you saw. But, be certain your evidence is accurate before you present it.

? Wouldn't You Rather Leave That Equipment Here?

Ask this question only when you are absolutely sure she has no reason to have the equipment in her briefcase. She is almost certain to answer, "What do you mean?" Say, "I watched as you put it in your briefcase fifteen minutes ago. That's put me in quite a spot. I can get in as much trouble as you can by not saying anything. How about helping us both by putting it back? If you do, I won't say a thing."

19-9

You Have to Break a Promise

Wholesale changes in your organization lately have resulted in chaos and uncertainty, especially among your employees. They're frustrated with new procedures and policies. In fact, the last time you announced the change in the company's hospitalization insurance, the only way you got them to calm down was to assure them that things were about to quiet down. You went one step further in promising that if they cooperated with the switch, you would outfit their break room with the microwave oven and refrigerator they had requested over a year ago. You were confident that your boss would support your request, and she would have, except that the employee cafeteria concessionaire just signed a new agreement with top management guaranteeing that employee break rooms will not be so equipped. You have no choice but to go back to your employees at the next staff meeting with egg on your face.

? Does Anyone Know How to Remove Egg Stains from Skin?

A question like this asked in front of a group is practically rhetorical. You'll not necessarily get an answer, and if you do, it won't matter. You have just opened the way to explain why you are unable to fulfill your promise, without giving them too much opportunity to attack you. Don't blame upper management. Be appropriately apologetic, but don't go overboard to blame yourself.

Several other questions might work in the same way. For example: "Does anyone here know what humble pie tastes like" and "How many ways can you say I blew it?" Use whichever one fits your personality and communication style.

? Do You Expect Your Boss to Do a Better Job of Keeping Promises Than a Politician Does?

Here's another semirhetorical question. This allows you to say how seriously you take the promises you make to your employees. You can also reassure them that the only thing that stopped them from getting the microwave oven and refrigerator was the surprise agreement with the concessionaire.

No matter which of these preliminary questions you ask, you'll want to close with the next one.

? What May I Do for You to Make Up for My
Unkept Promise?

This gesture enables you to maintain credibility with people you
disappoint with unkept promises. Your staff may answer by saying
that they don't want you to feel indebted to them and that they are
happy knowing you went to bat for them. Or, they may not be able
to think of anything at the time, in which case you can tell them to
take their time to think about it. If they do come up with a request
and you can agree to do your best to fulfill it, tell them so. If their
substitute request isn't practical, explain why and perhaps suggest
a compensation plan of your own.

Chapter

20

Handling Criticism
and Complaints

It's no fun when someone lashes out at you, and two responses to our actions that we especially don't want to hear are criticism and complaints. At the same time, few of us are adept at handling these two forms of negative feedback. Yet, you don't have the luxury of merely avoiding what may be inevitable responses from many of the people you work with and for. If your work environment is like most others across this country, job stress and competition are here to stay, and are motivating people to act in the ways described in the ten scenarios of this chapter.

When any of these outbursts occurs, the tendency is to feel attacked and to have the need to counterattack. If instead you use one of the questions we recommend, you'll get on top of each situation immediately, and you will put the criticizer or complainer on notice to deliver their feedback more carefully in the future.

20-1

You're Criticized Unfairly

One of your coworkers is a combination "dead weight" and back-stabber. She often ascribes her inadequacies and failures to others, as she has apparently just done to you with your boss. Believing the coworker's lies, your boss just accused you of something for which you share no blame. You listened carefully to the boss's complaint without interrupting to make certain that you understood it and to muster a succinct response.

? May I Take a Few Minutes to Reveal Some Information About This Situation That You Should Have?

It won't help to accuse your criticizer of being unfair, even if that's the case. Rather, you want the boss to remain open to the possibility that the discipline was unwarranted. Turn the focus to the situation that generated the remarks. First confirm the agreement you have with his reading of the situation. Then politely, yet firmly, correct any inaccurate information held by the criticizer. Say what you saw and what happened. Report the situation as objectively as you can. Don't get caught in embellishments or lies that will permanently damage your credibility. Thank the boss for the opportunity to share your perception. Don't blame the coworker who smeared you. Let the boss do that.

? How Do You Want Me to Handle This in the Future?

If you are really not at fault, you'll be able to respond to your boss's answer to this question by saying, "That's exactly what I did," and then elaborate on the situation as it happened. You can help to further discredit the perjured witness by ending with, "You may have received some bad information from someone."

20-2

You're Criticized in Public

You just suffered a humiliation that you're not likely to forget. The boss lost his temper with you in full view and hearing of half the office.

? What Can I Do to Ensure That We Have the Opportunity to Discuss My Performance in Private from Now On?

Calm down before you deal with this inexcusable indiscretion. Don't make the same mistake your boss did.

This question accomplishes a number of goals at once. First, it points out the error, making your perception of what happened very clear. (Believe it or not, the boss may not realize what was done.) Second, it puts the boss on notice for the future and makes your expectations clear. Third, it reduces the possibility of defensiveness by having you volunteer to take the responsibility for seeing that it doesn't happen again.

? How Are You Feeling Today?

At first, this may seem like a strange question to use after being pummeled in public, but consider its power. No matter what the answer, your response will be that the boss appears to be having a bad day because that's the only explanation you can find for what just happened.

Expect to hear, "What do you mean?" Now you can say something like, "Well, I don't think that you would have embarrassed me in front of half the office if you were feeling like yourself." Now that you have said your piece under the cover of the question, you can continue with a discussion of the circumstances that angered the boss in the first place.

20-3

You're Criticized Incessantly

You thought that by now every boss in the world had read *The One-Minute Manager*, that famous book that taught managers the value of devoting time to catching people in the act of doing something right. (Could your boss have read that last word as "wrong"?) Your boss couldn't find something nice to say to anyone. You're convinced that every time he enters your office he's looking for errors.

? Have You Ever Noticed Me Acting
Defensively at Your Comments
About My Work?

Whether he answers yes or no, report feeling defensive whenever you expect him to comment about your work. Indicate that this is because he rarely has anything good to say about your achievements. You're sure you deserve censure now and then, but you also suspect you deserve praise on occasion. Ask for more of a balance.

? When Was the Last Time I Did
Something Right?

A boss who criticizes excessively may need a question this blunt. Expect to hear, "What do you mean?" Respond by saying, "Well, according to my records, it's been quite a while since anything I did turned out well. At least you haven't told me that you've appreciated anything I've done." Explain that while you're not an egotist, you would like some feedback that signals when you're doing a good job. Tell him that a simple "thank you" will do.

? Is There Some Reason Why I Only Hear
from You When I've Done Something
Wrong?

This is the most direct of the three questions. Use it as a hard-hitting lead-in to either of the discussions recommended for the two previous questions.

20-4

You're About to Criticize Someone

Three months ago you hired a new receptionist who has been doing a good job, but today was an unfortunate exception. He failed to show up at the starting time of 9 A.M. By 9:10, with no receptionist yet in sight, the phones were ringing constantly and visitors were arriving in the waiting area. By 9:15 you were forced to recruit someone to cover the front desk. Peeking out your door at 9:26 you saw him arrive to assume his duties. You wait a few minutes for him to get settled and for you to calm down. Then you buzz his desk and, so that whatever you say to him will be in private, ask him to come in to see you. As you wait for him to arrive, ask yourself two critical questions; when he shows up, you'll ask him two even more important ones.

? What Exactly Do I Know About This
Situation? What Facts Are True Here?

One of the worst mistakes we could ever make is to be wrong in criticizing the behavior of others. Get your facts straight before you open your mouth. If you criticize in error, you'll lose credibility with the recipient that you may never recover completely.

? How Can I Phrase My Concern in Such
a Way That I'll Be Condemning the Deed
and Not the Doer?

Here are three tips for giving constructive criticism that focuses on the performance and not the performer. First, be certain that your motive in speaking up is to help the person become more effective rather than to punish him. Your true intent will be felt by the other person as he observes your body language and hears your tone of voice. Second, *say what you see.* Limit your comments to what you have observed or heard. Don't judge, interpret, or moralize. Third, never begin your criticism with the word "you." Use "I" rather than "you" statements.

? What Happened Today That Caused
the Front Desk Not to Be Covered from 9:00
to 9:26 A.M.?

At some point in your criticism you'll want to learn if there are any extenuating circumstances to explain his tardiness. Some people would begin the meeting with a question like this one. Others would hold off asking it until they had made a clear yet nonpunishing statement about what they observed and what was wrong with it (for example, "I had to pull Jan off her important job this morning because the phones were uncovered and visitors were not being greeted").

The danger of not asking a question like this one is that you might otherwise misspeak. If your receptionist has a good reason for not showing up on time this morning (for example, his dog was hit by a car and had to be taken to the animal hospital), you would feel foolish finding this out only after fully criticizing the incident.

? What Will It Take to Keep This
from Happening Again?

In most cases of critical feedback, you'll want to end the session with a commitment from the other person to corrective action. This question is one of the most assertive ways to get that commitment. It's also true that he is more likely to follow through with a solution that he—not you—has found.

20-5

You Hear a Complaint About Someone Else

You can't believe how often you get dragged into disagreements between your colleagues, and it's happening again. Standing in front of you is a member of your team, upset about another member of the team and complaining bitterly about that person's behavior. You don't want to be put into this position.

? Do I Have Your Permission to Share Your Feelings with Her?

This question demonstrates your belief that the next best step in this conflict is for the other person to find out how the complainer feels. Even though you're offering to communicate the complaint, your real intent is to sway the complainer to do it. (Note that you could have also chosen simply to ignore the complaint by not acknowledging it or by walking away. Indeed, it may be wiser to avoid antagonisms among your peers.)

If the answer to your question is yes, then say, "I have an idea. Why don't you be there with me and, since you feel so strongly about her behavior, you can do the talking with me there to facilitate the discussion."

If the answer to your question is no, say, "Then please stop telling me about your problems with her. When she and I work together I can't afford to have rumors about her compromise the success of our working relationship."

? Before You Go Any Further, Are You Willing to Share Your Feelings Later in Front of Her?

You may wish to interrupt the complaint with a question that makes your belief that this person has an obligation to state his or her concerns directly to the other person even clearer. Handle the responses to this as you would the original question.

? Have You Told Her How You Feel?

If the answer is no, say, "Then that's the next thing for you to do." Explain the danger of not getting to the point with people. Describe the perils of accumulated anger. Warn of the confusion people feel in response to negative feedback that is not clearly attributed to behavior they recognize in themselves. Witness to the destructive effects of dishonesty in work relationships.

If the answer is yes, you may want to offer, "What can I do to help the two of you work this out?"

20-6

A Customer Complains About Your Product or Service

An unhappy customer tells you that your service is inadequate and has not met her needs.

? What Can We Do to Make It Right?

Less than one in twenty unhappy customers complains. Yet, each will register dissatisfaction with as many as ten others, and over ninety percent will take their business elsewhere. A dissatisfied customer represents an opportunity to make it right and thereby win long-term loyalty.

Make certain your employees are trained to spot every instance of service failure and that they use this question as a prelude to corrective action. Empower them to give the generous compensation that is likely to convert a disturbed customer into one loyal for life (for example, "Let us redo that for you at our expense").

Better yet, ensure that the service they provide never fails. Train your employees, motivate them, and equip them to care for customers in a way that your competitors cannot.

? How Could We Have Done a Better Job
for You? Or, What Did You Hope to Get
Out of the Product That It Didn't Provide?

Use the first of these two choices to handle a service complaint, the second for a product. Notice that these two questions focus attention back to the problem rather than rush to a solution. This strategy can be quite effective to help you discover exactly what went wrong with the service or product. It is particularly recommended when it appears to you that the customer's complaint is invalid. In this case, respond to the customer's answer by gently yet assertively pointing out that her expectations are unrealistic, even though you might still choose to resolve the matter to the customer's complete satisfaction.

20-7

A Customer Screams or Otherwise Acts Abusively Toward You

Complaining customers sometimes get out of hand with their voice and their words, and responding effectively to what appears to be verbal abuse is an enormous challenge. It's difficult to balance the needs for objectivity, professionalism, and self-control with the absolute necessity to end the mistreatment you are witnessing or experiencing.

The first step in dealing with angry customers is to defuse their emotion by listening to them. This way you enable them to vent their anger without adding to it. As they calm down, you ask the right question.

? What Exactly May I Do to Help You?

Protesting customers either have a valid complaint, are misinformed, or are disagreeable people who enjoy being mean. Whatever the case, this question should bring an end to the harangue. You can offer a responsive solution to valid complainers, you can clear up the misconceptions of uninformed complainers, and trouble-making customers are likely to head for the door in disgust.

? May We Discuss This in a More Appropriate Location?

Use this question either to remove this confrontation from the hearing range of other customers or to relocate it to your office where the trappings of your authority may give you an edge. If the customer is too loud or offensive, you may not be able to wait for the customer to calm down before asking it.

? Are You Interested in a Solution?

If the customer becomes overly abusive, ask this question quickly and loudly to break the customer's emotional state. Once you succeed, offer a solution if you've heard enough to provide a good one. If you're not ready to solve the problem, ask the customer the right questions in a calm, soft tone of voice.

_____

? Can We Make a Deal?

Sharply ask the abusive customer this question. When the storm ends say, "I promise to make this situation right if you promise to stop swearing."

_____

? May I Suggest an Immediate Solution to This Problem?

This is an alternative way to state the first question. Use it when it's apparent that the customer is looking to you for a resolution or when you have a remedy you know will work. If the answer is no, fall back to the first question.

20-8

A Customer Threatens You

You have done everything within your power to satisfy an irate customer, with no success. In fact, she has turned downright menacing. She looks you directly in the eye and says, "I am going to have you fired." You know better than to argue with her, so you ask a defusing question.

_____

? Would You Like To Speak to My Supervisor?

You should do all you can to satisfy customers and to prevent your boss from having to intervene. Nevertheless, you won't be able to handle every difficult customer or every challenging situation. Even if the customer doesn't ask to speak to your superior, it may be clear to you that this is the strategy of choice.

Don't allow your ego or your insistence that you're right get in the way of asking this question. (Neither should you opt for it too quickly or too often.) Your supervisor may be in a better position to help, and you'll often find that your boss's presence will intimidate the customer into compliance.

Sometimes this question will cause the customer to back down.

? Will Having Me Fired Solve Your Problem?

The answer you receive to this question is not important. You ask it to show that you will not be intimidated. You might end the discussion with a statement of regret that the customer has chosen not to allow you to help solve her problem.

20-9
Employees Are Griping About Change

You work in an industry subject to government regulation, and lately those regulations have been multiplying furiously. The resulting chaos has been rough on employees. Just when they think they've caught on to a new requirement, it's updated or replaced. They feel a great deal of pressure and are having a hard time dealing with all the uncertainty. Their attitudes about a number of things have soured, and they seem to complain easily. In fact, they gripe about things that previously they would have accepted without question. You're really concerned about this because the last thing you feel you can do is introduce any new ideas to them, even those that will benefit them.

A management book you recently read extolled the virtue of the gripe session. You decide to have one, carefully following the recommended prescription of keeping the group relatively small, seating them around a U-shaped table, and recording their answers to your questions on a large flip chart. You preface your questioning by empathizing with them. You acknowledge the rapidity of the modifications they've been forced to live with, and you recognize the resulting pressure. Then you ask all four of these questions, probably in the order they appear.

? What Are Your Greatest Concerns About the Changes We've Been Forced to Accommodate?

Listen to the answers to this question with little or no rebuttal. Don't belittle their fears or concerns by saying, "You shouldn't feel that way." Get as many of their feelings out as possible so that you understand what's going on and why they've become so defensive. If the group doesn't express as much as you suspect they feel, be creative in encouraging them to respond. One way to do this is to present on a sheet of the flip chart a list of the concerns you suspect they harbor. Give them each a specific number of votes (about a third the number of suspected concerns on your list) to cast, perhaps with colored adhesive dots next to the listed items on the sheet, for their top concerns. When they see each other's votes, the discussion will open up.

? What Specific Problems Have Those Changes Caused for You Personally and for Your Ability to Perform Your Job?

Answers to both halves of this question are important. Allowing your employees to air their personal concerns—if they will—is cathartic. It enables them to blow off steam and air their grievances.

Responses evoked by the performance part of this question are critical for *you*. They may draw your attention to areas of waste or inefficiencies as well as to opportunities for eliminating them.

? What Could I or Top Management Have Done to Facilitate the Change Process?

Listen and record all suggestions before you respond. When you do, take great care not to be defensive. Some of the ideas you hear may appear ridiculous to you, but they make perfect sense to the people who suggest them. Thank them for their ideas, and then explain calmly and objectively why it wasn't done that way. In cases where it's the truth, admit that it might have been better had the change been implemented as suggested.

? What Can I Do to Improve Things Immediately?

This is perhaps the most useful question of the four. Once you collect their ideas, promise to get back to them within forty-eight hours with your response to each one.

For the great ideas that neither you nor your boss would have thought of, you can recognize the person who made the suggestion and report back on how and when the idea will be implemented. For the unworkable ideas, you can tell them why they won't be put into effect at this time. For ideas you may need more time to consider, tell them why and when you hope to report back. And make sure you do it, even if you must bring them bad news.

20-10

An Employee Insists You Don't Appreciate Her Efforts

You've always prided yourself on the consideration you show to your employees, and so the meeting you just had with your top assistant shocked you. She claims that in the years she has worked for you, you have rarely expressed praise or recognition for her considerable contributions to the team. Her comments floored you at first and then encouraged you to reflect on your history of working with her for proof that you've acknowledged her achievements, but you're drawing blanks. You're not sure how to respond, so you decide to keep her talking for a while to learn more about how she feels and to gain your composure.

? Can You Please Say More About That?

This might be a good starter question for half of the challenges presented in this book. It's particularly useful in this situation so you can understand your assistant's feelings better.

? Can You Give Me an Example of a Recent
Time When I Didn't Acknowledge One
of Your Accomplishments?

If she hasn't already given you specific examples, ask for some. Don't
be defensive when you hear them. If you agree that you were wrong,
thank her for the feedback and commit yourself to doing better in
the future. If you don't agree that you failed to acclaim the victories
she recalls (or that they were necessarily victories), say so, but vow
to make your applause more evident from now on. Thank her
sincerely for being willing to confront your behavior.

? What Do You Think I Should Have Done
in That Situation?

Listen completely to how your assistant thinks you should have
praised her work. Don't interrupt her for any reason. Don't even
judge her idea. Simply thank her for it, and indicate that it will help
you in the future.

Chapter
21

Responding to a Changing World

As the twenty-first century takes over we are witnessing techno-logical and societal transformations that no previous generation has endured. Our hand-held computers enable us to "mail" letters from airplanes. Laser surgery enables us to be operated on without being cut. The transplantation of animal organs into humans no longer makes headlines. We have achieved a demographic diversity in this country that was unimaginable just a few years ago. Geopolitically, the disintegration of the Soviet Union, the birth of the European Community, and the unification of Germany have changed the world forever.

We've also witnessed and experienced major changes in how we perform our jobs and where we perform them. Telecommuting, empowerment, affirmative action, self-managed teams, total quality management, and downsizing have resulted in new corporate struc-tures, new job descriptions, and new reporting relationships. For many in our workforce, the scope and pace of these changes have been threatening and traumatic. For others, these changes represent an opportunity. For all, they have brought challenge.

In this chapter we present scenarios of the kinds of tests you might expect in these times of change.

21-1

You're Asked to Telecommute

You've heard the term but you never really understood what it meant. Your boss called you into her office and said, "To cut down overhead costs we're asking all the employees in this department to telecommute. This means you'll work from home via a computer and modem that we'll provide. You'll receive the same pay and benefits you do now. We're going to phase this in next month. Do you have any questions?"

? What Do I Do When I Need
to Coordinate with You or Other People
in the Department?

Telecommuting can indeed save overhead costs such as utilities, office space, and maintenance. It can also motivate employees through individual initiative and empowerment. However, working alone at home may create another set of problems. With this question you're investigating perhaps the most significant problem: access to colleagues and supervision when needed.

Your boss may say that in addition to having a telephone everyone with whom you need to coordinate will be on your electronic mail network. If you find this acceptable, let the issue drop. However, you may want to follow with a probe: "Suppose I need face-to-face contact?" If your supervisor is unwilling to incorporate periodic face-to-face meetings into the telecommuting plan, you may wish to point out what communication experts claim: As much as ninety percent of the meaning people receive from each other is sent through their voices, apart from the words they speak, and from their body language.

? How Will My Work Be Monitored?

Both the good news and the bad news is that you'll be working without direct supervision. So, while no one will be looking over your shoulder to catch your errors, neither may anyone remain informed enough to keep track of your successes. Or, the monitoring may be via the computer, the same kind of electronic surveillance that checks your speed on the highway from an airplane you can't see. Before you take on the assignment get a clear understanding of how your work will be appraised. You don't want to be surprised during your next performance review.

? Will I Be Expected to Take on More Work Because I'm Doing It at Home?

Some telecommuting programs are used as a rationale for increasing workloads. These programs are based on the belief that since an employee saves the time of traveling to and from work, he or she should be able to get more done. Be wary of a plan that offers you the freedom of working at home at the cost of having to do more.

? Will My Out-of-pocket Expenses Be Compensated?

Be certain to get an understanding (in writing if possible) on this up front, whether it's the telephone, electricity, supplies, or any other cost you may incur. Some companies offer no reimbursement, insisting that you get all your supplies from the main office and rationalizing that the tax deduction you can take on your office space at home will cover the rest.

    Check with a tax advisor or the Internal Revenue Service on the requirements needed to deduct a portion of your mortgage or rent and utilities expense when you maintain a home office. Also note that a home office deduction taken by an employee may increase the probability of an IRS audit.

21-2

An Employee Wants to Telecommute

Aside from all the crises you've handled today, you've just received a precedent-setting request. One of your employees wants to work at home and communicate to you and the office via phone, fax, and computer, using her own equipment. Her job does have her working independently most of the time, yet you have misgivings about the request, but you don't want to alienate her by simply saying no.

? What Will Approval of Your Request Do for the Company?

If she answers, "Nothing," you'll ask, "Then why should I approve it?" Make it clear that her job and yours are directed at furthering the interests of the company, and that every decision made must keep that in mind. Send her back to the drawing board for justification for her request.

? What Risks or Potential Problems Do You See in Your Proposal?

The employee is probably considering only the benefits of telecommuting, not the drawbacks. This question forces her to look at both sides. You're opening the door for the negotiation that may be necessary for you to approve the request.

She may answer, "I don't see any risk" or "I haven't given that any thought." If so, suspend the discussion until she can get back to you with a detailed cost-benefit analysis. Promise that you'll study the analysis and be back to her in a few days with a decision. If she fails to acknowledge potential disadvantages apparent to you, add those to her list. In your response to her, tell her what will need to happen to minimize the risk, reduce the cost, and solve the problems the two of you have identified.

? If We Grant Your Proposal, What Changes
Should We Make in Job Requirements?

This question is not an implied threat of an increased workload. It simply reflects that the employee may have to give up certain responsibilities when she moves her work space to her home. For example, she may no longer be able to attend quality improvement meetings. If she'll be doing less of anything as a result of telecommuting, she should expect to take on compensatory duties she can discharge at home. You'll also want to insist that she make herself available in the office for certain functions (for example, quality improvement meetings).

Remain open to negotiations, but be certain that the employee understands that operational needs must remain paramount both as you consider the request and, if approved, as you implement it.

21-3

Two Employees Want to Job Share

Two of your best employees are sitting in front of you asking you to approve a request that has taken you by surprise. They say that because of personal lifestyle choices each wants to move from full-time to part-time employment, and they propose to share the responsibilities and compensation for the job. After your initial shock you compose your thoughts well enough to discuss your concerns.

? How Can I Be Sure That Your Proposal
Will Fill Both Your Needs and the Needs
of the Company?

The beauty of this question is that without denying the request you focus attention on effects and implications of the proposal. They probably haven't thought as fully about the significance of their request for the company as they have thought about its benefits for them personally. Whatever answer you receive, you'll want to tell them what assurances you need to endorse the request and take it to your boss for approval. A few of the expectations you'll have are as follows:

1. A written statement of who is accountable for what.

2. Each will be considered fully responsible for the success of the full position and will never be heard to say, "That's not my job."

3. There will be a daily overlap of at least fifteen minutes in their work schedules, on their own time, when the person going home will brief the person coming to work.

4. Coordination with other departments or other employees will continue at the highest level.

5. The three of you will meet three months after the new arrangement begins to decide whether it is working well enough to continue.

? What Are Your Ideas for Covering
for the One Full-Time Employee We'll
Lose If the Job Sharing Proposal
Is Approved?

Once you're assured that work will not suffer, that employees will not complain, and that no increased costs will be incurred, solicit their help in figuring out how to deal with the loss of the full-time equivalent of one employee. If they believe that it's your job, not theirs, to solve this problem, tell them two things: (1) Recruiting, selecting, and training a new employee who at first won't be as productive as either of them—and may prove never to be so—is an expensive and time-consuming activity caused by their request, and (2) they are so close to the job that they may have creative suggestions for how to handle the uncovered duties without having to incur all the expenses you anticipate. Let them know that resulting cost savings would definitely help their chances.

? How Can We Meet Both Your Needs
and Mine At the Same Time?

This is the bottom-line question for this scenario. Your employees have a need to job share. As the person in charge of this job, you have needs to meet the goals of the organization. Are they higher quality, more productivity, cost savings (see previous question), or less time spent supervising?

Look at this potential new arrangement as a change in the status quo that may afford you the opportunity to accomplish what you weren't able to realize in the past. Use your cooperation with them as leverage to get better results for the organization.

Let's say that you have an unfulfilled goal of convincing your employees to learn a new optional skill, and you might make your cooperation contingent upon theirs. Take great care to be certain that whatever you ask for in trade is reasonable, ethical, and legal.

21-4

An Employee Confides to You
That He Is Gay

No one ever said that being a manager was going to be easy. The person sitting across from you has just told you that after years of mental anguish, he has decided to come out of the closet. With obvious pain in his voice he told you that he's gay. You wish you could consult with your human resources director before taking another breath, but you can't put this employee off. Not knowing what to say, you decide, instead, to ask something.

? Why Are You Telling Me This?

This question will allow you to regain whatever composure you may have lost and solicit information to which you can respond. Whatever your personal feelings, you have a responsibility to help your employee remain productive. So you're looking for the opportunity to be supportive in some way.

Listen carefully and nonjudgmentally. You may hear a lot of personal pain, insecurity, and even anger. Keep the person talking as long as possible without rebuttal to allow for venting and to show your concern. Your best response (both sensitive and legal) is that as long as work does not suffer, his sexual orientation is irrelevant to you as his supervisor.

? Do You See Job Performance
Changing Because of What You've
Just Told Me?

You're paid to manage people and support goal achievement. With respect to this announcement, you are concerned with one issue and one issue only: How will this revelation affect his job performance or the performance of his coworkers?

Probe the likely consequences and implications of his decision to go public. Make sure that he understands that as long as his work meets expectations he will not be discriminated against. Stress that his sexual preference is his personal business and that it will create problems only to the extent that he might use his sexuality to harass or pressure other workers, the very same prohibition that faces heterosexual employees.

? What Can I Do to Help You Keep This
Revelation from Affecting Your
Performance?

This is a good question if you want to sidestep the issue of homosexuality completely. You're responding just as you would if this employee announced any problem that might hinder his effectiveness. If he denies any need for help, saying that he simply wanted you to know, thank him for his consideration. If he makes a reasonable request, fulfill it; if he asks for assistance you cannot provide, tell him why.

21-5

Your Company Wants to Screen You for Drugs

You've been asked to submit a urine sample as part of a random drug test of all employees. You don't want to jeopardize your job by refusing the request, but you don't like the idea that your rights to privacy might be violated. You also want to be sure that the testing procedure won't result in an error.

? What Safeguards Are in Place to Protect Employees from a False-positive Reading?

This is a reasonable question that deserves a response. It implies that you are willing to comply with the company drug policy as long as it has built-in safeguards for not being falsely accused. You have the right to ask for scientific data in support of the answer you get.

If the safeguards seem reasonable to you, you may wish to provide the sample. If your question is not answered, or if the answer you get is not reassuring, ask to speak to someone higher in the organization who is willing to answer your question and provide those safeguards.

Never be deterred by the response, "You're the only one who's complaining." Make it clear that you are not complaining, merely asking for reassurances that every employee wants, even if they don't all have the courage to ask for them.

? What Exactly Does "Random" Drug Testing Mean?

Again, you're seeking certification of procedures and a guarantee that your rights are protected. If the policy stipulated mandatory testing of all employees, you would know exactly what was expected. But the qualifier "random" suggests that some employees will be tested and others will not. You want to be sure that if there was reasonable cause for you to be tested (for example, erratic behavior, excessive absenteeism or tardiness, decreased productivity, a serious accident or injury) the cause be communicated directly to you. If, however, your selection was purely random, you have a right to know how you were selected to ensure that you weren't singled out.

? How Will Test Results Be Disseminated?

Insist that you learn about the results of your test at the same time that they are released to the company. Find out who in the company will have access to your results, and be certain that only those with a need to know are informed. You may wish to check with your human resource director for documentation that your company's dissemination procedures conform to the law.

21-6

You Want to Convince
Upper Management That It Should Invest
in a Childcare/Adultcare Program

You've set up a meeting with top management to discuss the need for funding a dependent-care program for full-time employees. You know it's going to be a hard sell because management sees most fringe benefits as a cost rather than as an investment. Moreover, you're fairly sure that top management lives in an ivory tower protected by their own affluent lifestyles. You decide to begin your pitch by asking them to answer a question.

? How Is Today's Work Force Different from Yesterday's, and How Will Tomorrow's Be Different from Today's?

A management team that does not perceive a need for change will resist it. A team that believes that work-force demographics have changed quantitatively but not qualitatively and that the past is like the present is like the future won't easily be persuaded to adopt the program you're proposing. This question encourages top managers to validate their assumptions and stereotypes about the work force. In particular, ask for their estimates of trends and statistics regarding ethnic, sexual, and marital status demographics.

Record their answers on a large sheet of flip chart paper for all to see. When their ideas are spent, reveal some real numbers that you garnered from research on the latest demographic work-force trends. You're likely to shock them. If you don't, congratulate them on their knowledge. Either way, show how the data support a dependent-care program.

? What's the Worst-case and Best-case
Scenarios of Not Funding the Program?
What's the Likelihood of Each Scenario?

This is a revealing two-part question. In the first, you're asking the team to speculate on consequences (both good and bad) of not funding the program. Naturally, they'd love to create the best case and prevent the worst case. You may have to coach them in being sensitive to the true worst case.

In the second question, you're asking them to judge the relative likelihood of each scenario. This simple exercise, initiated by your questions, should at least raise doubts about the prudence of rejecting your proposal. It may even end up selling the program.

? What Would You Like to See Employees
Give to This Company That They're Not
Giving Now? Or, What Are the Most
Important Current Contributions
from Employees That You Want to Be
Certain Not to Lose?

Be prepared to show top management how employee contributions will be enhanced as a result of being able to count on reliable care for their dependent children and parents.

? What Would It Take to Get You to Approve This Program?

This question is less risky than it may appear. There's a better chance than you may think that what they ask for (for example, "Improve the bottom line") is something you can claim *will* result from the program. By knowing the priorities of your top management team you can predict how they'll answer this question. Do your homework and have a well-documented argument prepared.

If you cannot show a relationship between what they ask for and the benefits of your program, tell them what contributions the program *will* make to the company.

21-7

An Employee Tells You That She's HIV Positive

It's been said that disease and illness are totally nondiscriminatory; they can strike anyone at anytime. The person sitting in front of you with tears in her eyes is proof of that saying. With deep sobs she said, "I just found out I'm HIV positive." You pause for a moment and ask these questions.

? Can I Do Anything to Help?

What do you say to someone who just told you that they have an incurable disease? Don't say anything. Ask how you can help. The person may cry; if so, console. The person may swear and get angry; if so, simply listen. The person may say absolutely nothing and simply stare at the floor or into space; if so, remain silent and avoid eye contact. The person may ask for a statement of the company's policy regarding employees with AIDS; if you have a policy, provide it and talk about it. If you don't have a policy, you now have a reason for developing one.

Remember two things. First, AIDS is not transmitted through casual contact at work, by drinking from water fountains, or from sharing bathroom facilities. Second, as long as a disease or handicap does not impair performance, the employee cannot be discriminated against.

? Has Your Doctor Given You Any Kind of Prognosis?

The answer to this question should tell you about the employee's personal plans for work. It's quite possible the employee may choose to quit work altogether and live the remaining years in personal pursuits.

If the employee chooses to remain, this question allows you to discuss the job pressures the employee is likely to experience and to develop a strategy for dealing with those pressures.

21-8

Your Boss Doesn't Realize That His Thinking Is Out of Date

You've just returned from a marvelous management seminar. You can't wait to begin applying all the wonderful ideas you learned there for motivating your employees. You're especially excited about an idea called "servant leadership," which points to the need for managers to support their employees, putting them first and asking themselves what employees need to give top performance.

By contrast, your boss comes from the old school. You were a bit concerned about how he would react to your post-seminar report, but it's worse than you expected; he even said that had he known you were learning such foolishness, he never would have paid for the seminar. In his words, "Employees should not have to be pampered into giving the day of hard work they owe in return for a day of fair pay." He went one step further in prohibiting you from "practicing such foolishness." Rather than buckling under, you decide to resist without antagonizing him.

? Do You Believe That Most Employees Have More to Give to This Company Than They're Giving Right Now?

The answer is likely to be yes. Respond with, "Well, so do I. That's why I want to implement the ideas from the seminar. They may prove to be as imperfect as you think they are, but if they have a chance to increase productivity, I believe they are worth trying, and I hope you'll support me in that attempt."

If the answer is no, say, "I feel that employees *can* work both harder and smarter, and I'd like to prove it by experimenting with the motivational techniques I learned in the seminar." If you received a book or other materials at the seminar, this would be a good time to offer them to the boss to read.

? Do You Agree That Each Manager Has His or Her Own Style That Works Best for That Person?

If you get the yes you're hoping for, say that you learned in the seminar that your most effective style is probably the servant leadership approach. Add that you'd like to use it with your employees for a time to see if it works as well as you believe it will.

If you are disappointed with a no response, you may wish to challenge your boss with evidence to the contrary within your company or from society. You can probably point to authoritarian managers who succeed alongside equally effective participative ones, each managing in the way they know best. In World War II, Generals Omar Bradley and George Patton were both respected by a majority of their followers even though Bradley was a "teddy bear" and Patton was fearfully referred to as "blood and guts."

Get the okay from your boss to use what works best for you and the company.

Index